WITHDRAWN

THE ROUGH GUIDE TO
SINGAPORE

ROUGH
GUIDES

written and researched by
Richard Lim

Contents

Introduction to
Singapore

"The handiest and most marvellous city I ever saw", wrote the natural historian William Hornaday of Singapore in 1885, " as well planned and carefully executed as though built entirely by one man. It is like a big desk, full of drawers and pigeonholes, where everything has its place, and can always be found in it." This succinct appraisal seems apt even now, despite the tiny island's transformation from an endearingly chaotic colonial port, one that embodied the exoticism of the East, into a pristine, futuristic shrine to consumerism. In the process, Singapore acquired a largely deserved reputation for soullessness, but these days the place has taken on a more relaxed and intriguing character, one that achieves a healthier balance between Westernized modernity and the city-state's traditional cultures and street life.

The foundation for Singapore's prosperity was its designation as a tax-free port by Sir Stamford Raffles, who set up a British trading post here in 1819. The port plays a key role in the economy to this day, though the island city-state now also thrives on high-tech industry, financial services and tourism, all bolstered by a super-efficient infrastructure. All these achievements were accompanied by a major dose of paternalism, with the populace accepting state interference in most aspects of life in exchange for levels of affluence that would have seemed unimaginable a couple of generations ago. Thus it is that since independence much of the population has been resettled from inner-city slums and rustic kampongs (villages) into new towns, and the city's old quarters have seen historic buildings and streets bulldozed to make way for shopping malls. Even visitors will soon notice that this remains a country that neither knows how to sit still nor when it's best leave things well alone: museums close to completely restyle their galleries, metro stations mushroom almost cheek by jowl, and migrant workers constantly attend to seemingly faultless footpaths and floral borders.

Yet although Singapore lacks much of the personality of some Southeast Asian cities, it has more than enough elegant temples, fragrant medicinal shops and imposing

TOP 5 DISHES

Singapore has no national dish – but that's because it has any number of dishes that could happily qualify for that title. It's definitely worth sampling a few things beyond the predictable fried rice and noodle plates – here is our selection of five of the best things to try.

Satay A mainly Malay dish of mini-kebabs, barbecued over coals and eaten dipped in a peanut-based sauce, accompanied by glutinous rice cakes and cucumber and onion slices.

Fish-head curry Many Indian restaurants offer this fiery stew containing a large fish head – eyes and all; the cheeks are the best bits.

Chicken rice Widely available at hawker centres, this Hainanese Chinese speciality features steamed chicken served atop rice cooked in chicken stock, and is served with chicken consommé – simple but incredibly satisfying.

Chilli crab Whole crabs wok-fried and served in a thick gravy made with tomato, chilli, garlic and a little egg. It's mainly served at seafood outlets, though some ordinary Chinese restaurants offer it too.

Laksa A Peranakan classic of rice noodles, prawns and other morsels steeped in a rich, spicy, curried coconut soup; not hard to find at hawker centres and food courts.

colonial and modern architecture to captivate visitors. Much of Singapore's fascination springs from its **multicultural population** of around five-and-a-half million, predominantly Chinese, with significant Malay and Indian minorities (English, Chinese, Malay and Tamil are the official languages). This ethnic make-up can make a short walk across town feel like a hop from one country to another, and endows the island with a range of mouthwatering cuisines – a major highlight of any visit. The city also rejoices in a clutch of fine **museums**, plus a lively **arts scene** featuring no shortage of international talent and local creativity.

What to see

Shaped like a diamond, Singapore's main island is 42km from east to west and 23km from north to south, compact enough to explore in just a few days. The southern corner of the diamond is home to the main part of the city – "downtown", or just "town" to locals – which centres on the **Singapore River**, the creek where Raffles first landed here in 1819. After a full day's sightseeing, the riverside is undoubtedly the top place to unwind, lined with former warehouses that are now home to buzzing restaurants and bars.

The main draws for visitors are the city's historic ethnic enclaves, particularly **Little India**, a couple of kilometres north of the river. Packed with gaudy Hindu temples, curry houses and stores selling exotic produce and spices, the district retains much of its original character, as does nearby **Arab Street**, dominated by the golden domes of the **Sultan Mosque**. South of the river, **Chinatown** is a little sanitized though it still has a number of appealing shrines, an immaculately restored Chinese mansion – the **Baba House** – plus a heritage centre documenting the hardships experienced by past generations of Chinese migrants to Singapore. Wherever you wander in these old quarters, you'll see rows of the city's characteristic **shophouses**, compact townhouse-like buildings that are the island's traditional architectural hallmark.

Of course, the British left their distinctive imprint on the island as well, most visibly just north of the Singapore River in the **Colonial District**, It was around the grand Neoclassical buildings here and nearby – including the famed **Raffles Hotel** plus City Hall and the old Supreme Court, now jointly converted into Singapore's lavish **National Gallery** – that the island's British residents used to promenade. Also here are the **National Museum**, showcasing Singapore's history and culture, and **Fort Canning Hill**, a lush park that's home to a few historic remains. All these are somewhat upstaged, however, by the newest part of town, **Marina Bay**, built on reclaimed land around a man-made reservoir into which the Singapore River now drains. Around it are arrayed the three-towered **Marina Bay Sands** casino resort, the spiky-roofed **Esplanade – Theatres on the Bay** arts centre and **Gardens by the Bay**, with its two huge arch-shaped conservatories.

Nearly as modern as Marina Bay, but steeped in tradition as far as Singaporean consumerism is concerned is **Orchard Road**, a parade of shopping malls that begins just a few minutes' walk inland from the Colonial District. Just beyond is the finest park on the whole island, the UNESCO-listed **Botanic Gardens**, featuring a little bit of everything that makes Singapore such a verdant city and a ravishing orchid section.

SINGLISH

Singapore is the only country with an ethnic Chinese majority not to use Chinese as its main language of education and business. English enjoys that role – but here it's often upstaged by the entertaining, though often baffling, **Singlish**, a mash-up of English together with the grammatical patterns and vocabulary of Chinese and Malay. Pronunciation is staccato, with final consonants often dropped, so "cheque book" would be rendered "che-boo". In two-syllable words the second syllable is lengthened and stressed by a rise in pitch: ask a Singaporean what they've been doing, and you could be told "slee-PING".

Conventional **English syntax** is twisted and wrung, and tenses and pronouns discarded. If you ask a Singaporean if they've ever seen a Harry Potter film, you might be answered "I ever see", while enquiring whether they want to go out to buy something might yield "Go, come back already". Responses are almost invariably reduced to their bare bones, with words often repeated for stress; ask a shopkeeper whether they have something in stock and you'll hear "have, have", or "got, got".

Exclamations drawn from **Malay** and **Hokkien Chinese** complete this pidgin, the most ubiquitous being the Malay suffix "lah", used to add emphasis to replies, as in: "Do you think we'll get in for free?" "Cannot lah!" If Singlish has you totally confused, try raising your eyes to the heavens and crying "ay yor" (with a drop of tone on "yor") – an expression of annoyance or exasperation.

Although lexicographers have recognized Singlish as a distinct variety of English and started adding its terms to mainstream dictionaries, in Singapore there is much official hand-wringing that poor English could compromise the country's ability to do business globally, so much so that a government-backed **Speak Good English** movement has been set up to try to shore up standards.

Downtown Singapore is probably where you'll spend most of your time, but the rest of the state has its attractions too. North of downtown is the island's last remaining pocket of primary rainforest, the **Bukit Timah Nature Reserve**, and the splendid **zoo**, where the animals are confined in naturalistic enclosures rather than cages. There's more fauna of the avian kind on show in the west of the island at the excellent **Jurong Bird Park**, while eastern Singapore is home to some sandy beaches and a museum recalling the infamous **Changi Prison**, where so many soldiers lost their lives in World War II. Among the many smaller islands and islets that lie within Singapore waters, the only one close to being a must-see is **Sentosa**. Linked to the main island by causeway and cable car, it boasts Southeast Asia's only **Universal Studios** theme park and several slick beach hotels.

When to go

Singapore's **climate** is simplicity itself: hot and humid. The island experiences two monsoons, from the southwest (June–Sept) and the northeast (Nov–March), the latter picking up plenty of moisture from the South China Sea. Consequently, December and January are usually the rainiest months, though it can be wet at any time of year; during the southwest monsoon, for example, there are often predawn squally showers sweeping across from the Straits of Malacca. The inter-monsoon months have a tendency to be especially stifling, due to the lack of breezes. At least it's easy enough to prepare for the conditions – have sun cream and an umbrella with you at all times.

SINGAPORE'S CLIMATE

The table below shows the average maximum and minimum **temperatures** in Singapore, and average **monthly** rainfall.

	Jan	Feb	Mar	Apr	May	Jun	Jul	Aug	Sep	Oct	Nov	Dec
Max/min (°C)	30/24	32/24	32/25	32/25	32/25	32/25	31/25	31/25	32/25	32/25	31/24	30/24
Max/min (°F)	86/75	90/75	90/77	90/77	90/77	90/77	88/77	88/77	90/77	90/77	88/75	86/75
Rainfall (mm)	235	113	170	155	171	131	154	159	157	155	259	319

20

things not to miss

Unless you're in town for a while, it's not possible to see everything Singapore has to offer in one trip. What follows is a selective taste of the city-state's highlights – the most vibrant neighbourhoods, best museums and most captivating events. Each entry has a page reference to take you straight into the Guide, where you can find out more.

1 CHINATOWN

See page 62

Chinatown's once characterful shophouses have been rendered improbably perfect by restoration, but the area is still home to many shrines and shops specializing in Chinese food, medicine and other products.

2 BUKIT TIMAH NATURE RESERVE

See page 92

Crisscrossed by several easy trails, this pocket of primary rainforest offers an authentic jungle experience, minus leeches but with the prospect of coming face-to-face with hyperactive macaques.

3 THE S.E.A. AQUARIUM

See page 116

Packed with stunningly vast tanks showcasing marine life, mostly hailing from the waters around Asia.

4 THE ARTS SCENE

See page 154

From ballet in the ultramodern Esplanade complex to street performances of Chinese opera, Singapore's entertainment scene has something for everyone.

5 THE BUDDHA TOOTH RELIC TEMPLE

See page 66

Chinatown's biggest and brashest temple has its own museum, roof garden and, most memorably, thousands upon thousands of Buddha figurines.

6 LITTLE INDIA
See page 52

Little India is easily the most atmospheric of Singapore's historic quarters, with colourful south Indian-style shrines, spice shops and outlets blaring Tamil music.

7 ARAB STREET
See page 56

Dominated by the golden-domed Sultan Mosque, the area around Arab Street is a fascinating mix of carpet-sellers, curio shops and alternative boutiques.

8 MARINA BAY SANDS
See page 80

The striking Marina Bay Sands hotel and casino includes its own museum and a vast rooftop deck where you can eat or drink while enjoying eye-popping views back to the Colonial District.

9 BOAT QUAY
See page 72

Boat Quay is alfresco dining at its best; the reflected lights of its myriad riverside bars and restaurants dancing on the waters of the Singapore River by night.

10 THE NATIONAL GALLERY
See page 35

Nowhere better epitomizes Singapore's artistic ambitions than the National Gallery, presenting East Asian art and world-class travelling exhibitions.

11 CHANGI MUSEUM
See page 102

Reopening in 2020, this is a hushed and moving memorial to the horrors perpetrated in Singapore during World War II.

12 ASIAN CIVILISATIONS MUSEUM
See page 38

A tip-top museum of cultural artefacts from all over Asia, noteworthy in particular for the treasures in its Tang Shipwreck Gallery.

13 THE BABA HOUSE
See page 74

A gloriously restored shophouse, recreating how a prosperous family of Baba-Nonyas – an ethnically and culturally mixed local community – might once have lived.

14 ZOO NIGHT SAFARI AND RIVER SAFARI
See page 96

Spot polar bears and Malayan tigers at these three adjacent zoos; one section is entirely devoted to nocturnal animals and open, appropriately, at night.

15 TEKKA MARKET
See page 53

The closest thing Singapore has to a central produce market, selling everything from halal goat meat to exotic vegetables, and featuring its own superb food centre.

14

15

16 LEE KONG CHIAN MUSEUM OF NATURAL HISTORY

See page 110

Fossilized dinosaur skeletons, thousands of creepy-crawlies and other zoological and botanical specimens, plus the low-down on Singapore's own flora, fauna and geology.

17 THIMITHI

See page 63

The annual fire-walking festival is centred on the Sri Mariamman temple, a Hindu shrine that, in true multicultural Singapore style, happens to be in the heart of Chinatown.

18 AN ORCHARD ROAD SHOPPING SPREE

See page 162

Think Oxford Street, Fifth Avenue or Ginza: Orchard Road has enough famous brands to impress even the most jaded shopaholic.

19 THE BOTANIC GARDENS

See page 86

Genuinely world-class, Singapore's Botanic Gardens feature everything from ornamental tropical shrubs and jungle to a dazzling collection of orchids.

20 STREET FOOD

See page 132

Enjoy Malay and south Indian curries and a bewildering range of Chinese rice and noodle dishes – mainstays of Singapore's delightful and inexpensive street food – in myriad food markets called hawker centres and in the *kopitiam* diner.

16

17

Tailor-made trips

These itineraries aren't meant to be followed rigidly – you may have to leave out one or two suggestions if you choose to linger at a museum or cool off at one of the air-conditioned malls, for example, and Singapore's excellent public transport makes it feasible to chop and change routes. The trips below give a flavour of what Singapore has to offer and what we can plan and book for you at www.roughguides.com/trips

LITTLE INDIA TO THE COLONIAL DISTRICT

❶ **Tekka Market** A terrific place for food at any time of day, and home to an engaging produce market. See page 53

❷ **Indian shops** Small stores at the start of Serangoon Road sell flower garlands, foodstuffs, music and jewellery. See page 54

❸ **The Sri Veeramakaliamman temple** Probably the most engaging of Serangoon Road's Hindu shrines. See page 53

❹ **The Sakaya Muni Buddha Gaya Temple** Explore the inside of the Buddha statue at this Thai temple. See page 56

❺ **Kampong Glam** Visit the Sultan Mosque, with its golden domes, then browse the souvenir and craft shops of the surrounding area or take in the Malay Heritage Centre. See page 56

❻ **Colonial District museums** Spend the whole afternoon at the National Gallery or a couple of hours at the Asian Civilisations Museum. See pages 35 and 38

❼ **Raffles Hotel** With its striking whitewashed facade, Raffles exudes colonial elegance. Splash out on a Singapore Sling at the Long Bar, where the gin-based cocktail was invented. See page 42

❽ **The Singapore River** Take in the river's restaurants and nightlife on an evening river cruise, then dine and drink at Boat Quay. See pages 39, 138 and 150

CHINATOWN TO MARINA BAY

❶ **The Chinatown Heritage Centre** A museum that examines the struggles of the area's migrant pioneers. See page 62

❷ **Sri Mariamman Temple** Singapore's most high-profile Hindu shrine. See page 63

❸ **The Buddha Tooth Relic Temple** A mammoth affair packed with Buddha figurines, worth seeing from its ground-floor halls right up to its roof garden. See page 66

❹ **Thian Hock Keng**. An immaculately restored historic temple, now something of a museum piece. See page 69

You can book these trips with Rough Guides, or we can help you create your own. Whether you're after adventure or a family-friendly holiday, we have a trip for you, with all the activities you enjoy doing and the sights you want to see. All our trips are devised by local experts who get the most out of the destination. Visit **www.roughguides.com/trips** to chat with one of our travel agents.

FORT CANNING HILL

❺ **Maxwell Food Centre** Lunch at this old-school hawker centre, where the quality of the food makes up for the hot, sweaty atmosphere. See page 137

❻ **Bukit Pasoh Road** A conservation area with terraces of ornate shophouses. See page 67

❼ **Baba House** Book in advance to tour this restored shophouse, once the residence of a wealthy Peranakan family. See page 74

❽ **Marina Bay Sands** Head up to one of the rooftop restaurants and bars for superb views back towards downtown. See page 80

❾ **Gardens by the Bay** Evening is a good time to visit, with the Supertree grove magically lit and both giant conservatories still open. See page 81

THE SOUTHERN RIDGES AND SENTOSA

With an early start, you can combine the hilltop walks of the Southern Ridges with an afternoon and evening at Sentosa. If you need to freshen up at your hotel after the walk then scale down your plans at Sentosa.

❶ **Haw Par Villa** Endearingly kitsch prewar relic of a park packed with tableaux depicting scenes from Chinese folklore. See page 108

❷ **Walk the Southern Ridges** A series of hilltop parkland walks, all linked by bridges. See page 107

❸ **Universal Studios** The most popular target at Sentosa, with oodles of rides and film-set recreations. See page 114

❹ **The S.E.A. Aquarium** A superb marine life showcase. See page 116

❺ **Fort Siloso** An old British base, now a museum of past attempts at defending Singapore and its capture by the Japanese. See page 117

❻ **Siloso beach** Sentosa's most broadly appealing beach has a few beachside restaurants and bars for sundowners. See page 118

THE BOTANIC GARDENS, ORCHARD ROAD AND BEYOND

Singapore's fine botanic gardens lie not far from the Orchard Road shopping precinct; once you've seen both it's easy to head out to more distant attractions.

❶ **The Botanic Gardens** Spend the cool of the morning here, being sure to see the ravishing orchid gardens. See page 86

❷ **Orchard Road** Some malls are extremely upmarket, others quite pedestrian – a good middle-of-the-road place for lunch and a small dose of retail therapy is Plaza Singapura. And for a tipple, check out the bars of Emerald Hill. See pages 84 and 162

❸ **Fort Canning Hill** This likeable park hosts Battle Box – an old military bunker revitalized as a museum of the fall of Singapore during World War II. See page 46

❹ **The Night Safari** Head out to northernmost Singapore to see what is deservedly the most popular section of the zoo. See page 96

MARINA BARRAGE

Basics

Getting there

Reaching Singapore by air is straight-forward: the island is one of the main air hubs of Southeast Asia and is often a stopover on the extremely busy long-haul route between Europe and Australasia, so fares can be much more competitive than you might expect. There are also budget flights linking the country with the rest of Southeast Asia, India and Australia.

Fares climb by at least ten percent for travel during **high season** – from mid-June to early September, and over Christmas and New Year. It's also a little more expensive to fly at the weekend; the sample fares below are for midweek travel and include taxes. Whenever you fly, you generally get the best fares by booking as early as possible.

Flights from the UK and Ireland

There are daily flights to Singapore from the UK. Singapore Airlines, British Airways and Qantas both offer **nonstop** flights out of London Heathrow (13hr), Singapore Airlines also flying several days a week from Manchester. Many European, Middle Eastern and Asian airlines offer **indirect** flights to Singapore, which involve a change of plane at their hub airport en route. Although these take at least a couple of hours longer, they are generally also cheaper if you're starting from one of the London airports. Conveniently, airlines such as Air France, KLM or Lufthansa can get you to Singapore from a UK regional airport or from Ireland.

Fares from London to Singapore start at around £450 during low season, climbing to at least £550 in high season. From the Republic of Ireland, reckon on €600 in low season, and at least €700 in high season.

Flights from the US and Canada

Singapore is roughly halfway around the world from North America, which means that whichever way you head to Southeast Asia, you have a long journey ahead of you – at least 21 hours from the east coast, 18 hours from the west. Setting off from the west coast, you'll invariably fly across the Pacific; it's faster to fly the transatlantic route if you're departing from the east coast, though sometimes it can cost less to fly via the Pacific.

Unsurprisingly, the most comprehensive service is provided by Singapore Airlines, which operates **nonstop flights** from Los Angeles, San Francisco, Houston plus (from Sept 2019) Seattle. New York flights normally involve one stop, although from Newark airport there's also the option of the nonstop flight 22 (business class only; 18–19hr), the longest scheduled passenger flight in the world. United Airlines flies nonstop from San Francisco, too.

Fares start at around US$800 or Can$1100 from major airports on either coast.

Flights from Australia and New Zealand

The **budget carriers** JetStar and Scoot (an offshoot of Singapore Airlines) offer some of the best deals **from Australasia** to Singapore. JetStar has the better coverage, with flights from several cities in both Australia and New Zealand; Scoot serves only Sydney, Melbourne, Perth and the Gold Coast. Otherwise, the usual full-cost airlines operate to Singapore from major cities. Flights from Auckland to Singapore take just over ten hours nonstop, while from Sydney and Perth the journey takes eight and five hours respectively.

Fares in high season are generally up to a third higher than in low season. In general, a low-season return ticket from Melbourne to Singapore can start from as little as Aus$450 on JetStar. From Auckland, you're looking at fares of around NZ$1000 in low season with JetStar.

Flights from South Africa

There are flights **from Cape Town** to Singapore via Johannesburg with Singapore Airlines, taking around thirteen hours from Cape Town. These tend to be

---

A BETTER KIND OF TRAVEL

At Rough Guides we are passionately committed to travel. We believe it helps us understand the world we live in and the people we share it with – and of course tourism is vital to many developing economies. But the scale of modern tourism has also damaged some places irreparably, and climate change is accelerated by most forms of transport, especially flying. We encourage our authors to consider the carbon footprint of the journeys they make in the course of researching our guides.

expensive though, costing around twenty percent more than indirect flights with a Middle Eastern airline, for which you can expect to pay around R10,000 in low season.

From Southeast Asia

It's easier than ever to visit Singapore as part of a wider Southeast Asian trip. Between them, AirAsia, JetStar, Scoot and others provide low-cost links with many Malaysian cities. There are also plenty of flights, not just on budget airlines, between major cities in the region and Singapore.

Buses and trains

Travelling to Singapore by land or sea might seem more interesting than flying, but the range of places you can do this from is surprisingly limited. There's a plethora of buses from Peninsular Malaysia, with no major town more than twelve hours from Singapore. The largest of the Malaysian bus companies is Transnasional (W transnasional.com.my), which is the only one with services to Singapore from both coasts of Peninsular Malaysia (other firms only go so far as Johor Bahru, the border city on the north side of the Causeway). Other companies worth trying include Sri Maju (W srimaju.com), which serves the main west-coast cities. Finally, there are also buses from Hat Yai in southern Thailand, a fourteen-hour slog.

The Malaysian **rail** network is best described as mixed. Much of the important west coast line is modernized and speedy, but elsewhere – including, importantly, the southern part of the network – trains are infrequent and actually slower than the buses. Schedules change often (check the latest timetables at W www.ktmb.com.my) but, for the time being, it is basically impractical to catch a train from Singapore or Johor Bahru to Kuala Lumpur. Paradoxically, it is possible to catch a slow, antiquated train between the rural east coast of Malaysia and Johor Bahru via the jungled interior, a journey that takes eighteen hours end-to-end.

For the intricacies of navigating the border crossings between southern Malaysia and Singapore, see page 24.

Ferries

No long-distance international **ferries** serve Singapore at all. The only ferries that exist operate from nearby Indonesian islands, including Bintan and Batam, plus the small southern Malaysian town of Kampung Pengerang in Johor, all of which are mainly visited from Singapore rather than being on the tourist trail in their own country. You can get an overview of the Indonesian ferry services on W www.singaporecruise.com.sg.

Arrival

Singapore's Changi International Airport is gleaming, modern and ridiculously efficient – the country in microcosm. Arriving by bus or train is a slightly less streamlined experience thanks to border formalities and occasional jams at the two land crossings connecting Singapore to the southernmost Malaysian state of Johor. Wherever you arrive, the island's well-oiled infrastructure means that you'll have no problem getting into the centre.

By air

Changi Airport (W changiairport.com) is at the eastern tip of Singapore, 16km from the city centre, and has three terminals connected by free Skytrains, with a fourth connected to terminal 2 by bus. There are the usual exchange facilities and ATMs, plus shops selling local SIM cards. Chances are you'll not linger long – baggage comes through so swiftly that you can be heading to the city centre within twenty minutes of arrival.

SINGAPORE ADDRESSES

Premises within high-rise towers, shopping complexes and other buildings generally have an address containing two numbers preceded by #, as in "#xx-yy". Here xx refers to the floor (ground level is 01, the next floor up 02, and so on) while yy refers to the unit number. So a restaurant whose address includes #04-08 can be found in unit 8 on the building's fourth storey. Note that the term "ground floor" is also used in some older buildings to refer to the floor at street level. It's also worth noting that all buildings within municipal housing estates have a block number displayed prominently on the side, rather than a number relating to their position on the street on which they're located.

To look up an address on a **map**, enter it (or just the street, building name or six-digit postal code) into W onemap.sg and you will usually get a precise fix on the location.

The airport's **MRT** (metro) station is beneath terminals 2 and 3. Between 6am and 11.15pm, trains run to Tanah Merah station, two stops away, where you transfer to the main East West line into town (see page 24). Note that the last downtown train leaves from here around 11.30pm. The half-hour downtown trip costs around $2.50, less if you buy a stored-value EZ-Link card (see page 25).

All the terminals are served by the **#36 or #36A bus** (every 10min, 6am–midnight; around $2), which passes through the suburb of Katong and then Marina Centre before heading to the Orchard Road area.

Whether you take the MRT or a bus, lack of room for luggage (especially on the bus) may be a hindrance. One solution is to use **airport shuttle** buses, which serve most downtown hotels and hostels ($9; 24hr). **Taxis** are plentiful (see page 25); one to downtown costs at least $20 and takes up to half an hour; note that there's an airport surcharge of $3–5, and a fifty percent surcharge between midnight and 6am.

If you happen to be arriving on a short-haul, propeller-driven flight, then you may find yourself at **Seletar Airport**, which was rebooted in 2018 with a new passenger terminal. Once a British airfield, it is situated in the northern fringes of the island – effectively Timbuktu, even for many locals.

At the time of writing, Malaysia's Firefly was the sole airline using Seletar, operating daily flights here from Kuala Lumpur's Subang airport.

The only public transport from this airport is bus #102 to Sengkang or Buangkok MRT stations.

By bus

Most buses from Malaysia and Thailand use the Causeway to reach Singapore from Johor, and terminate at one of three locations. Local buses from **Johor Bahru** (JB) in **Malaysia** arrive at the Queen Street terminal, a couple of minutes' walk from Bugis, Jalan Besar and Rochor MRT stations. In the absence of a long-distance bus station, buses from further afield in Malaysia and from **Thailand** mostly terminate at the **Golden Mile Complex** or the adjacent **Golden Mile Tower** on Beach Road (Nicoll Highway MRT is less than a 10min walk away, or catch bus #100, which passes close to *Raffles Hotel* and City Hall MRT before heading to the financial district).

However, Golden Mile Complex was on the market at the time of writing, and could well be largely demolished if the sale goes through, in which case bus firms are likely to disperse to other commercial buildings.

Arriving at the Causeway, you will have to get off the bus on the Malaysian side to clear immigration and customs, then get back on board – if you're on a local bus, hang on to your ticket and use it to continue on any vehicle on this route – to reach the Singapore side of the bridge, where you go through the same rigmarole. When jams build up at the Causeway, as they often do, follow the crowd and get off the bus a little way before the checkpoints; it's much faster to walk.

Just to complicate matters further, Golden Coach services and some local buses do not use the Causeway at all. Instead, they cross into Singapore using the much less busy **Second Link** bridge at the western tip of the island.

By train

Trains run by the Malaysian rail operator, **KTM**, do not serve downtown Singapore, terminating at JB Sentral station in Johor Bahru. From there, two dozen shuttles a day make the meaningless five-minute trip to and from Singapore's Woodlands station near the Causeway checkpoint. It's far better to exit from JB Sentral, and cross between the two countries by local bus.

By sea

Boats from Indonesia's **Riau archipelago** dock either at the HarbourFront Centre, off Telok Blangah Road at the southern tip of Singapore, or at the Tanah Merah Ferry Terminal in the east of the island. The former is on the MRT's North East and Circle lines, while the latter is linked by bus #35 to Tanah Merah and Bedok MRT stations. Most ferries from the resort island of Batam end up at HarbourFront Centre, though a few of these boats plus all services from the other resort island, Bintan, use the Tanah Merah terminal.

Any mentions of "RFT" in schedules (W www.singaporecruise.com.sg) refer to the HarbourFront Centre.

Cruise ships serving Southeast Asian ports dock either at HarbourFront Centre or at the **Marina Bay Cruise Centre** south of Gardens by the Bay, with Marina South Pier MRT less than ten minutes' walk away.

The only ferry service from **Malaysia** comprises humble "bumboats" from Kampung Pengerang just northeast of Singapore in the Straits of Johor. These moor at Changi Point, beyond the airport, from where bus #2 travels to Tanah Merah MRT station.

Transport

Downtown Singapore is best explored on foot and is compact enough to be tackled this way: for example, Orchard

LEAVING SINGAPORE

Leaving Singapore presents no special issues except that if you wish to head to Malaysia or Indonesia around the time of a major festival or during the school holidays, try to buy your tickets at least a couple of weeks in advance.

BY AIR

Unless using the MRT to reach Changi airport (flight enquiries ☎6542 4422, ⓦchangiairport. com), be sure to set off early during rush hour to allow for traffic congestion. Air tickets can be purchased online or from a travel agent such as STA Travel, #B1-46 Singapore Management University, 70 Stamford Rd (near the National Museum; ☎6737 7188, ⓦstatravel.com.sg) or Chan Brothers, #07-01 Fook Hai Building, 150 South Bridge Rd (Chinatown; ☎6438 8880, ⓦchanbrothers.com).

BY RAIL

Malaysian rail tickets can be bought at ⓦktmb.com.my.

BY BUS

Long-distance bus companies are mostly based on Beach Road – though it's worth asking what the latest situation is – or at their own offices scattered around downtown. Starmart (☎6295 2103, ⓦstarmartonline.com) and Sri Maju (☎6294 8228, ⓦsrimaju.com) have good coverage of the west coast of Malaysia, while Grassland Express (☎6293 1166, ⓦgrassland. com.sg) serves the west coast as well as southern Thailand. The most comprehensive services to both coasts of Malaysia are operated by Transnasional at The Plaza on Nicoll Highway, close to Arab Street (☎6294 7034, ⓦtransnasional.com.my). It is also possible to buy bus tickets on ⓦeasybook.com.

If you simply want to pop across to Malaysia briefly, perhaps to get a fresh visa upon your return or take advantage of much lower prices in the shops, the easiest way is to head to **Johor Bahru** on the local #170 bus, the Singapore–Johor Express bus or a yellow Causeway Link #CW2 service; all of these leave fairly frequently between 6am and 11.30pm from the Queen Street bus terminal (near Bugis MRT), with tickets costing $2 to $3.50 one-way. Having cleared Malaysian formalities at the Causeway, you can head into the city on foot rather than get back on the bus unless you wish to end up at the Larkin Terminal outside the centre, from where there are buses to all parts of the country. You can head back on the #170 or #CW2 at the Causeway.

Road is only just over 2km end to end, and it's a similar distance from the Padang to the middle of Chinatown. Of course you'll need a high tolerance for muggy heat to put in the legwork, and tourists often rely on the underground MRT trains. At some point you may also end up taking buses, which are just as efficient as the trains but a little bewildering, such is the profusion of routes. Both trains and buses are reasonably priced, as are taxis.

Most of the public transport network is in the hands of two firms: **SBS Transit** (☎1800 287 2727, ⓦwww. sbstransit.com.sg) – historically a bus company, though it's now responsible for two MRT lines – and **SMRT** (☎1800 336 8900, ⓦsmrt.com.sg), which runs the rest of the MRT network and has some buses of its own. Ostensibly to promote competition, some bus services are now in the hands of two London-based operators.

Note that moves are afoot to turn the entire public transport system **cashless**. If things go to plan, by 2020 buses will cease to accept cash fares, and ticket machines at MRT stations will require plastic to pay for journeys or to top up stored-value cards.

The MRT

Singapore's **MRT** (Mass Rapid Transit) metro network is a marvel of engineering – the island's remarkably soft subsoil makes it a real challenge to drill train tunnels – and of cleanliness, efficiency and value for money, though often overcrowded. In many parts of downtown, so close together are stations and so sprawling are they that you're seldom more than ten minutes' walk from a station entrance.

The system has five **lines** (see map page 204), with a sixth, the Thomson-East Coast line, opening in stages from north to south between 2019 and 2021; its stations are included in travel advice in this guide. Note that the Circle line isn't a full circle – the "missing" section being unfortunately within downtown. To journey between two stations on either side of this break, use the North East line between Dhoby Ghaut and HarbourFront. Note also that the Downtown line does a bizarre loop under itself midway. To travel between the northern and eastern legs of the line, it's faster (and cheaper) to walk between Rochor and Jalan Besar stations – only 400m apart – than stay on board while the train calls at eight more central stops.

Trains run every five minutes on average from 6am until midnight downtown, but, as you'll soon discover, seats are hard to come by – and not just during rush hour. Your mobile phone will work in stations and on trains, even in the tunnels, but you aren't allowed to eat, drink or smoke (the signs that appear to ban hedgehogs from the MRT actually signify "no durians").

The easiest and cheapest way of getting about is to buy a stored-value card (see page 25). Otherwise, while cash fares last, MRT **tickets** will cost between $1.40 and $2.70, and can be bought from ticket counters or from automated machines at stations. Note that every physical ticket can be used for up to six journeys – just present it at the machine when paying for a new ride.

Buses

Singapore's **bus network** is comprehensive and slightly cheaper than the MRT system for short trips. Most buses operate from 6am, with services tailing off between 11pm and 12.30am. Both double- and single-decker buses are in use, and you always board at the front.

Fares rise in tiny steps with the distance travelled (cash fares are between $1.40 and $2.50, except on express or night services), so if paying cash you may well have to consult the driver on the precise fare for your destination. Cash should be dropped down the metal chute next to the driver; change isn't given, so have plenty of coins to hand to avoid frittering money away – or buy an EZ-Link card or tourist pass. With an EZ-Link card, you must touch the card on the electronic reader not only on entering but also **at the exit**, otherwise the maximum fare will be deducted.

Some buses have **fixed fares**, chiefly services within new towns, a few premium services (which run nonstop for much of their route) and **night buses**, which operate late on Fridays, Saturdays and before a public holiday and connect downtown with the new towns. SMRT's night buses (11.30pm–2am; $4.50) start from Resorts World Sentosa, Marina Centre or Boat Quay, while SBS night buses (midnight–2am; $4.40) operate from Marina Centre; they can be useful for downtown travel after the MRT shuts, but note that they may run express in certain parts of town.

Both the SBS Transit and SMRT websites have break-downs of their bus routes, including journey planners and maps; alternatively, try the MyTransport.sg app (see page 33).

Taxis

Singapore's **taxis** are seemingly without number; indeed some locals joke that in uncertain economic times the authorities probably license yet more taxis to keep jobless figures down. While this means flagging down a taxi generally isn't a problem, it can be tricky at night or during a storm. If you have difficulty finding a cab, it's best to join the queue at the nearest **taxi rank** – hotels and malls are your best bet. Note that in the downtown area, queuing at a taxi rank is supposed

---

EZ-LINK CARDS AND TOURIST PASSES

You can avoid the rigmarole of buying tickets for every bus or MRT ride by purchasing a stored-value **EZ-Link card** (Ⓦ ezlink.com.sg), available at some MRT stations, bus interchanges and 7-11 stores. Besides offering convenience, the card can nearly halve the price of short trips and shave at least twenty percent off the cost of longer ones; what's more, a journey involving up to five transfers (using trains, buses or both within 2hr) is treated as one extended trip if you use the card, again saving you money. The cards can be bought for $10–12, of which $5 is the actual cost of the card and the remainder is credit. Cards can be topped up with $10 or more of credit at ticket offices or ticket machines, and stay valid for at least five years. Note that in order to board a train, you need to have at least $3 credit on the card.

Alternatively, the **Singapore Tourist Pass**, valid for up to three days' unlimited travel, can be bought at Visitor Centres and around 15 MRT stations, including the one at the airport. It costs $10/$16/$20 for 1/2/3 days, plus a $10 refundable deposit. Once the pass expires, it can be topped up and used like an EZ-Link card, with the cost of trips deducted from the stored value. To claim the deposit back, be sure to return the card within five days of purchase. For more, see Ⓦ thesingaporetouristpass.com.sg.

to be compulsory during the day (specifically Mon–Sat 7.30am–8pm), though some drivers will ignore this rule to pick up passengers on quieter roads. To book a taxi (surcharges of several dollars apply), either call ☎ 6342 5222, which represents all of the taxi operators, or try individual firms such as Trans Cab (☎ 6555 3333) or SMRT Taxis (☎ 6555 8888).

Taxis come in various colours, but all are clearly marked "TAXI" and have a sign or display on top indicating if they are available for hire. Regular cabs (as opposed to premium/"limousine" vehicles) **charge** $3–4 for the first kilometre and then 22c for every 400m travelled, with a slightly lower tariff kicking in after 10km.

There are **surcharges** to bear in mind: 25 percent extra on journeys during rush hour (which, for taxis, means Mon–Fri 6–9.30am & 6pm–midnight, Sat & Sun 6pm–midnight), and fifty percent extra between midnight and 6am. Then there are charges arising from Singapore's **electronic road pricing** (**ERP**) scheme, which means a $3 surcharge on taxi journeys starting from the ERP zone downtown between 5pm and midnight, plus passengers being liable for the actual road use their trip has incurred (shown on the driver's ERP card reader). Journeys from Changi Airport, Sentosa and Gardens by the Bay incur additional charges of several dollars (some firms also charge extra for Sunday daytime trips from Marina Bay Sands). Fares can be paid using plastic as well as cash.

On the whole, Singaporean taxi drivers are friendly and honest, but older drivers may not be that fluent in English, so if you are heading off the beaten track, it's worth having the address (including the postal code, for the benefit of GPS) written down for them to digest. If a taxi displays a destination sign or "Changing shift" above, it means the driver is about to head home or that a new driver is about to take over the vehicle, and that passengers will be accepted only if they are going in the right direction for either to happen.

Traditional taxis aside, there are **ride-hailing vehicles** operated by the homegrown Uber-style upstart **Grab** (which actually drove Uber to sell up and quit Singapore) and the Indonesian giant **Go-Jek**. Grab operates its own taxis, with the same tariffs as traditional firms, while the unmetered GrabCar calculates fares based on your pick-up point and destination; they generally work out a bit cheaper than taxis, unless only a few drivers are bidding for your journey. Download their respective apps to explore their options and book.

River taxis

River taxis are commuter boats along the Singapore River (Mon–Fri 8–10am & 5–7pm; $5; EZ-Link cards only). They are operated by the firms that do river sightseeing trips (see page 27), namely River Cruise (plying between Esplanade and Robertson Quay) and WaterB (from Clifford Pier to the *Grand Copthorne Waterfront* hotel, slightly upriver from Robertson Quay). Although a little pricey, the rides are an entertaining alternative to buses and the sightseeing trips themselves. For more details, enquire at the jetties/kiosks of either company, easily spotted along the river.

Driving

Given the efficiency of public transport, there's hardly any reason to **rent a car** in Singapore, especially when it's a pricey business. Major disincentives to driving are in place in order to combat traffic congestion, including huge fees for a permit to even own a car and tolls to drive into and within a large part of downtown. This being Singapore, it's all done in the most hi-tech way using electronic road pricing (**ERP**): all Singapore cars have a gizmo installed that reads a stored-value card or EZ-Link card, from which the toll is deducted as you drive past an ERP gantry. **Parking** can be expensive, although at least every mall has a car park (displays all over town will tell you how many spaces are left in the vicinity) and many car parks offer the convenience of taking the fee off your ERP card, failing which you will have to purchase coupons from a licence booth, post office or shop. If you are still keen to rent a car, you can contact Avis/Budget (🌐 avis.com.sg) or Hertz (🌐 hertz.com), both of which have offices at Changi Airport – and note that in Singapore, you drive on the left.

Cycling

The Singapore government has been talking up the environmental and health benefits of cycling for the past few years, but has dragged its feet when it comes to delivering the infrastructure needed. Availability of dockless **bikes to rent** shrank in 2018 and prices rose after firms were hit with new licensing fees, meant to combat the problem of recklessly discarded bikes. More to the point, Singapore has spent decades investing in wide, modern roads suited to furious traffic; drivers' supremacy over roads remains unchallenged because of a dearth of cycle lanes and facilities such as traffic lights that would give cyclists a head start. For now, much of the commuter cycling seems to be taking place in the new towns, where residents can relatively easily pedal to their nearest MRT station.

That said, roads in and around the **Colonial District** (notably Bencoolen St and the newly pedestrianized Armenian St) are slowly being made more bike-friendly, and much of the area, plus the financial district, go **car-free** on designated Sundays (🅦 facebook.com/carfreesundaysg). Certain main roads downtown are more manageable than you might assume, if you keep to bus lanes outside rush hour. Much of the **Marina South** area, around Gardens by the Bay and the Marina Barrage, also lends itself to two wheels. If your hostel has bikes to rent, it is well worth seeking any advice they can give on suitable routes. Wherever you are, exercise caution on unfamiliar roads.

Where bikes really come into their own, in theory, is in out-of-town recreational or rural areas, such as Changi Beach and Pulau Ubin, both of which have bike rental outfits. Although much of Singapore is pancake flat, you'll need a tolerance for the muggy weather, and be prepared to get drenched if you're caught in a downpour.

A limited supply of bikes are available to hire. Rules and guidelines for cyclists were still evolving at the time of writing; for the latest, see 🅦 lta.gov. sg. Dockless bikes are available to rent from SG Bike (🅦 sgbike.com.sg) and Anywheel (🅦 anywheel.sg), among others. Find out more by downloading the mobile apps.

Organized tours and trips

Singapore is so easy to navigate that there's little reason to do an organized **tour**, which is perhaps why the offerings are limited. To engage a guide for a more personalized look at, say, Singapore's architecture or historical districts, try the directory at 🅦 guides-on-line.yoursingapore.com.

If you will be staying in Singapore for any length of time and have an interest in Singapore's wilder side, consider joining the Singapore Nature Society (🅦 nss.org.sg). This veteran group undertakes conservation projects and organizes guided walks for birdwatchers, plant lovers and so forth, sometimes in areas genuinely off the beaten track. Similarly, the Singapore Heritage Society (🅦 singaporeheritage.org) organizes regular talks on history and conservation as well as tours of buildings of architectural interest.

TRIPS AND OPERATORS

Betel Box ☎ 6247 7340, 🅦 betelboxtours.com. Run by the people behind the *Betel Box* hostel, these tours cover the usual downtown historic neighbourhoods plus the Geylang Serai area where the hostel is located, and aim to offer more context than you might get from rival offerings.

DuckTours ☎ 6338 6877, 🅦 ducktours.com.sg. Tour the Colonial District and Marina Bay on an amphibious vehicle; fun for families. Hourly 10am–6pm; $43/$23.

Geylang Adventures 🅦 geylangadventures.com. Night-time guided walks around Geylang, inevitably touching on the red-light character of the district but also taking in food, long-established businesses and the lives of the local migrant worker community, run by an activist who has been giving support to migrants for a number of years (see page 99).

Jane's Singapore Tours 🅦 janestours.sg. Some of the most thoughtfully constructed tours of the island you can find, from small-group walks to – their strong point – specialist architectural tours taking in "Tropical Tudor" colonial houses (with interior access) or modern buildings designed by the likes of Zaha Hadid.

The Original Singapore Walks ☎ 6325 1631, 🅦 singaporewalks.com. Guided walks of the historic downtown areas and Changi (the latter with a wartime focus), generally lasting 2hr 30min. From $38/18, although the Changi walks are much pricier.

Singapore River Cruise ☎ 6336 6111, 🅦 rivercruise.com.sg. See the city from river level in tarted-up versions of bumboats, taking In Marina Bay too. Probably the most popular trip with tourists; tickets from any of their booths en route. Evening trips that coincide with Marina Bay Sands' show Spectra (see page 80) cost more. Tours run every 15–20min from 9am to 10.30pm; 40min; $25/$15.

Trishaw Uncle Booth on Queen St, close to Bugis MRT ☎ 6337 7111, 🅦 trishawuncle.com.sg. This cooperative charges $39/$29 for a half-hour cycle-rickshaw ride around the immediate vicinity and Little India, or $49/$39 to go to Chinatown (45min). Daily 11am–8pm.

WaterB ☎ 6509 8988, 🅦 waterb.com.sg. Singapore River trips similar to those of Singapore River Cruise. Tickets online or from riverside booths. Roughly twice an hour from 9am to 10pm; 40min; $25/$15.

The media

In the 2018 World Press Freedom Index, issued by the pressure group Reporters Without Borders, Singapore was way down the rankings at no. 151 out of 180 nations – some distance below much poorer nations not exactly noted as exemplars of free speech, such as Afghanistan and Zimbabwe. The country boasts an abundance of newspapers, TV channels and radio stations in the four official languages, but hard-hitting, healthily sceptical coverage of domestic politics is in short supply.

The media are kept on their toes by a legal requirement that they must periodically renew their licence to publish. Most newspapers have actually been herded into a conglomerate in which the state has a major stake. Likewise radio and TV are dominated by Mediacorp, a company that is effectively state-owned; satellite dishes are banned, and, while many international broadcasters are available on cable, the sole cable provider is a company in which Mediacorp is a major shareholder.

The advent of **independent news websites** and **blogs** has, at least, been a breath of fresh air in recent years. However, even these can in theory be required, once their domestic audience reaches a certain threshold, to stump up a $50,000 "performance bond" to continue to operate – a provision that the government clearly wants in reserve to keep them in check. Singapore's leaders have a long history of winning defamation suits against foreign publications and local bloggers in the island's courts, and criticism of the integrity of the legal system is in itself criminalized as a contempt.

NEWSPAPERS, MAGAZINES AND ONLINE NEWS

Straits Times Ⓦ straitstimes.com. This venerable broadsheet was founded in 1845, though, sadly, its pedigree isn't matched by the candour of its journalism; not so dull when it comes to foreign news, however.

Today Ⓦ todayonline.com. A free e-paper from the state-owned broadcaster Mediacorp, *Today* is less bland than the *Straits Times* and carries worthwhile long-form analyses at the weekend.

The Online Citizen Ⓦ theonlinecitizen.com. Delivers a rather less sanguine picture of Singapore than you'll find in the mainstream media. Its days may be numbered as its editor was being tried for "criminal defamation" at the time of writing.

RADIO AND TV

BBC World Service Ⓦ bbcworldservice.com. 88.9FM, 24hr.
Channel News Asia Ⓦ channelnewsasia.com. Mediacorp's CNN-like diet of rolling TV news, via cable.
Channel 5 Ⓦ tv.toggle.sg/en/channel5. The main terrestrial channel for English programming, with plenty of imported shows.
Mediacorp Radio Ⓦ meradio.sg. Several English-language radio stations, including the speech-based 938 LIve (93.8FM) and Symphony (92.4FM) for classical music.

Health

The levels of hygiene and medical care in Singapore are higher than in much of the rest of Southeast Asia. Tap water is drinkable everywhere except at Pulau Ubin, where you should rely on bottled water.

No inoculations are required for visiting Singapore. However, it's a wise precaution to visit your doctor no later than four weeks before you leave to check that you are up to date with your polio, typhoid, tetanus and hepatitis A inoculations.

It pays to use mosquito repellent in Singapore, particularly if you're in a nature reserve or beach area. This isn't because Singapore is malarial – it isn't – but because mosquitoes may carry **dengue fever**, an illness that is seldom fatal but can be debilitating while it lasts. Note that repellents based on **DEET** are not available in Singapore, so if you prefer these you will have to buy them abroad.

The mosquito species that transmits dengue also spreads the **Zika virus**, and a number of cases have been reported in Singapore. Symptoms are mild, flu-like and can involve rashes, but the infection matters because it can affect foetal development. Pregnant women should therefore seek medical advice on whether to defer travelling to the country.

In general, **air quality** is not a major health issue. However, the region is vulnerable to what's euphemistically called "**the haze**", most recently in 2015 when peat forest fires in Indonesia burned out of control for months; major outdoor events in Singapore had to be cancelled and locals donned surgical masks to venture outside. If and when the haze recurs, people with respiratory health issues should monitor pollution levels using apps such as myENV (see page 33) and seek medical advice on whether to travel.

To avoid **sunburn** and **dehydration**, use high-factor sunscreens, drink plenty of water, and wear sunglasses and a hat. **Heatstroke** is more serious: it is indicated by fatigue or dizziness, a fast pulse and nausea, and can require hospitalization.

Medical services in Singapore are excellent, with staff almost everywhere speaking good English. **Pharmacies** are well stocked with familiar brand-name drugs, although only the largest outlets have pharmacists; the two main chains are Guardian and Watsons, both ubiquitous. If you need a prescription drug, you should see a doctor, at whose discretion the hospital's or clinic's own dispensary may be able to supply it.

Private clinics are found throughout the city, charging consultation fees of at least $50. You can find a list of dentists at Ⓦ yellowpages.com.sg. If you require emergency treatment, dial ☎ 995 or get to one of the **hospitals** listed below, all of which have **24-hour casualty/emergency facilities**. Don't forget to keep any receipts for insurance claim purposes.

HOSPITALS

Gleneagles Hospital 6A Napier Road ☎ 6575 7575, Ⓦ gleneagles.com. Private; by the Botanic Gardens.
Raffles Hospital 585 North Bridge Rd ☎ 6311 1111, Ⓦ rafflesmedicalgroup.com. A stone's throw from Bugis MRT; private.

Singapore General Hospital (SGH) Outram Rd ☎ 6222 3322, ⓦ sgh.com.sg. The main state-run hospital, near Outram Park MRT.

MEDICAL RESOURCES FOR TRAVELLERS

UK AND IRELAND
Hospital for Tropical Diseases Travel Clinic ☎ 020 3456 7891, ⓦ thehtd.org.
MASTA (Medical Advisory Service for Travellers Abroad) ☎ 0330 100 420, ⓦ masta.org. Travel clinics throughout the UK.
Travel Medicine Clinic Northern Ireland ☎ 028 9031 5220.
Tropical Medical Bureau Ireland ☎ 01 271 5200, ⓦ tmb.ie.

US AND CANADA
Canadian government travel health ⓦ travel.gc.ca/travelling/health-safety. Includes list of travel health centres.
CDC ⓦ cdc.gov/travel. Official US government health advice.
International Society for Travel Medicine ⓦ istm.org. Has a full list of travel health clinics.

AUSTRALIA AND NEW ZEALAND
The Travel Doctor ☎ 1300 658 844, ⓦ traveldoctor.com.au. Travel clinics in Australia and New Zealand.

SOUTH AFRICA
Netcare Travel Clinics ⓦ www.travelclinic.co.za.

Travel essentials

Costs

Singapore consistently makes headlines for coming at or near the top of lists of the world's most expensive cities, but that is somewhat misleading from the tourist point of view, as it's actually not hard to visit on a modest budget. If you stay in a dormitory accommodation, eat at food courts and hawker centres, eschew alcohol, buy a three-day Singapore Tourist Pass for unlimited use of public transport and confine yourself to sights with no admission fees, you can in principle get by on just £25/US$37 a day. Move up to a shared double room in a lower-mid-range hotel and treat yourself to one restaurant meal a day in addition to hawker food, and your budget is likely to climb to £60/US$90. Realistically, of course, you will need to allow additional outlay for **sightseeing**, which is the most elastic aspect of budgeting: major public museums levy fees of around just over £10/US$14, but some attractions are much more expensive; the various components of the zoo and Sentosa, for example, can burn a considerable hole in your pocket.

EMERGENCY NUMBERS
Police ☎ 999
(Freephone police hotline ☎ 1800 255 0000)
Ambulance and Fire Brigade ☎ 995

Note that Singapore has a 7 percent Goods and Services Tax **(GST)**, levied by all companies except small businesses. Prices in shops include GST, though refunds are possible for tourists (see page 162), but it's not uncommon for hotels and restaurants to leave it out, quoting prices with **"++"** at the end. In this case, the first plus indicates that they levy a ten percent **service charge** (as all mid-range and upmarket hotels and many restaurants do) and the second plus indicates GST levied on your bill plus the service charge, that is, a 17.7 percent surcharge in total.

Where two prices are given for a museum or other attraction in this book, the second price is for a **child ticket** unless otherwise stated.

Crime and personal safety

If you lose something in Singapore, you're more likely to have someone running after you to hand it than running away. Nevertheless, you shouldn't be complacent – muggings have been known to occur and theft from dormitories by other tourists is not unknown. Singapore's police, recognizable by their dark blue uniforms, keep a fairly low profile but are polite and helpful when approached.

Singapore is notorious for the **fines** that people who have committed various misdemeanours are liable to pay. Though these fines are seldom enforced – their severity has the intended deterrent effect on an already compliant public – it reveals something of the micro-managed state the island has become that, in principle, someone can be fined hundreds of dollars for smoking in certain public places and shopping malls, "jaywalking" (crossing a main road without using a designated pedestrian crossing or overhead bridge less than 50m away) and littering. Even the sale of **chewing gum** (with the exception of gum containing prescription medication) has been banned for the mess its improper disposal creates; it is, however, perfectly fine to bring in gum for your own use. That concession does not apply to **e-cigarettes** and **vaping liquids**: they are banned outright. On a related note, visitors should be aware that the legal age for **smoking** and buying tobacco products is rising: it is 19 in 2019, 20 in 2020 and will end up at 21 in 2021. It is also worth noting that most of the Orchard Road shopping precinct is a no smoking zone, and that there are some restrictions on consuming **alcohol** in public (see page 149).

Most importantly, the penalties for possessing or trafficking in **illegal drugs** are non-trivial; foreigners have been executed in the past. If you are arrested for drugs offences, you can expect little sympathy and that diplomatic intervention may not bear fruit.

Culture and etiquette

The rules of thumb often trotted out concerning behaviour in Asia apply much less to Singapore, given how Westernized the island can be. Nonetheless, appearances are deceptive, and it pays to bear a few points in mind to avoid causing offence.

Although Singaporeans are not especially prudish when it comes to **dress**, they may well frown upon public displays of affection, which aren't really the done thing. It's also not appropriate to pat children (or even friends, for that matter) on the head – the head being considered sacred in Buddhist culture. Conversely, the soles of the feet and, by extension, the soles of your shoes, are regarded as unclean, hence the need to **remove footwear** before stepping over the threshold when visiting people at home, at just about every guesthouse and before entering a temple or mosque.

One cliché about Asia that does still hold in Singapore concerns the importance of not losing face. A mistake or problem that might be regarded as trifling elsewhere might, here, be rather humiliating for the person responsible. The most likely situation in which visitors might need to bear this particular sensitivity in mind is when making a **complaint**. Rather than raising your voice and making a scene, it's best to state your case politely but firmly; this will help preserve the dignity of whomever you are complaining to, and improve the chances of a speedy resolution.

To avoid losing face yourself, note that when it comes to **punctuality**, the old Singaporean habit of nonchalantly showing up half an hour late for social and other engagements has been replaced by pretty stringent timekeeping, so be sure to set off early.

Finally, while there are few restrictions about what you can and can't **photograph**, staff at some temples and other places of worship take a dim view of snapping pictures on their premises; when in doubt, always ask.

Electricity

Singapore's **power supply** is at 230 V/50 Hz, and British-style sockets – taking plugs with three square pins – are the standard.

Entry requirements

Singapore reserves the term "visa" for travel permits that must be obtained in advanced. British nationals, and those of the Republic of Ireland, the US, Canada, Australia, New Zealand and South Africa, are simply given a **visit pass** upon arrival in Singapore. The duration of the pass is at the discretion of the immigration officer, but is usually at least thirty days. There is a formal procedure for extending it, but it's usually much easier to simply do a day-trip by a bus to Johor Bahru just inside Malaysia and be given a fresh pass on returning to Singapore.

For a list of nationalities that require visas, along with how to apply and how to extend a visit pass within Singapore, see Ⓦ ica.gov.sg. Full details of Singapore's embassies abroad are at Ⓦ mfa.gov.sg.

Customs

Upon entering Singapore from anywhere other than Malaysia, you can bring in up to three litres in total of spirits, wine and beer **duty-free**; duty is payable on all tobacco. For up-to-the-minute customs information, including how the alcohol allowance works in practice, go to Ⓦ customs.gov.sg. Under certain conditions, tourists can reclaim the Goods and Services Tax (GST) of seven percent on the cost of items they have bought in Singapore (see page 162).

Insurance

Before you set off, it's a good idea to arrange **travel insurance** to cover medical expenses as well as loss of luggage, cancellation of flights and so on. A typical policy usually provides cover for the **loss of baggage**, tickets and – up to a certain limit – cash or cheques, as well as cancellation or curtailment of your journey. Most of them exclude so-called dangerous sports unless an extra premium is paid. When securing baggage cover, make sure that the per-article limit will cover your most valuable possession. If you need to make a claim, you should keep receipts for medicines and medical treatment, and in the event that you have anything stolen, you must obtain an official statement from the police.

ROUGH GUIDES TRAVEL INSURANCE

Rough Guides has teamed up with **WorldNomads.com** to offer great travel insurance deals. Policies are available to residents of over 150 countries, with cover for a wide range of adventure sports, 24-hour emergency assistance, high levels of medical and evacuation cover and a stream of travel safety information. Roughguides.com users can take advantage of their policies online 24/7, from anywhere in the world – even if you're already travelling. And since plans often change when you're on the road, you can extend your policy and even claim online. Roughguides.com users who buy travel insurance with WorldNomads.com can also leave a positive footprint and donate to a community development project. For more information, go to ⓦroughguides.com/travel-insurance.

Internet access

Internet cafés have largely died out except in Little India, where a few cling on, charging as little as $2/hr. Most accommodation will have free wi-fi, though, and there is also the free **Wireless @SG/SGx** wi-fi service available at public buildings, including at most MRT platforms, plus some parts of Sentosa and several shopping malls. Unfortunately it's not always reliable, and signing up may require a code to be sent to your mobile phone, which doesn't always work. The core of Chinatown, around Smith Street, has its own public wi-fi network, once again not always reliable. Otherwise, you can always take advantage of some good deals offering tourists a local SIM card with a data allowance (see page 32).

Mail

Singapore's **postal system** is predictably efficient. The island has dozens of **post offices** (typically Mon–Fri 9.30am–6pm & Sat 9.30am–2pm). For more on the mail system, contact SingPost (☎1605, ⓦsingpost.com).

Maps

The most up-to-date road **maps** of Singapore are those at ⓦonemap.com (app available; see page 33), produced by the Singapore Land Authority. The maps are totally up to speed with the constant rebuilding and reshaping of Singapore, and also show real-time bus information. They do not, however, show small businesses like shops and restaurants; for those, you can try ⓦstreetdirectory.com – also locally produced, it is less up to date than it once was – and the usual mapping services run by the Silicon Valley giants. Otherwise, the maps in this book should be sufficient for most of your exploration, and you can back them up with free foldout maps available from the Singapore Tourism Board.

Money

Singapore's **currency** is the Singapore dollar, divided into 100 cents. Notes are issued in denominations of $2, $5, $10, $20, $50, $100, $500, $1000 and $10,000; coins are in denominations of 1, 5, 10, 20 and 50 cents, and $1. Note that two sets of coins are presently in use, the older of which is – annoyingly for anyone also visiting Malaysia – uncannily similar in size and feel to Malaysian coins of the same denominations. Exchange rates are generally around $1.80 to £1 and $1.35 to US$1. All dollar prices in this book are in local currency unless otherwise stated.

Singapore **banking hours** are generally Monday to Friday 9.30am to 4pm, Saturday 9.30am to 12.30pm. Outside of these hours, currency exchange is available at moneychangers, whose rates are comparable to those at banks. Major hotels also offer currency exchange, though don't expect their rates to be competitive.

ATMs are plentiful around Singapore, although note that the most common ones, operated by DBS/POSB, may not accept international cards as they focus on the local NETS debit system; other banks' machines take the usual international credit and debit cards, as do larger retailers and businesses. **Contactless** payments may be referred to by the card companies' own trade names – so a waiter may call a Visa contactless payment "WavePay".

Opening hours and public holidays

Shopping centres are open daily 10am to 9.30pm, while offices generally work Monday to Friday 8.30am to 5pm and sometimes on Saturday mornings. In general, Chinese temples open daily from 7am to around 6pm, Hindu temples 6am to noon and 5 to 9pm, and mosques 8.30am to noon and 2.30 to 4pm.

Singapore has numerous **public holidays**, reflecting its mix of cultures. Dates for some of these vary (see page 32).

It's worth noting the dates of local **school holidays**, at which time Sentosa and other places of interest to kids can be inordinately crowded: schools take a break for one week in March and September, throughout June and from mid-November until the end of December.

PUBLIC HOLIDAYS

January 1 New Year's Day
January/February Chinese New Year (2 days)
March/April Good Friday
May 1 Labour Day
May Vesak Day
May/June Hari Raya Puasa (the end of Ramadan; Eid al-Fitr)
August 9 National Day
July/August Hari Raya Haji (Eid al-Adha)
October/November Deepavali (Diwali)
December 25 Christmas Day

Phones

Local calls from private phones in Singapore cost next to nothing; calls from public payphones, of which few still exist, cost 10c for three minutes. Nearly all phone numbers have eight digits (except for a few free or premium-rate numbers, which start with 1800 or 1900 respectively). Land-line numbers always begin with 6 and mobile (cell) numbers with 8 or 9; there are no area codes.

Local **SIM cards** are available from any 7-11 store or shop run by the three major cell providers, Singtel, Starhub and M1; bring your passport to complete the registration process, and be aware that only **3G** or more recent devices will work in Singapore. Prices vary depending on what packages are being promoted – the cheapest prepaid SIMs can cost just a few dollars but will include very little data, while one with over a gigabyte might set you back closer to $10. Be aware that a generous data allowance may come with a catch, for instance, that part of it is only usable from midnight

---

DIALLING CODES

To call home **from Singapore**, dial ☎00 plus the relevant country code, then the number (omitting any initial zero).
Australia ☎61
Ireland ☎353
New Zealand ☎64
South Africa ☎27
UK ☎44
US & Canada ☎1

---

to 6am. Note also that with a Singapore SIM, there is a small charge for answering a call and receiving SMSes.

Sports

Singapore has a good range of sports facilities, including one of the best networks of **swimming** pools anywhere – almost every new town has its own open-air 50m pool, charging less than $2 for a swim. A full list of state-run sports centres appears at ⓦ myactivesg.com; some venues, including privately run facilities, are listed below.

SPORTS FACILITIES

Golf The Marina Bay Golf Course at 80 Rhu Cross ☎ 6345 7788, ⓦ mbgc.com.sg. Next to the Bay East garden, this is one of the most central golf facilities, and as such it tends to get booked up quickly – best to reserve a slot at least a couple of weeks in advance (mornings are less busy). Nine holes costs $100 on weekdays, including use of a golf buggy. Bus #11 from Stadium MRT.
Gyms The main private operators are Fitness First (ⓦ fitnessfirst. com.sg) and Pure Fitness (ⓦ pure-fitness.com.sg). Both have gyms downtown, though you will need to take out membership to use them.
Swimming The most conveniently located of the island's many Olympic-sized pools is at the Jalan Besar Swimming Complex on Tyrwhitt Rd (daily 8am–9.30pm, Wed from 2.30pm; ☎ 6293 9058; Lavender or Bendemeer MRT).
Tennis Farrer Park Tennis Centre, 1 Rutland Rd (daily 7am–7pm; ☎ 6299 4166; Farrer Park or Little India MRT); Kallang Tennis Centre, 8 Stadium Boulevard (daily 7am–10pm; ☎ 6348 1291; Mountbatten MRT).

Time

Singapore is eight hours ahead of Universal Time (GMT) year-round, and therefore two hours behind Sydney (when daylight saving time is not in effect there) and thirteen hours ahead of Eastern Standard Time.

Tipping

There are a few cases where you might want to tip someone offering you a personal service, for example a hairdresser or barber, but these are the exception rather than the rule – tipping is seldom the custom in Singapore. The cheaper restaurants don't expect tips (see page 130), nor do taxi drivers.

Tourist information

In a place as organized and cyber-savvy as Singapore, it's usually straightforward to get hold of up-to-date information of use to travellers.

SINGAPORE APPS

A variety of mobile apps can help you get the most out of your visit to Singapore. At the time of writing, all of the following were free and available for both iOS and Android devices.

Chope *Chope* is a Singlish term that roughly means to reserve a place by proxy – parking one of your acquaintances or possessions (typically pocket tissues) there. This app achieves the same result for restaurant reservations island-wide.

myENV Official weather forecasts, flood and dengue fever alerts, plus – so Singaporean – a hawker-centre locator.

MyTransport.SG Service information and journey planner for all of Singapore's transport system.

One Map Constantly updated home-grown maps, including real-time bus information and taxi ranks, but not covering small business.

Singapore Heritage Trails Guided walks for Singapore neighbourhoods old and new, though not always totally up to date.

Visit Singapore The Singapore Tourism Board's website in app form.

The **Singapore Tourism Board** (**STB**; information line Mon–Fri 9am–6pm; ☎1800 736 2000, ⓦvisitsingapore.com) has its main Visitor Centre at 216 Orchard Road, across from the 313@Somerset mall (daily 8.30am–9.30pm). STB's website is comprehensive and is also packaged for smartphones in the form of the Visit Singapore app. Three smaller information points are located on the ground floor of the ION Orchard mall (above Orchard MRT; daily 10am–10pm), behind the Buddha Tooth Relic Temple in Chinatown (daily 9am–9pm) and at 55 Bussorah St in Kampong Glam (daily 8am–6pm).

A number of **publications** offer entertainment listings plus reviews of restaurants and nightlife, the best of which is the free weekly *SGnow* (ⓦsg.asia-city.com). It's also worth consulting STB's free quarterly booklet *SG Insider* (online at their website), and the expat-geared free monthly *The Finder*, available at some downtown bars and restaurants and on ⓦthefinder.com.sg.

SINGAPORE TOURIST OFFICES ABROAD

UK First floor, Southwest House, 11a Regent St, London ☎020 7484 2710, ⓔstb_london@stb.gov.sg.
US 589 Fifth Avenue Suite 1702, New York ☎212 302 4861, ⓔnewyork@stb.gov.sg.
Australia Level 11, AWA Building, 47 York St, Sydney ☎02 9290 2888.

Travellers with disabilities

Singapore is a moderately **accessible** city for **travellers with disabilities**. Many hotels and even a handful of guesthouses make provision for disabled guests, though often there will be only one accessible room in the smaller establishments – always call ahead and book in plenty of time.

Getting around Singapore is relatively straightforward. MRT stations and trains are built to assist passengers using wheelchairs or with impaired sight or hearing. Around four-fifths of buses are now claimed to be wheelchair accessible, although some stops may not be suitable for wheelchair users. One annoyance for visually impaired people is that few buses have automated voice systems that call out the name or location of the next stop. If you can afford to use taxis all the time, so much the better; SMRT Taxis (☎6555 8888) has wheelchair-accessible vehicles that you can book.

The best people to talk to for pre-trip advice are the Disabled People's Association of Singapore (ⓦdpa.org.sg), which has a tourist FAQ section on its website, or the Singapore Tourism Board. You may also want to consult one local tour operator, the Asia Travel Group (ⓦasiatravelgroup.com.sg), which can arrange tours of the island in suitably equipped minibuses.

NATIONAL GALLERY

The Colonial District

On the north bank of the Singapore River is what might be termed the Colonial District, its core peppered with venerable reminders of British rule set back from the vast lawn that is the Padang. The area still feels like the centrepiece of downtown, even though modern edifices in the surroundings constantly pull focus from it. The district also has a viable claim to be the island's museums quarter, home to the lavish National Gallery, the National Museum, the Asian Civilisations Museum and Peranakan Museum. Also worth a look are verdant Fort Canning Hill, the dignified St Andrew's Cathedral and the diminutive Armenian Church of St Gregory the Illuminator. By far the most famous building hereabouts, however, is the grand old Raffles Hotel.

The Padang

Bounded by St Andrew's Rd to the west and Stamford Rd to the north • City Hall or Raffles Place MRT

The **Padang** ("field" in Malay) lies at the heart of what Singapore's city planners mundanely refer to as the civic district, a name that signally fails to evoke its status as the very essence of colonial Singapore. Earmarked by Raffles as a recreation ground shortly after his arrival, the Padang itself has never been encroached upon by speculators and it remains much as it was in 1907, when G.M. Reith wrote in his *Handbook to Singapore*: "Cricket, tennis, hockey, football and bowls are played on the plain". Once the last over of the day had been bowled, the Padang assumed a more social role: the image of Singapore's European community hastening to the corner once known as Scandal Point to catch up on the latest gossip is pure Somerset Maugham.

The brown-tiled roof and whitewashed walls of the **Singapore Cricket Club**, at the southwestern end of the Padang, have a nostalgic charm. Founded in the 1850s, the club was once the hub of colonial British society; today its membership is more diverse, though the place remains a fairly exclusive affair, catering not just to cricket but also to rugby and, less strenuously, bridge. Right at the opposite end of the Padang is another clubhouse, the grandiose **Singapore Recreation Club**, founded in 1883 by Eurasians who were barred from the Cricket Club by the prejudices of the era.

The National Gallery

1 St Andrew's Rd (main entrance on Coleman St) • Sat–Thurs 10am–7pm, Fri 10am–9pm • $20, temporary exhibitions ticketed separately • ☎ 6271 7000, ⓦ nationalgallery.sg • City Hall MRT

Taking up the Padang's entire west side, two of Singapore's most imposing colonial edifices are united by bridges to form the gigantic National Gallery. Some ten years in the making, it finally provides Singapore with what could become a world-class art showcase, hosting occasional tip-top travelling exhibitions. The permanent galleries focus on the art of Southeast Asia and are a mixed bunch, in truth, taking in romanticized jungle and colonial-era scenery, portraiture and more lacklustre contemporary conceptual art.

The DBS Singapore Gallery (City Hall)

To the right as viewed from the Padang is **City Hall**, witness to momentous events in the island's history. It was here – in a wood-panelled chamber, preserved on level 3 – that Japanese forces in Singapore surrendered to the Allies in 1945, an event announced from the Padang-facing steps by Louis Mountbatten, then supreme Allied commander in Southeast Asia. Fourteen years later, Lee Kuan Yew chose the self-same steps for his address at a rally celebrating self-government for Singapore.

The main entrance on Coleman Street brings you into the expansive foyer, one floor up from which is the **DBS Singapore Gallery**, kicking off with nineteenth-century watercolours of flora, fauna and landscapes. These are but a brief prelude, though, to the gallery's main theme of twentieth-century art by artists born or at some point resident in Singapore. There's a notable emphasis on the **Nanyang style** (*nanyang* being Mandarin for the South China Sea, which Chinese migrants to these parts would have sailed), an umbrella term for art featuring a fusion of Western and Chinese techniques. Two exemplars are **Xu Beihong**, whose work spanned portraiture and more traditional art (as in his *A Painting in the Spirit of Six Dynasties Poetry*, in which a man on a donkey looks enviously at another on a white charger, then back at a muscly peasant straining with a handcart); and **Georgette Chen**, whose elegant *Lotus in a Breeze* bears the hallmarks of Neo-impressionism, yet

1

was only painted in 1970. Even more recent, **Tan Choe Tee**'s 1981 *Singapore River* is proof – if any were needed – that today's river is but a shadow of its former fetid, chaotic self (see page 39).

The UOB Southeast Asia Gallery

Much smaller than City Hall but looming over it with its domed roof of green lead, Singapore's erstwhile **Supreme Court** was built in Neoclassical style in the 1930s on the site of the exclusive *Hotel de L'Europe*, whose drawing rooms apparently provided Somerset Maugham with inspiration for many of his Southeast Asian short stories. Today its courtrooms and chambers house the **UOB Southeast Asia Gallery**, which attempts to put a hotchpotch of art from the region into some kind of context. The exhibits may not grab you, but the architecture probably will: this is the most lovingly conserved part of the National Gallery, retaining black-and-white marbled floors and wooden ceilings. An internal domed **rotunda** still houses a collection of legal books,

THE COLONIAL DISTRICT

DRINKING AND NIGHTLIFE		SHOPPING	
Aura Sky Lounge	4	Arch	4
Crazy Elephant	5	Funan SG Mall	6
Timbre	1, 6	Museum Label	1
Wine Connection		Raffles City	2
Cheese Bar	2	Roxy Records	5
Zouk	3	True Blue Shoppe	3

EATING		ACCOMMODATION	
Cedele	4	The Capitol Kempinski	3
Coriander Leaf	2	Fort Canning	4
The English House	5	Peninsula Excelsior	5
Flutes	1	Robertson Quay Hotel	6
Privé	6	Swissôtel The Stamford	4
Sushi Tei	3	YMCA	1

while erstwhile **holding cells** for detainees can be glimpsed at the small Parliament Place entrance.

Amid all the art, look out for the entrance – opposite the rotunda doorway – to **Law of the Land**, a small but remarkable exhibition of documents from Singapore's history. Taking pride of place is a copy of the 1819 treaty between Stamford Raffles and Johor's Malay rulers, allowing the British to set up shop on the island, plus two floridly lettered manuscripts from September 1963; one declares that Singapore "shall be forever a part" of the newly formed federation of Malaysia, while the other proclaims the birth of the new country. Starkly typewritten is the signed draft treaty nearby, signalling Singapore's divorce from Malaysia in August 1965.

The roof garden

By day or by night (when bars like *Aura* remain open; see page 149), it's worth heading up to the National Gallery's **roof** for a fine **panorama** out over the Padang, with *Marina Bay Sands* directly opposite; you can even peer down to City Hall's foyer through the glass-floored decorative pools. Turn around and face west to take in the flying-saucer-like crown of the Norman Foster-designed **New Supreme Court** on North Bridge Road, which opened in 2006.

The Victoria Theatre and Concert Hall

11 Empress Place • ☎ 6908 8810, ⓦ vtvch.com • Raffles Place or City Hall MRT

Across from the southern end of the Padang are two more fine examples of colonial architecture, the **Victoria Theatre** and, to the right, the **Victoria Concert Hall** (also called the Victoria Memorial Hall). The former was completed in 1862 as Singapore's town hall, while the concert hall was added in 1905. The two venues now boast plenty of glass walls and ceiling panels, added as part of a major refit. Both also host many prestigious cultural events.

During the Japanese occupation, the concert hall's clock tower was altered to Tokyo time, while the statue of Raffles in front of it narrowly escaped being melted down. Sent to the National Museum, it was then hidden by the newly installed Japanese curator, who reported it destroyed. The statue has long been returned to its original spot, but a copy (in white) attracts more attention by the river nearby at **Raffles' landing site** where, in January 1819, the great man apparently took his first steps on Singapore soil.

The old and new parliament houses

Old Parliament House/The Arts House 1 Old Parliament Lane • Daily 10am–10pm • ☎ 6332 6900, ⓦ theartshouse.sg • **New Parliament House** 1 Parliament Place • To watch a debate check ⓦ parliament.gov.sg • Raffles Place or City Hall MRT

The dignified white Victorian building up Parliament Lane, somewhat overshadowed by the Victoria Concert Hall, is the **Old Parliament House**. Designed by Singapore's pre-eminent colonial architect, the Irishman George Drumgoole Coleman, it was originally built as a home for a rich merchant in 1827, so is probably the oldest extant building in the country. The bronze elephant in front was a gift to Singapore from King Rama V of Thailand (whose father was the king upon whom *The King and I* was based) after his trip to the island in 1871 – the first foreign visit ever made by a Thai monarch. Relieved of its legislative duties, the building is now home to a contemporary arts centre called **The Arts House**. Backing on to it is the rather soulless **New Parliament House**, where it is possible to watch parliamentary debates in progress.

1

Asian Civilisations Museum

1 Empress Place • Sat–Thurs 10am–7pm, Fri 10am–9pm • $8/$4 (half-price Fri after 7pm); prices may alter during special exhibitions •
☎ 6332 7798, ⓦ acm.org.sg • Raffles Place or City Hall MRT

The **Empress Place Building**, very close to the mouth of the Singapore River, is a robust Neoclassical structure named for Queen Victoria and completed in 1865. Once government offices, it is now home to the fine **Asian Civilisations Museum**, tracing Asia's many and varied cultures.

The museum's glassy riverside extension is also its highlight, housing the **Tang Shipwreck Gallery**, a dazzling trove of ninth-century Chinese goods purchased by Singapore after being commercially salvaged – to the ire of some archeologists, concerned about scientific rigour and profits being made – from a sunken Arab dhow discovered off the coast of Sumatra in 1998. There's a profusion of ceramic bowls, mostly stoneware, but what really sticks in the memory are the few specimens of gold and silverware: cups, dishes decorated with swastikas or birds, and flasks for wine. Incidentally, a recreation of the dhow can be seen at Sentosa's Maritime Experiential Museum (see page 114). Next door, a maritime trade gallery continues the theme with fine specimens of luxury goods that would often have been exported, such as Indian chests inlaid with mother-of-pearl.

Much of level two is taken up by galleries of **religious artefacts**, including some quirky examples of cross-cultural pollination such as a lacquered Chinese wood cabinet with a crucifix at its centre. Also here is the underwhelming **Chinese Scholar Gallery**, a collection of antiques that an imperial scholar might have at hand. Its centrepiece is an ornate **opium bed** of a kind commissioned by merchants with intellectual aspirations, although you wonder how they would ever have got any studying done while under the influence.

Cavenagh Bridge

The elegant suspension struts of **Cavenagh Bridge** are one of the Colonial District's irresistible draws. Named after Major General Orfeur Cavenagh, governor of the Straits Settlements from 1859 to 1867, the bridge was constructed in 1869 by Indian convict labourers using imported Glasgow steel. Times change, butnot necessarily here, where a police sign maintains: "The use of this bridge is prohibited to any vehicle of which the laden weight exceeds 3cwt and to all cattle and horses." Cross the footbridge to reach Singapore's former General Post Office, now the luxurious *Fullerton Hotel* (see page 125), with Boat Quay (see page 72) and Raffles Place (see page 75) just a couple of minutes' walk away.

Esplanade Park

Connaught Drive, on the east side of the Padang • Unrestricted access • City Hall, Esplanade or Raffles Place MRT

Esplanade Park feels somewhat overlooked today, though back in 1907 G.M. Reith recommended it as "a strip of green along the sea wall, with a footpath, which affords a cool and pleasant walk in the early morning and afternoon". Even a few decades ago, it drew flocks of locals to its seafront promenade, **Queen Elizabeth Walk**. Now it's the fresh water of man-made Marina Bay that's on view, and the vista is slightly spoilt by the new Esplanade Bridge in the foreground.

The park itself has a handful of minor monuments, the most prominent of which is the central **Cenotaph**, commemorating the dead of World War I and somewhat reminiscent of the Cenotaph in central London. Rather more attractive is the cast-iron **Tan Kim Seng fountain** to the north, erected in tribute to the wealthy merchant who helped fund the island's first water treatment works. A delightful blue-and-white assembly of Roman mythological figures, it looks like it could have been purloined from a minor central European palace, though it was actually manufactured in northern England in the 1880s.

St Andrew's Cathedral

St Andrew's Rd, with a small visitor centre on North Bridge Rd · Mon–Sat 9am–5pm; free volunteer-led tours Mon–Fri 10.30am & 3pm · ☎ 6337 6104, ⓦ cathedral.org.sg · City Hall or Esplanade MRT

Gleaming even brighter than the rest is the final building of note close to the Padang, **St Andrew's Cathedral**. Built in high-vaulted, neo-Gothic style using Indian convict labour, it was the third church on this site and was consecrated by Bishop Cotton of Calcutta on January 25, 1862. The exterior walls were plastered using Madras *chunam* – an unlikely composite of eggs, lime, sugar and shredded coconut husks which shines brightly when smoothed – while the small cross behind the pulpit was crafted from two fourteenth-century nails salvaged from the ruins of Coventry Cathedral in England, bombed during World War II. During the Japanese invasion, St Andrew's became a makeshift hospital; today, it remains a pleasantly understated period piece with, oddly, closed-circuit TVs which allow the whole congregation a close-up view of proceedings at the altar. Scrutinize the three stained-glass windows in the apse to spot Stamford Raffles' coat of arms, near the top of the central one.

Raffles City

252 North Bridge Rd · City Hall or Esplanade MRT

Dwarfing St Andrew's Cathedral is **Raffles City**, a huge development occupying a block between Bras Basah and Stamford roads and comprising two hotels – one of which is the 73-storey **Swissôtel The Stamford** – and a shopping mall. The complex was designed by Chinese-American architect I.M. Pei (the man behind the Louvre's glass pyramid) and required the highly contentious demolition of the venerable Raffles Institution, a school established by Raffles himself and built in 1835 by George Drumgoole Coleman. The *Swissôtel* holds an annual vertical marathon, in which hardy athletes

THE SINGAPORE RIVER

Little more than a creek, the Singapore River became the main artery of Singapore's growing trade in the nineteenth century. **Bumboats** – traditional houseboat-sized vessels, with eyes painted on their prows as if to see where they were going – ferried coffee, sugar and rice to warehouses called **godowns**, where coolies loaded and unloaded sacks. In the 1880s the river itself was so busy it was practically possible to walk from one side to the other without getting your feet wet. Of course bridges were built across it as well, mostly endearingly compact and old-fangled, apart from the modern Esplanade Bridge at the mouth of the river.

Walk beside the river today, all sanitized and packed with trendy restaurants and bars, some occupying the few surviving godowns, and it's hard to imagine that in the 1970s this was still a working river. It was also filthy, and the river's current status as one of the leading nightlife centres of Singapore ultimately stems from a massive clean-up campaign launched back then, which saw cargo traffic moved west to new facilities at Pasir Panjang within the space of a few years. It succeeded admirably, but as an old exhibition at the Asian Civilisations Museum put it: "[the project] also washed away … [the river's] vibrant history as a trade waterway. Its newly cleaned waters now appeared characterless and sterile." Both this museum, the National Museum and the Singapore Maritime Gallery (see page 45) have small displays covering the river's evolution, while various **boat rides** and water taxis offer a view of the restaurants and city skyline from down at water level (see page 27).

1

SIR STAMFORD RAFFLES

Despite living and working in a period of imperial arrogance and land-grabbing, Sir Stamford Raffles maintained an unfailing concern for the welfare of the people under his governorship, and a conviction that British colonial expansion was for the general good. He believed Britain to be, as Jan Morris says in her introduction to Maurice Collis's biography of Raffles, "the chief agent of human progress… the example of fair Government".

Fittingly for a man who was to spend his life roaming the globe, Thomas Stamford Raffles was born at sea on July 6, 1781 on the *Ann*, whose master was his father Captain Benjamin Raffles. By his 14th birthday, the young Raffles was working as a clerk for the **East India Company** in London, his schooling curtailed because of his father's debts. Even at this early age, Raffles' ambition and self-motivation was evident as he stayed up through the night to study and developed a hunger for knowledge which would later spur him to learn Malay, amass a vast treasure-trove of natural history artefacts and write his two-volume *History of Java*.

Raffles' diligence and hard work showed through in 1805, when he was chosen to join a team going out to Penang, then being developed as a British entrepôt. Once in Southeast Asia, he enjoyed a meteoric rise: by 1807 he was named **chief secretary to the governor in Penang**. Upon meeting Lord Minto, the governor general of the East India Company in India, in 1810, Raffles was appointed **secretary to the governor general in Malaya**, a promotion quickly followed by the **governorship of Java** in 1811. Raffles' rule of Java was liberal and compassionate, his economic, judicial and social reforms transforming an island bowed by Dutch rule.

Post-Waterloo European rebuilding saw the East Indies returned to the Dutch in 1816 – to the chagrin of Raffles. He was transferred to the **governorship of Bencoolen** in Sumatra, but not before he had returned home for a break. While in England he met his second wife, Sophia Hull (his first, Olivia, had died in 1814), and was knighted. Raffles and Sophia sailed to Bencoolen in early 1818. Once in Sumatra, Raffles found the time to study the region's flora and fauna as tirelessly as ever, discovering **Rafflesia arnoldii** – "perhaps the largest and most magnificent flower in the world" – on a field trip. By now, Raffles felt strongly that Britain should establish a base in the Straits of Melaka and in late 1818 he was given leave to pursue this possibility. The following year he duly sailed to the southern tip of the Malay Peninsula, where his securing of **Singapore** was a daring masterstroke of diplomacy.

For a man whose name is inextricably linked with Singapore, Raffles spent a remarkably short time on the island. His last visit was in 1822; by August 1824, he was back in England. Awaiting news of a possible pension award from the East India Company, he spent his time founding the London Zoo. But the new life Raffles had planned never materialized. Days after hearing that a Calcutta bank holding £16,000 of his capital had folded, his pension application was refused; worse still, the Company was demanding £22,000 for overpayment. Three months later, in July 1826, the brain tumour that had caused Raffles headaches for several years took his life. He was buried at Hendon in north London with no memorial stone – the vicar had investments in slave plantations in the West Indies and was unimpressed by Raffles' friendship with the abolitionist William Wilberforce. Only in 1832 was Raffles commemorated, with a statue in Westminster Abbey.

attempt to run up to the top floor in as short a time as possible: the current record stands at under seven minutes. Lifts transport lesser mortals to admire the view from the sumptuous bars and restaurants on the top floors.

CHIJMES

30 Victoria St • ⓦ chijmes.com.sg • City Hall, Bras Basah or Esplanade MRT

Two venerable Catholic institutions lie almost immediately north of St Andrew's Cathedral, although one of them no longer serves its original purpose. What was the Convent of the Holy Infant Jesus is now a complex of bars and restaurants named **CHIJMES** (pronounced "chimes"), popular with expats. Its neo-Gothic husk, complete with courtyards, fountains and a sunken forecourt, made it an obvious choice for the

1

filming of the wedding scenes in *Crazy Rich Asians*. Look out for the Gate of Hope on its Victoria Street flank, where nuns once took in foundlings.

Cathedral of the Good Shepherd

Corner of Queen St and Bras Basah Rd • Mon–Fri 8am–9pm, Sat & Sun 7am–9pm; Heritage Gallery daily 9am–10pm • ☎ 6337 2036, ⓦ cathedral.catholic.sg • Bras Basah or City Hall MRT

Opened on June 6, 1847, the Catholic **Cathedral of the Good Shepherd** is more modest in scale than its Anglican rival and yet more refined. Neoclassically styled, the building has regained its lovely chequerboard flooring and white, cream and gold colour scheme, thanks to a hugely expensive recent restoration. Upstairs, the 1912 organ is similarly immaculate, having been completely overhauled by specialists from the Philippines. An annexe houses the Heritage Gallery, a mini-museum of the cathedral's history.

The Civilian War Memorial

In the green space east of Beach Rd and north of the Padang • Esplanade or City Hall MRT

The open plot east of Raffles City is home to four 70m-high white columns, nicknamed "the chopsticks" but actually the **Civilian War Memorial**, commemorating those who died during the Japanese occupation. Each column represents one of Singapore's four main ethnic groups – the Chinese, Malays, Indians and Eurasians – while beneath the structure are remains reinterred from unmarked wartime graves around the island.

Raffles Hotel

1 Beach Rd • ☎ 6337 1886, ⓦ raffleshotel.com • Esplanade or City Hall MRT

Though utterly dwarfed by the modern metal-clad towers of the South Beach development opposite (see page 60), **Raffles Hotel** has lost none of its legendary charm. With its lofty halls, restaurants, bars and peaceful gardens, it was practically a byword for colonial indulgence, prompting Somerset Maugham to remark that it "stood for all the fables of the exotic East". Oddly, though, this most inherently British of hotels started life as a modest seafront bungalow belonging to an Arab trader. In 1886, the property was bought by the Armenian Sarkies brothers, who came to control a trio of quintessentially colonial lodgings: the *Raffles*; the *Eastern and Oriental* in Penang, Malaysia; and the *Strand* in Rangoon, Burma.

The brothers commissioned Regent Bidwell of local architecture firm Swan & MacLaren to convert the house into what became the *Raffles Hotel*, which opened for business on December 1, 1887. Despite a guest list heavy with politicians and film stars over the years, the hotel is proudest of its literary connections: Joseph Conrad, Rudyard Kipling, Herman Hesse, Somerset Maugham, Noël Coward and Günter Grass all stayed here, and Maugham is said to have penned many of his Asian tales in the garden.

The hotel's heyday was during the first three decades of the last century, when it established its reputation for luxury – it was the first building in Singapore with electric lights and fans. In 1902, according to a (probably apocryphal) tale, the last tiger to be killed on the island was supposedly shot here. Thirteen years later bartender Ngiam Tong Boon created another *Raffles* legend, the Singapore Sling cocktail (still served for the princely sum of $37).

During World War II, the hotel served as officers' quarters for the Japanese, then as a transit camp for liberated Allied prisoners following the war's end. A subsequent slow decline earned it the soubriquet "grand old lady of the East", and the hotel was little more than a shabby tourist diversion when it was declared a national monument in 1987. After a hugely expensive facelift, the hotel reopened in 1991 with a new extension that some felt diluted its character.

History aside, the hotel's Beach Road facade remains one of Singapore's most arresting sights, beautifully whitewashed, elegantly proportioned and flanked by palms and frangipani trees. Inside, the grounds still give a sense of being at one remove from the hubbub of the city, and with several restaurants and bars to choose from, notably the *Tiffin Room* (see page 132) and the *Long Bar* (see page 150), you don't need to be staying here to partake of the hotel's atmosphere.

Hill and Coleman streets

A couple of blocks west of the Padang, **Hill Street** leads south along the eastern side of Fort Canning Park to the river. The brash building at no. 47 with the striking Chinese-temple-style roof is the **Singapore Chinese Chamber of Commerce**, dating from 1964 though remodelled since. Along its facade are two large panels, each depicting intricately crafted porcelain dragons flying from the sea up to the sky.

The Armenian Church of St Gregory the Illuminator

60 Hill St • Daily 9am–6pm • Ⓦ armeniansinasia.org • City Hall, Bras Basah or Clarke Quay MRT

Possibly the second-oldest building in Singapore, the **Armenian Church of St Gregory the Illuminator** was designed by George Drumgoole Coleman and completed in 1835. It's an appealingly intimate affair, with four porticos and a white circular interior that holds a marble altar topped by a painting of the Last Supper. Also on display is a framed photo of the few dozen Armenians who lived in Singapore in 1917, for whom this tiny church would have been room enough.

Among the handful of graves in the tranquil garden is that of Agnes Joaquim, a nineteenth-century Armenian resident of Singapore. Today she is remembered as the person after whom the national flower, the delicate, purple *Vanda Miss Joaquim* orchid is named; she discovered it in her garden and had it registered at the Botanic Gardens.

Central Fire Station

Junction of Coleman and Hill streets • Galleries Tues–Sun 10am–5pm • Free • Ⓣ 6332 2996 • City Hall, Bras Basah or Clarke Quay MRT

The **Central Fire Station**, a stone's throw from the Armenian Church, across Coleman Street, is a pleasing red-and-white-striped edifice. When it was built in 1908, the watchtower was the tallest building in the area and made it easy for firemen to scan for fires. Part of the station is now taken up by the **Civil Defence Heritage Gallery**, which traces the history of fire-fighting in Singapore from the formation of the first Voluntary Fire Brigade in 1869. The galleries display old helmets, extinguishers and steam fire engines, all beautifully restored. Of more interest, though, are the accounts of some of the island's most destructive fires. One, not far from Chinatown in 1961, ripped through a shanty district destroying sixteen thousand homes, a disaster which led directly to a public-housing scheme that spawned Singapore's new towns.

The Freemasons' Hall

23A Coleman St, behind the Central Fire Station • City Hall, Bras Basah or Clarke Quay MRT

Singapore's compact **Freemasons' Hall** features a proud Palladian facade bearing the masonic compass-and-square motif. The building dates from the 1870s and remains in use. It's worth noting that Stamford Raffles himself was apparently a mason.

1

Singapore Philatelic Museum

23B Coleman St • Dailiy 10am–7pm • $8/$6 • ☎ 6337 3888, ⓦ spm.org.sg • City Hall, Bras Basah or Clarke Quay MRT

The **Singapore Philatelic Museum** is clearly a niche destination, but manages to use its stamp collections imaginatively to highlight facets of the multicultural history and heritage of Singapore. It also hosts special exhibitions with a stamp connection, however tenuous; one recent example featured stamps and other ephemera connected with the famed tale *The Little Prince* and its author, Antoine de Saint-Exupéry.

Peranakan Museum

39 Armenian St • Closed until 2021 for a major revamp • ☎ 6332 7591, ⓦ peranakanmuseum.org.sg • City Hall, Bras Basah or Clarke Quay MRT

Dating from 1910, the beautifully ornamented three-storey building just west of Hill Street was once the venerable Tao Nan School, and is now the worthy **Peranakan Museum**. Once reopen in 2021, it should whet your appetite not only for the Baba House (see page 74) but also the Peranakan heritage of the Katong area (see page 99).

Singaporean Peranakans are **Baba-Nonyas** (see page 44), and the galleries focus on their possessions (theirs was always a largely material culture) and customs, such as the traditional twelve-day wedding – needless to say, hopelessly impractical today. Other typically Peranakan items to look out include *kamcheng*, colourful Chinese-made storage jars; *kerosang*, brooches used as clothes-fasteners; furniture inlaid with mother-

---

THE BABA-NONYAS

It's often glibly said that the **Baba-Nonyas** are the product of Chinese/Malay intermarriage, though this ignores the practical difficulties of taking a Muslim spouse without converting to Islam. What can be said with confidence is that they are a Chinese subgroup with deep roots in the Malay Peninsula and a distinctive hybrid culture. Male migrants, arriving from China from at least the sixteenth century onwards, married local women, some Malay, others from the region's various communities such as Orang Asli (the original inhabitants of the Malay Peninsula) or ethnic Thais. Eventually their descendants became a community in their own right – the menfolk known as **Babas**, the women **Nonyas** (or Nyonyas) – although confusingly the terms **Straits Chinese** and **Peranakan** are also used for both sexes, and Peranakan can refer to other mixed-race groups such as the partly Indian Chitty people of Melaka in Malaysia.

The Baba-Nonyas clung to aspects of Chinese culture while absorbing local influences, most notably in their dress – Nonyas wore Malay-style batik clothes and were renowned for beadwork such as slippers – and cooking (see page 142). Their **language** was also distinctive: many spoke Chinese dialects, notably Hokkien, as well as their own Malay dialect. With British rule, they mastered English too, and Baba-Nonyas became the bridge between Westerners and the *sinkeh*, the newly arrived Chinese migrants. Many *sinkeh* married Nonyas and the resulting family businesses flourished; choice residential areas such as Katong (see page 99) were packed with Peranakan mansions.

It wasn't to last. In the interwar years, the British loosened the immigration rules to allow migrants to bring their wives with them, and earlier migrants were, by then, often giving their children a Western education. Now the Baba-Nonyas became far less useful to the new blood from China, who viewed them with disdain as being not properly Chinese. They were even labelled "OCBC" after the name of a local bank, though in their case the acronym meant "*orang Cina bukan Cina*", Malay for "Chinese [yet] not Chinese". In a country where ethnicity is stated on everyone's ID cards, it's worth noting that "Peranakan" isn't deemed a valid category – meaning the Baba-Nonyas were inevitably lumped together with the wider Chinese community and became subsumed into it. Although their traditions have largely died out, they are at least now showcased in museums in both Singapore and Malaysia, and their culinary heritage shows no signs of going away.

of-pearl; beautiful repoussé silverware, including betel-nut sets used to prepare mildly psychoactive betel nuts and leaves for chewing in bygone days; and *pintu pagar*, tall, carved swing doors used at the entrance to a house.

Stamford Road

From the northern edge of the Padang, **Stamford Road** zigzags its way past the Colonial District's most important sight, the National Museum, passing three grand surviving examples of colonial commercial architecture: the 1930s **Capitol Building**, at the corner of North Bridge Road; **Stamford House**, built in 1904 at the corner of Hill Street; and the red-and-white **Vanguard House**, completed in 1908 at the corner of Armenian Street. Each has had an illustrious past – the Capitol Building as a cinema, Stamford House as an annexe to the *Raffles Hotel* (they were designed by the same architect) and as a shopping centre, and Vanguard House as the headquarters of the Methodist Publishing House, then much later as home to the flagship store of the MPH bookshop chain. Today the Capitol and Stamford House have been fused and transformed into a mall and luxury hotel, while various unremarkable shops roost at Vanguard House.

The National Museum

93 Stamford Rd • Daily 10am–7pm • $15/$10 • ☎ 6332 3659, ⓦ nationalmuseum.sg • Bras Basah, Dhoby Ghaut or Bencoolen MRT

You can't fail to spot the eye-catching dome, seemingly coated with silvery fish scales, of the **National Museum of Singapore**. Its forerunner, the Raffles Museum and Library, opened in 1887 and soon acquired a reputation for its botanical and zoological specimens, now relocated to the marvellous Lee Kong Chian Natural History Museum (see page 110). In the 1960s, following independence, the place was renamed the National Museum and subsequently altered its focus to local history, an emphasis retained after a 2005 extension saw the original Neoclassical building gain a hangar-like rear counterpart larger than itself. The exhibits were completely overhauled then, a process repeated to coincide with Singapore's fiftieth anniversary celebrations in 2015. It hasn't been an altogether successful affair. A lack of significant artefacts is always going to be an issue for such a young country, but there are few items of as much import as the documents on display at the National Gallery (see page 35), for instance, and its scale aside, this can feels like a provincial museum with a parochial mindset.

Level 1

Almost the entire lower level of the museum is taken up by the **Singapore History Gallery**, which provides an adequate primer of its subject. Initially the focus is on Temasek, as the Malays called precolonial Singapore. Look out here for the mysterious **Singapore Stone**, all that survives of an inscribed monolith which once stood near where the *Fullerton* hotel is today, though more memorable is the beautiful gold **jewellery** excavated at Fort Canning in 1928 and thought to date from the fourteenth century.

With the colonial era come portraits of Stamford Raffles, his sidekicks and later officials, most notably one of **Frank Swettenham**, governor of the Straits Settlements in the 1900s, by the American artist John Singer Sargent. There's also a look at the lives of colonial housewives, including an amusing Malay phrasebook for transacting with servants, which has phrases such as "I want to inspect the kitchen to-day" and "This meat is tainted!".

A replica Japanese tank heralds what is perhaps the most interesting section for foreigners, dealing with the British collapse during **World War II**, and the massacres of Operation Sook Ching (see page 173). Also interesting are the displays on postwar politics, including the abortive marriage with Malaysia. From today's perspective it seems hard to believe that up until around the early 1970s, much was still up for grabs in Singapore politics, and the museum deserves credit for devoting space to former opposition figures. Thereafter things degenerate into a forgettable wander through the rapid development of recent decades.

Level 2

Upstairs are four galleries of varying quality; the best is the **Modern Colony Gallery**, kitted out in Art Deco style to explore the prosperous Singapore of the 1920s. Also worth a look is **Desire and Danger**, a gallery featuring flora and fauna artworks famously commissioned by William Farquhar – one or two are also on display at the National Gallery (see page 35) – with a few biological specimens on show and even odour-dispensing jars for an even more back-to-nature experience. Then there is **Surviving Syonan**, on the privations of the Japanese occupation, and – least successful of the lot – **Voices of Singapore**, a collection of old cinema posters and other cultural ephemera.

Fort Canning Park

Entrances include River Valley Rd, Hill St or from behind the National Museum • Unrestricted access • Dhoby Ghaut, Bras Basah or Fort Canning MRT

When Raffles first caught sight of Singapore, the hill now taken up by **Fort Canning Park** was known as Bukit Larangan (Forbidden Hill). Malay annals tell of the five ancient kings who ruled the island from here six hundred years ago, and unearthed artefacts prove it was inhabited as early as the fourteenth century. The last of the kings, Sultan Iskandar Shah, reputedly lies here, and it was out of respect for – and fear of – his spirit that the Malays decreed the hill off-limits. Singapore's first Resident (colonial administrator), William Farquhar, displayed typical colonial tact by promptly having what the British called Government Hill cleared and erecting a bungalow, Government House, on the summit; the fateful Anglo-Dutch treaty of 1824 was probably signed here. The building was replaced in 1859 by a fort named after Viscount Charles Canning, governor-general of India, but only a gateway, guardhouse and adjoining wall remain.

The park is packed with mature trees offering welcome shade (but also putting paid to views over the Singapore River), beneath which nestle more substantial reminders of colonial rule. The building in the northwest was constructed in the 1920s for British army administrators and was later used as a military training academy; these days it is occupied by the swish *Hotel Fort Canning*. More centrally placed and just as squat and sturdily built is the **Fort Canning Centre**, a former British barracks. By the time you read this, an exhibition on the hill's history should be up and running here, and the park itself will feature new gardens and archeological displays – all to mark the bicentenary of Singapore's founding.

The Battle Box

Cox Terrace • Ticket office daily 9.30am–5.30pm; timings for compulsory tours online • Standard 1hr 15min tour $18/$9 • ☎ 6338 6133, ⓦ battlebox.com.sg

At the northern end of the Fort Canning Centre, a path leads to the 1939 bunkers from which the Allied war effort in Singapore was masterminded. Now restored and called the **Battle Box**, it holds dioramas bringing to life the events leading up to the British surrender in February 1942.

The keramat and Raffles Terrace

At Fort Canning Centre, turn left to reach a **keramat** ("auspicious place"), the supposed site of Iskandar Shah's grave, which attracts a trickle of local Muslims. Continue round the hill and you meet the staircase from Hill Street at **Raffles Terrace**, where there are replicas of a colonial flagstaff and a lighthouse – the hill was the site of an actual lighthouse that functioned up until the 1950s.

1

Along River Valley Road

Fort Canning Park's southern boundary is defined by **River Valley Road**, which skirts below the park from Hill Street. At its eastern end is the **Old Hill Street Police Station**, with shuttered windows in striking bright colours. It is home to two government ministries, including that for culture, which perhaps explains why it also features a handful of private art galleries.

G-MAX and GX5

Daily 11am till late • Each ride $45 • ☎ 6338 1146, ⓦ gmaxgx5.sg • Clarke Quay or Fort Canning MRT

Close to the Coleman Bridge is **G-MAX**, billed as a "reverse bungy jump" though it's really more like a metal cage suspended from steel cables, allowing several screaming passengers to be tossed around in the air. Neither it nor the adjacent **GX5** "extreme swing" are best sampled if you've just indulged at one of the many bars and restaurants nearby.

Clarke Quay

3 River Valley Rd • ⓦ clarkequay.com.sg • Clarke Quay or Fort Canning MRT

The nineteenth-century godowns of **Clarke Quay**, painted in gaudy colours and housing flashy eating and nightlife venues, feel about as authentic as the translucent plasticky canopy built over them for shelter; nearby Boat Quay (see page 72) feels more down-to-earth even when at its busiest. Further up the north bank is **Robertson Quay**, offering more of the same, though more pleasant and less hectic.

Chettiar Temple

15 Tank Rd, off River Valley Rd • Daily roughly 8.30am–12.30pm & 5.30–8.30pm • Free • ☎ 6737 9393, ⓦ sttemple.com • Fort Canning MRT or bus #143 from Orchard Rd or Chinatown

Just west of Fort Canning Park and close to Robertson Quay is what is often still called the **Chettiar Temple** (officially the Sri Thendayuthapani Temple). Featuring a large, attractive gopura, it was built in 1984 to replace a nineteenth-century temple constructed by Indian *chettiars* (moneylenders) and is dedicated mainly to the worship of the Hindu deity Lord Murugan. It's also the target of every participant in the procession that accompanies the annual Thaipusam festival (see page 159).

ABDUL GAFFOOR MOSQUE

Little India and Arab Street

Head a little way north of the Colonial District and you arrive at two of Singapore's most atmospheric old quarters. Centred on Serangoon Road, Little India has retained far more of its cultural integrity than Chinatown: here Indian pop music blares from shops, the air is perfumed with incense, spices and jasmine garlands, Hindu women promenade in bright saris, a wealth of restaurants serve up superior curries – and there are a handful of temples to visit, too. No more than a ten-minute stroll east is Arab Street, also known as Kampong Glam. Dominated by the domes of the Sultan Mosque, it's one of the island's more appealing little enclaves, an odd mix of old-fashioned textile shops and hip cafés and boutiques.

Walking to either of these areas from the Colonial District means heading northeast across **Bras Basah Road**. The Singapore Art Museum aside, the surrounding area seems an uninteresting jumble of commercial towers at first, but look closer and you'll discover that a fair number of old buildings have survived, including a sprinkling of churches, temples and shophouses.

Bras Basah Road to Rochor Road

Bras Basah Road – the main thoroughfare between Orchard Road and Marina Centre – supposedly got its name because rice arriving on cargo boats used to be brought here to be dried (*beras basah* means "wet rice" in Malay). The zone between it and **Rochor Road** at the edge of Little India has a transitional sort of feel, sitting as it does between the Colonial District and what were intended to be "ethnic" enclaves to the northeast. These days it's a nexus for the arts, with many distinguished old properties on and around Waterloo Street being turned over to creative organizations, including the **Singapore Art Museum**. The country's leading institutes in the field have also been lured here, among them the **Nanyang Academy of Fine Arts** (NAFA) on Bencoolen Street; and the **School of the Arts**, in a striking building next to the Cathay cinema.

Singapore Art Museum

71 Bras Basah Rd plus SAM at 8Q Annexe at 8 Queen St • Main museum closed until 2021; SAM at 8Q hosts special exhibitions Sat–Thurs 10am–7pm, Fri 10am–9pm • $5 • ☎ 6589 9580, ⓦ singaporeartmuseum.sg • Bras Basah, City Hall or Bencoolen MRT

It's hard not to feel a little sorry for the **Singapore Art Museum**. Launched in 1996 in the skilfully renovated former premises of St Joseph's Institution, Singapore's first Catholic school, it was meant to be the premier state-run art showcase on the island – until the government swung its weight behind the idea of the National Gallery (see page 35). Although now utterly overshadowed, the museum still has a *raison d'être*: officially, it will promote cutting-edge and emerging artists from around the region while the National Gallery leans toward more established practitioners.

The museum is of some architectural interest, retaining the school's silver dome and chapel; its closure until 2021 is meant to allow a rejig of the interior to create even larger display spaces. There's also an annexe, **SAM at 8Q**, housing more art in another former Catholic school around the corner at 8 Queen Street.

Waterloo Street

Head up Waterloo Street from the Singapore Art Museum and almost immediately you encounter one of the area's many places of worship, the peach-coloured **Maghain Aboth Synagogue**, looking for all the world like a colonial mansion except for the Stars of David on the facade. The surrounding area was once something of a Jewish enclave – you'll see another building prominently bearing the Star of David midway along nearby Selegie Road – though the Jewish community, largely of Middle Eastern origin, never numbered more than around a thousand. The synagogue, which dates from the 1870s, can be visited, though this must be arranged in advance by calling ☎6337 2189.

A couple of minutes' walk on, at the intersection with Middle Road, the tiny yellow building bearing a striking resemblance to a church was erected in the 1870s as the Christian Institute. Soon after, it became the focal point of Singapore's Methodist missionaries before becoming a Malay-language church for the Peranakan community in 1894. The building has served as an art space in recent years, although its future was uncertain at the time of writing. An adjacent building sharing the site holds the excellent *Artichoke* restaurant (see page 131).

LITTLE INDIA AND ARAB STREET

The Sri Krishnan Temple

152 Waterloo St • ☎ 6337 7957 • Rochor or Bugis MRT

Just outside the pedestrianized section of Waterloo Street, the **Sri Krishnan Temple** began life in 1870, when it amounted to nothing more than a thatched hut containing a statue of Lord Krishna under a banyan tree. The present-day temple is a fine example of Southeast Asian religious harmony and syncretism in action, with worshippers from the neighbouring Buddhist Kwan Im Temple often seen praying outside.

The Kwan Im Temple

178 Waterloo St • Daily 6am–6.30pm • ☎ 6337 3965 • Rochor or Bugis MRT

The best-known sight on Waterloo Street is the **Kwan Im Temple**, named for the Buddhist goddess of mercy. The current version dates only to the 1980s – hence its substantial and rather slick appearance – and draws many devotees daily; it can be filled to overflowing during festivals. As you might anticipate, fortune-tellers, religious artefact shops and other traders operate in a little swarm just outside.

Albert Street

Intersecting Waterloo Street just before it meets Rochor Road is **Albert Street**, which half a century ago was lined with shophouses offering some of Singapore's finest street eating. Now the street is dominated by modern complexes and has been so remodelled it doesn't even appear in its entirety on some maps, though its past is hinted at in the few restaurants trading at ground level. If you do head this way, try to take in the zigzagging glass facades of the **Lasalle College of the Arts** between Albert and McNally streets.

Bugis Street and Bugis Junction

Until the 1980s, **Bugis** (pronounced "boogis") **Street**, was one of the most notorious sites in Singapore, crawling with rowdy sailors, prostitutes and ladyboys by night. Today, the name applies to a claustrophobic bunch of market stalls and snack sellers crammed into two alleyways, occupying what was the southern end of Albert Street. It recaptures something of the bazaar feel Singapore markets had of old, and amid the T-shirt vendors is at least one outlet selling sex aids – about the only link to the area's seedy past. The original Bugis Street was eventually redeveloped, partly because it was anathema to the government and partly so that the Bugis MRT station could be built. In its place today, on the south side of Victoria Street, is the **Bugis Junction** development, where the shophouses have been gutted, scrubbed clean and encased under glass roofs as part of a modern mall and hotel, the *InterContinental*.

Little India

Of all the old districts of Singapore, the most charismatic has to be **Little India**, noticeably less slick and gentrified than its nearest rival, Chinatown. The original occupants of this downtown niche were Europeans and Eurasians who established country houses here, and for whom a racecourse was built in the 1840s on the site of today's Farrer Park. Many of the roads in Little India started out as private tracks leading to these houses, and their names – Dunlop, Cuff, Desker, Norris – recall these early colonial settlers. Only when Indian-run **brick kilns** began to operate here did a markedly Indian community start to evolve (although the name "Little India" was actually coined for a 1970s tourist board campaign).

Indians have featured prominently in the development of Singapore, though not always out of choice: from 1825 onwards, convicts were transported here from the subcontinent and by the 1840s there were more than a thousand Indian prisoners labouring on buildings such as St Andrew's Cathedral and the Istana. Today, migrant Tamil and Bengali men labour to build the island's MRT stations, shopping malls and villas, and on weekends they descend on Little India in their thousands, making the place look like downtown Chennai or Calcutta after a major cricket match.

The district's backbone is **Serangoon Road**, dating from 1822 and hence one of the island's oldest roadways. Its southwestern end is a kaleidoscope of Indian life, packed with restaurants and shops selling everything from nose studs and ankle bracelets to incense sticks and *kumkum* powder (used to make the red dot Hindus wear on their foreheads). To the southeast, stretching as far as Jalan Besar, is a tight knot of roads that's good for exploration. Parallel to Serangoon Road is **Race Course Road**, at whose far end are a trio of noteworthy temples. Note that **buses** serving Serangoon Road make their return journey along Jalan Besar.

Tekka Market

At the start of Serangoon Rd, on the left (western) side of the road • Little India MRT

Tekka Market combines many of Little India's commercial elements under one roof. It's best to arrive in the morning when the **wet market** – as Singaporeans term a traditional produce market where the floor is periodically cleaned by hosing it down – is at its busiest. More sanitary than it once was, the market is nevertheless hardly sanitized – halal butchers push around trolleys piled high with goats' heads, while at seafood stalls live crabs, their claws tied together, shuffle in buckets. Look out also for a couple of stalls selling nothing but banana leaves, used to serve up delicious curry meals all over Singapore but especially in Little India. The cooked food at the **hawker centre** here is excellent, and though the outlets upstairs selling Indian fabrics and household items are mundane, there are great views over the market from here.

Buffalo Road

Buffalo Road, along the northern side of Tekka Market, sports a few provisions stores with sacks of spices and fresh coconut, ground using primitive machines. Its name, and that of neighbouring Kerbau ("buffalo" in Malay) Road, recall the latter half of the nineteenth century when cattle and buffalo yards opened in the area, causing the enclave to grow as more Indians were lured here in search of work. Nearby on Bukit Timah Road is Singapore's largest gynecological/pediatric hospital, called KK (short for *kandang kerbau*, "buffalo pen").

Kerbau Road

Kerbau Road is noteworthy for its meticulously renovated shophouses and for being, like Waterloo Street 1km to the south, a designated "arts belt", home to theatre companies and other creative organizations. Curiously, the road has been split into two, with a pedestrianized bit of greenery in the middle. Here, at no. 37, you can't miss the gaudily restored **Chinese mansion**, built by one Tan Teng Niah, a confectionery magnate, in 1900 and now used as commercial premises. Look out also for the traditional Indian picture framer's shop at no. 57, packed with images of Hindu deities.

The Sri Veeramakaliamman Temple

141 Serangoon Rd, just beyond Belilios Lane • ☎ 6295 4538, ⓦ sriveeramakaliamman.com • Little India MRT

Recently refurbished, the **Sri Veeramakaliamman Temple** is the most prominent shrine on Serangoon Road and just as worthwhile as the larger and more famous Sri Mariamman Temple in Chinatown. The temple is dedicated to Kali, the Hindu goddess of power or energy, and she occupies the central part of the three-doored sanctum inside the *mandapam* (prayer hall), with her sons, the deities Ganesh and Murugan, to the left and right respectively. One of many other notable deities here is the ten-armed figure to the left of the sanctum, Lord Shiva, shown trampling a moustachioed demon of ignorance.

Hastings Road to Cuff Road

Across from Tekka Market on the other side of Serangoon Road, the restored block of shophouses comprising **Little India Arcade** is a sort of Little India in microcosm: behind its pastel-coloured walls and green shutters you can purchase textiles and tapestries, bangles, religious statuary, Indian sweets, tapes and CDs, and even Ayurvedic herbal medicines. Exiting the arcade on to Campbell Lane leaves you opposite the riot of colours of **Jothi flower shop** where staff thread jasmine, roses and marigolds into garlands for prayer offerings. Campbell Lane itself, recently pedestrianized, is now a nucleus for shops selling souvenirs of variable quality.

The Indian Heritage Centre

5 Campbell Lane • Tues–Thurs 10am–7pm, Fri & Sat 10am–8pm, Sun 10am–4pm • $6/$4; free guided tours daily (times online) • ☎ 6291 1601, ⓦ indianheritage.org.sg • Rochor, Little India or Jalan Besar MRT

Only the massive wooden doors, like those found at many Indian temples, give away that the ultramodern honeycombed facade of metal and glass belongs to Singapore's new showpiece for Indian culture. The **Indian Heritage Centre** is the latest in a string of top-down initiatives to manage the island's arts and heritage, although it still feels like a building in search of a purpose. Until its abundant event spaces are matched by a packed calendar, the main attraction is the underwhelming **museum**. Start on the top floor for a general look at Indian traditions via some impressive statuary and carvings, then descend to sections dealing with diverse themes such as stereotypical occupations once pursued by Indian migrants (rubber tappers, policemen and the like) and the activities of the Indian nationalist **Subhas Chandra Bose**, who made a base for himself in Japanese-occupied Singapore.

Dunlop Street

Dunlop Street is defined by beautiful **Abdul Gaffoor Mosque** (no. 41; daily 8am–8pm, closed Fri noon–2.30pm), with a green onion dome and cream interior walls decorated with stars and crescent moons. The mosque also features an unusual 25-pointed sundial bearing the names of 25 Islamic prophets in Arabic script.

A couple of streets along is **Cuff Road**, where a tiny, traditional spice grinder's shop can still be seen at no. 2, open mainly at weekends. At the eastern end of Cuff Road,

---

DEEPAVALI

Never dull, Little India springs even more gloriously to life over the colourful Hindu festival of **Deepavali** (or Diwali), which falls in October or November. Local Hindus mark the festival by lighting oil lamps (*diyas*) or candles in their homes – this is, after all, the Festival of Lights. The festival marks Lord Krishna's slaying of the demon Narakasura, who ruled the kingdom of Pradyoshapuram by terror, torturing his subjects, and kidnapping the women and imprisoning them in his palace. Lord Krishna destroyed the demon, and Hindus across the world have given praise ever since. More universally, the festival celebrates the triumph of light over darkness, and of good over evil.

For Hindus, Deepavali is a period of great excitement, a time to dress up in colourful new clothes, deck their houses out in multi-hued decorations, prepare festive delicacies, exchange cards and gifts, and pay respects to their elders. On the morning of the festival itself, worshippers bathe themselves in oil, then proceed to the temple to thank the gods for the happiness, knowledge, peace and prosperity they have enjoyed in the year past, and to pray for more of the same in the coming year.

If you visit Little India in the run-up to Deepavali, you'll find all of Serangoon Road decked out in lights. Special **markets** are set up selling decorations, confectionery, garlands and clothes on Campbell Lane and also in the open areas close to the Angullia Mosque further up Serangoon Road.

the simple white **Kampong Kapor Methodist Church** is just one of many unsung examples of Art Deco that you'll see in downtown Singapore.

Rowell and Desker roads

Both **Rowell and Desker roads** mark a noticeable shift from the South Indian flavour of much of Little India. Here Bengali features prominently on some shops signs, and at weekends the streets throng with Bengali migrant workers. However, both roads have another claim to fame – or infamy: they have long been synonymous in Singapore with vice, and there's something about the openness of goings-on that's almost radical on this strait-laced island. Between the two roads, running along the backs of the shophouses, is an alleyway whose doorways are illuminated in pink at night. Here sex workers sometimes solicit openly or more often sit indoors looking outwards while being watched by huddles of men, as if the whole thing were some weird form of street entertainment.

2

Race Course Lane

One striking building stands out on **Race Course Lane**, on the west side of Serangoon Road just before Rowell Road. Here the **Mahatma Gandhi Memorial Building**, at no. 3, bears the great man's image to one side of its mainly brick exterior. Although it looks like it might be a museum, it is in fact the offices of the Singapore Hindi Society, which runs Hindi languages classes here and in schools around the island.

Syed Alwi Road to Petain Road

Little India takes on a more Islamic feel around **Syed Alwi Road**, across from whose northern end is the **Angullia Mosque**, but the road is better known for being the hub of the shopping phenomenon that is the **Mustafa Centre**. Just "Mustafa" to locals, it's an agglomeration of department store, moneychanger, travel agent, jeweller, fast-food joint and supermarket, much of the place open 24/7. The business started modestly and somehow knew no bounds, growing into the behemoth that occupies several interlinked buildings. You'll probably find a visit here much more appealing than Orchard Road, as you rub shoulders with Indian families salivating over confectionery from Delhi; Chinese and Malays seeking pots and pans or luggage; and even African businessmen buying consumer goods that are hard to find back home.

Running along the back of the Mustafa Centre is **Sam Leong Road**, worth a detour for its attractive **Peranakan shophouses**, their facades decorated with depictions of stags, lotuses and egrets.

North of Rangoon and Kitchener roads

Rangoon and Kitchener roads more or less mark the northern boundary of Little India, but it's worth venturing beyond to discover a couple of temples and yet more restored **Peranakan shophouses** on **Petain Road**, which are covered with elegant ceramic tiles reminiscent of Portuguese *azulejos*. There's more Peranakan architecture on display on Jalan Besar – turn right at the end of Petain Road.

The Sri Srinivasa Perumal Temple

397 Serangoon Rd • Daily 6.30am–noon & 6–9pm, though usually visitable at other times • ☎ 6298 5771 • Farrer Park MRT

On Serangoon Road, opposite the start of Petain Road, is the **Sri Srinivasa Perumal Temple**, dedicated to Lord Perumal (Vishnu), the Preserver of the Universe. The temple dates from the late nineteenth century but, like many of Singapore's Hindu shrines, is remodelled periodically, which explains why everything looks so pristine – the gopura and other features were redone in 2017. The chariots and trolleys you may see lying about the grounds are used whenever deities need to be transported from their sanctums to preside over ceremonies, at which time the colourful parasols are used to shade them. The temple is best known as the starting point for the gruesome melee of activity at Thaipusam (see page 159).

The Sakya Muni Buddha Gaya Temple

366 Race Course Rd • Daily 8am–4.30pm • Farrer Park MRT

Just beyond the Sri Srinivasa temple, a small path leads northwest to Race Course Road, where the **Sakya Muni Buddha Gaya Temple** (or Temple of the Thousand Lights) is a slightly kitsch affair that betrays a strong Thai influence – not surprising, since it was built by a Thai monk. On the left of the temple as you enter is a huge Buddha's footprint, inlaid with mother-of-pearl, and beyond it a 15m-high Buddha ringed by the thousand electric lights from which the temple takes its alternative name. Twenty-five dioramas depicting scenes from the Buddha's life decorate the pedestal on which he sits. It is possible to walk inside the statue, through a door in its back; inside is yet one more diorama, depicting the Buddha in death. One wall of the temple features a sort of wheel of fortune, decorated with Chinese zodiac signs. To discover your fate, spin it (for a small donation) and take the numbered sheet of paper that corresponds to the number at which the wheel stops.

The Sri Vadapathira Kaliamman Temple

555 Serangoon Rd • Daily roughly 8am–noon & 6–9pm • ☎ 6298 5053, ⓦ srivadapathirakali.org • Farrer Park or Bendemeer MRT

The **Sri Vadapathira Kaliamman Temple** is the least visited of Serangoon Road's Hindu shrines, but no less attractive than the rest. Unusually it lacks a towering gopura, but compensates with an especially wide facade bristling with characters from the Hindu pantheon, including the green, monkey-faced figure of the god Hanuman on the far right. He is one of no fewer than eleven deities worshipped at a temple believed to date back to 1830, although refurbished and extended many times since.

The Thekchen Choling Temple

2 Beatty Lane • Daily 24hr • ☎ 6466 3720, ⓦ thekchencholing.org • Bendemeer or Lavender MRT

From Petain Road, it's just a couple of minutes' walk on to the surprisingly gaudy **Thekchen Choling**, one of a handful of Tibetan Buddhist temples in Singapore. Nestled in a fast-gentrifying neighbourhood, it boasts an array of impressive gilt statuary, including a multi-armed Chenrezig – the Bodhisattva better known as Avalokiteshvara – as well as its own giant prayer wheel.

Arab Street (Kampong Glam)

The area surrounding **Arab Street**, known as **Kampong Glam**, is the most achingly hip enclave in Singapore – quite literally so for some members of the Muslim community. Its lanes packed with boutiques and modern cafés, the district is also home to the venerable Sultan Mosque, and has traditionally had an Islamic and Malay character. Of late, gentrification has come out on top as slick upstart restaurants have edged out venerable textile stores, craft shops and traditional curry houses. Some members of the local community have mounted a rearguard battle against the quarter's increasing booziness, and although the authorities made assurances about fewer licenses for new restaurants and bars in the area, the damage to the cultural fabric has already been done. This backstory shouldn't detract from any visit, with the mosque and the **Malay Heritage Centre** as the obvious sights, but it's as well to be aware that the area remains in a state of flux, even more so than the rest of perennially evolving Singapore.

As for how the area acquired its original character, that is explained by the presence of a Malay village named Kampong Glam in the time before Raffles' arrival; *glam* may have been the name of a type of tree or of a group of local sea gypsies. After signing

his dubious treaty with the newly installed Sultan Hussein of Johor, Raffles designated the zone around the village as one for Muslim settlement. Soon the zone was attracting Sumatrans and Javanese as well as traders from what is now eastern Yemen. Today, the descendants of those Yemeni traders make up Singapore's **Arab community**. They number perhaps fifteen thousand, though they are something of an invisible minority, having intermarried with the wider population and being resident in no particular area.

2 Arab Street

While Little India is memorable for its fragrances, it's the vibrant colours of the shops of **Arab Street** and its environs that stick in the memory. Textile stores and outlets selling Persian carpets are the most prominent, but you'll also see leather, perfumes, jewellery and baskets for sale. It's easy to spend a couple of hours weaving in and out of the stores, though don't expect a quiet window-shopping session – some traders are old hands at persuasion and will have you loaded up with sarongs and whatnot before you know it.

Haji and Bali lanes

South of Arab Street, **Haji Lane** and tiny **Bali Lane** – the latter petering out into the wide walkway next to Ophir Road – are where the quarter's clash of cultures is most evident. Both have something of London's Brick Lane about them, with traditional shops rubbing shoulders with trendy clothes shops and the odd hipster barber's. Haji Lane, with its brash street art and informal DJ set-ups (eves and weekends), might as well be renamed "selfie lane", for reasons that will be clear the moment you arrive.

Parkview Square

600 North Bridge Rd • Bugis MRT

It's worth taking a brief look at the **Parkview Square** office building, just across from Bali Lane on North Bridge Road. Although the tower was built in the Noughties, its styling just screams 1930s Art Deco (à la Batman's Gotham City), and there's a stunning ground-floor bar in the same vein, *Atlas* (see page 149). Great care was taken to site the building dead between the twin towers of **The Gateway** one block south (see page 60) – for the sake of feng shui, of course. Two non-identical honeycombed towers now flank Parkview Square itself, forming the new Duo commercial development, effectively a joint venture between the governments of Singapore and Malaysia.

Sultan Mosque

3 Muscat St • Sat–Thurs 9.30am–noon & 2–4pm, Fri 2.30–4pm • ☎ 6293 4405, ⊕ sultanmosque.sg • Bugis MRT

With its golden onion domes, the **Sultan Mosque** or Masjid Sultan represents the beating heart of the Muslim faith in Singapore. An earlier mosque stood on this site, finished in 1825 and constructed with the help of a $3000 donation from the East India Company. The present building was completed a century later to a design by colonial architects Swan and MacLaren. Look carefully at the base of the main dome and you'll see a dark band that looks like tilework; it actually consists of the bottoms of thousands of glass bottles. The prayer hall is decked out in green and gold, but non-Muslims must look on from just inside the entrance.

Bussorah Street to the south offers the best view of the mosque and still has a couple of worthwhile souvenir outlets, although it's dominated by noisy Middle Eastern restaurants touting for business – hardly any of whom were here just ten years ago. During the Muslim fasting month, the area around the mosque is thronged with stalls of the Ramadan bazaar from mid-afternoon, selling biriyanis, murtabak, dates and cakes for consumption by the faithful after dusk.

The Malay Heritage Centre (Istana Kampong Glam)

85 Sultan Gate • Tues–Sun 10am–6pm • $6/$4; free guided tours most days (times online) • ☎ 6391 0450, ⓦ malayheritage.org.sg • Bugis or Nicoll Highway MRT

Between Kandahar and Aliwal streets, the colonially styled **Istana Kampong Glam** was built as the royal palace of Sultan Ali Iskandar Shah, the son of Hussein who negotiated with Raffles to hand over Singapore to the British. Until a few years ago the house was still home to the sultan's descendants, though it had fallen into disrepair. Then the government acquired it together with the similar, smaller yellow house in the same grounds, which belonged to the heirs of a wealthy merchant. That house, **Gedung Kuning**, is now home to an attempt at an upmarket Malay restaurant, while the *istana* has mutated into the over-smart **Malay Heritage Centre**, a rather hit-and-miss museum. The best displays celebrate the rural boat-building and fishing lifestyle of yore, plus Singapore's unjustly overlooked Malay literary and pop-culture scene of the postwar period. But there's a deafening silence on the building of new towns – a mixed blessing for all who experienced upheaval and relocation, especially for the Malays, who saw every one of their villages erased and communities broken up.

North of Sultan Mosque

The stretch of **North Bridge Road** between Arab Street and Jalan Sultan has a less touristy feel, and though gentrification is spreading even here, the strip's shops tend to be geared more towards locals than tourists, stocking items such as the *songkok* hats worn by Malay men, *miswak* twigs used by some locals to clean their teeth, and Islamically compliant women's swimwear.

Several roads run off the western side of North Bridge Road, including Jalan Kubor (Grave Street), which, across Victoria Street, takes you to an unkempt Muslim **cemetery** where, it is said, Malay royalty are buried. Turn right here up Kallang Road to reach Jalan Sultan and the blue **Malabar Mosque**, built for Muslims from the South Indian state of Kerala and a little cousin of the Sultan Mosque, with more golden domes. Its traditional styling belies its age – the mosque was completed in the early 1960s.

Beach Road

Mostly easily visited together with Arab Street, **Beach Road** still has shops that betray its former proximity to the sea – ships' chandlers and fishing tackle specialists – until land reclamation created the Marina Centre district that juts into the northwest of Marina Bay. There are no attractions of note here other than the famed **Raffles Hotel**, a stone's throw from the Padang.

Raffles Hotel

1 Beach Rd • Fully reopens mid-2019 after restoration • ☎ 6337 1886, ⓦ raffleshotel.com/singapore • Esplanade or City Hall MRT

Though utterly dwarfed by the modern metal-clad towers of the South Beach development opposite (see page 60), **Raffles Hotel** retains its legendary charm. With its lofty halls, restaurants, bars and peaceful gardens, it was practically a byword for colonial indulgence, prompting Somerset Maugham to remark that it "stood for all the fables of the exotic East". Despite a guest list heavy with politicians, film stars and musicians over the years, the hotel is proudest of its literary connections: Joseph Conrad, Rudyard Kipling, Herman Hesse, Somerset Maugham, Noël Coward and Günter Grass all stayed here, and Maugham is said to have penned many of his Asian tales in the garden.

This most inherently British of hotels started life as a modest seafront bungalow belonging to an Arab trader (coincidentally, the hotel is in Arab hands once again, being Qatari-owned). In 1886, the property was bought by the Armenian Sarkies brothers, who came to control a trio of quintessentially colonial lodgings: the *Raffles*; the *Eastern and Oriental* in Penang, Malaysia; and the *Strand* in Rangoon, Burma. The brothers commissioned Regent Bidwell of local architects Swan & MacLaren to convert the house into what became the *Raffles Hotel*, which opened for business on December 1, 1887.

The hotel's heyday was during the first three decades of the last century, when it established its reputation for luxury – it was the first building in Singapore with electric lights and fans. In 1902, according to a (probably apocryphal) tale, the hotel was where the last tiger to be killed on the island was shot. Thirteen years later bartender Ngiam Tong Boon created another *Raffles* legend, the Singapore Sling cocktail, on the menu now for a rather plump $37.

During World War II, the hotel served as officers' quarters for the Japanese, then as a transit camp for liberated Allied prisoners following the war's end. A subsequent slow decline earned it the soubriquet "grand old lady of the East", and the hotel was little more than a shabby tourist diversion when it was declared a national monument in 1987. After a hugely expensive and sometimes controversial facelift, the hotel reopened in 1991 with a new extension that some felt diluted its character. The most recent restoration has attracted less scrutiny, bringing upgrades to all the suites and new restaurants helmed by big-name chefs.

Today, the hotel's Beach Road facade remains one of Singapore's most arresting sights, beautifully whitewashed, elegantly proportioned and flanked by palms and frangipani trees. Inside, the grounds and lobby still give a sense of being at one remove from the hubbub of the city, although they are largely off limits to non-guests. With several restaurants and bars to choose from, though, notably the *Long Bar* (see page 150), you don't need to be staying here to partake of the hotel's atmosphere. It's also possible to drop by a small history gallery celebrating the hotel's distinguished past; it's within the Raffles gift shop.

South Beach

30 Beach Rd • Esplanade or City Hall MRT

One of the more startling additions to the Singapore skyline of late is the **South Beach development**, its two towers looking like box graters from a giant's designer kitchen. A combination of luxury hotel, apartments and office space, it was partly designed by [Norman] Foster + Partners, and repurposes a couple of colonial-era buildings. One of these is the old Singapore Volunteer Corps Headquarters, an understated Art Deco affair in white and dark brown – look out for the 1950 plaque outside memorializing "all ranks…who lost their lives in the Malayan campaign and as prisoners of war 1941–1945".

The Gateway

150 & 152 Beach Rd, southwest of Arab St • Nicoll Highway MRT

The two logic-defying office buildings that together comprise **The Gateway** rise magnificently into the air like vast razor blades. Designed by I.M. Pei – who was also behind the Raffles City complex (see page 39) – they appear two-dimensional when viewed from certain angles.

The Hajjah Fatimah Mosque

4001 Beach Rd, just east of the junction with Jalan Sultan • Nicoll Highway MRT

Not only does the minaret of the **Hajjah Fatimah Mosque** resemble a steeple (perhaps because its architect was European), it also has a visible six-degree tilt; locals call it Singapore's Leaning Tower of Pisa. The mosque is named after a wealthy businesswoman from Malacca who amassed a fortune through her mercantile vessels, and whose family home formerly stood here. Fatimah upped sticks after two break-ins and an arson attack on her home, then funded the construction of a mosque on the vacated site.

正法久住

不振宗風

BUDDHA TOOTH RELIC TEMPLE

Chinatown and the Financial District

The two square kilometres of Chinatown, west and south of the Singapore River, were never a strict Chinese enclave in what is, after all, a Chinese-majority country, but did once represent the focal point of the island's Chinese life and culture. More so than the other old quarters, however, Chinatown has seen large-scale redevelopment and become a bit of a mishmash. Even so, a wander through the surviving nineteenth-century streets still unearths musty and atmospheric temples and clan associations, and you might hear the rattle of a game of mahjong being played. To the southwest, the adjacent district of Tanjong Pagar has yet more old terraces of shophouses and one major museum of Peranakan heritage, the Baba House. There's no such subtlety about the skyscrapers of the area to the southeast, Singapore's Financial District.

Chinatown

Chinatown, Telok Ayer, Outram Park, Clarke Quay or Tanjong Pagar MRT • Buses run southwest along North Bridge Rd, South Bridge Rd and New Bridge Rd, returning along Eu Tong Sen St

The area now known as **Chinatown** was first earmarked for Chinese settlement by Raffles, who decided in 1819 that Singapore's communities should be segregated. As immigrants poured in, the land southwest of the river took shape as a place where new arrivals from China, mostly from Fujian (Hokkien or Fukien) and Guangdong (Canton) provinces and to a lesser extent Hainan Island, would have found temples, shops with familiar products and, most importantly, *kongsi*s – clan associations that helped them find lodgings and work as small traders and coolies.

This was one of the most colourful districts of old Singapore, but after independence the government chose to grapple with its tumbledown slums by embarking upon a redevelopment campaign that saw whole streets razed. As Lee Kuan Yew himself acknowledged: "In our rush to rebuild Singapore, we knocked down many old and quaint buildings. Then we realized that we were destroying a valuable part of our cultural heritage, that we were demolishing what tourists found attractive." Not until the 1980s did the remaining shophouses and other period buildings begin to be conserved (see page 70), though restoration has often rendered them improbably perfect. Furthermore, gentrification has seen the clan houses and religious and martial arts associations often replaced by hotels, design agencies and upmarket (or sometimes not so salubrious) bars. Ironically, getting a taste of the old ways of Chinatown now often means heading off the main streets into the concrete municipal housing estates, where older trades linger.

Even so, as in Little India, the character of the area has had a bit of a shot in the arm courtesy of recent immigrants. As regards sights, the Thian Hock Keng, Buddha Tooth Relic and Sri Mariamman temples are especially worthwhile, as is the Chinatown Heritage Centre museum, and there's plenty of shophouse architecture to justify a leisurely wander.

Chinatown Heritage Centre

48 Pagoda St • Daily 9am–8pm, last admission 7pm • $15/$11 • ☎ 6224 3928, ⓦ chinatownheritagecentre.sg • Chinatown MRT

One of the exits from the Chinatown MRT station leads straight up into the thick of Pagoda Street's tacky souvenir stalls. To understand how different the area once was, head to the **Chinatown Heritage Centre**. Occupying three whole shophouses, it's a museum enshrining the difficult experiences of Chinatown's inhabitants over the past couple of centuries, a theme somewhat at odds with the touchscreens and full air-conditioning installed during a recent makeover.

The postwar tailor's shop is not the most promising way to begin, but things soon perk up at the living cubicles, recreating the cramped conditions in Chinatown's shophouse slums, with trishaw drivers, clog-makers and prostitutes living cheek by jowl. Landlords once shoehorned as many as forty tenants into a single floor; if you think it couldn't possibly happen today, spare a thought for the thousands of mainly Indian and Bangladeshi migrant workers on building sites all over Singapore, many of whom are crammed into fairly basic dormitories.

Other sections take you back to the sadly vanished nightlife venues of postwar Chinatown and then right back to the privations of sailing the South China Sea aboard junks. Once the *singkeh* (literally "new guests") came ashore at Bullock-Cart Water (as Chinatown's Chinese name translates), they formed or joined clan associations, as covered in another section. The final two galleries deal with the death houses of Sago Street (see page 67) and, commendably, the Indian minorities of the area.

Along South Bridge Road

Head down Pagoda Street from the Chinatown Heritage Centre and you come to South Bridge Road, one of Chinatown's main thoroughfares, with the Pinnacle@Duxton (see page 75) looming over its far end. At no. 218, on the corner of Mosque Street, is the pastel-green **Jamae Mosque** (also called the **Chulia Mosque**), established by South Indian Muslims in the 1820s. Its twin minarets appear to contain miniature windows while above the entrance stands what looks like a tiny doorway, all of which makes the upper part of the facade look strangely like a scale model of a much larger building.

One street northeast, at the junction with Upper Cross Street, the Japanese screened locals for signs of anti-Japanese sentiment in the infamous Sook Ching campaign of World War II (see page 173). That tragic episode is commemorated by a simple, signposted monument outside the **Hong Lim Complex**, a housing development whose walkways are lined with medical halls, makers of chops (rubber stamps), stores selling dried foodstuffs and so forth – much more representative of the area's original character than more recent arrivals.

To top up your blood-sugar level while wandering the area, try the venerable **Tong Heng** pastry shop (daily 9am–10pm) at no. 285, which sells takeaway custard tarts, lotus seed paste biscuits and other Chinese sweet treats.

3

The Sri Mariamman Temple

244 South Bridge Rd • Daily 7am–9pm, though the main sanctum is usually closed noon–6pm • Free, cameras $3 • ☎ 6223 4064 • Maxwell, Chinatown or Telok Ayer MRT

Singapore's oldest Hindu shrine, the **Sri Mariamman Temple**, dates back to the 1820s, when a wood and palm-thatch shrine was erected here on land allotted to Naraina Pillay, a government clerk who had arrived together with Stamford Raffles on his first visit to Singapore. The present temple is derived in large part from a reconstruction in the 1960s.

Inside, walk around the courtyard to admire the gaudy but somewhat sun-bleached friezes depicting a host of Hindu deities. The main sanctum is devoted to Mariamman, a goddess worshipped for her healing powers. Smaller sanctums include one dedicated to the goddess Periachi Amman with a queen lying on her lap, whose evil child she has ripped from her womb; it's perhaps odd, then, that Periachi Amman is the protector of children, to whom month-old babies are brought.

Once a year, during the festival of **Thimithi** (Oct or Nov), a patch of sand to the left of the main sanctum is covered in red-hot coals that male Hindus run across to prove the strength of their faith. The participants, who line up all the way along South Bridge Road waiting for their turn, are supposedly protected from the heat of the coals by the power of prayer.

The Eu Yan Sang Medical Hall

269 South Bridge Rd • Mon–Sat 9am–6.30pm • ☎ 6223 6333 • Maxwell, Chinatown or Telok Ayer MRT

The beautifully renovated **Eu Yan Sang Medical Hall** is one of the oldest Chinese herbalists in the area. The smell in the store is the first thing you'll notice (a little like a compost heap on a hot day); the second is the weird assortment of ingredients on the shelves, which to the uninitiated look more likely to kill than cure. Besides the usual herbs and roots favoured by the Chinese, there are various dubious remedies derived from exotic and endangered species. Circulation problems and wounds are eased with centipedes and insects, crushed into a "rubbing liquor"; the ground-up gall bladders of snakes or bears apparently work wonders on pimples; and deer penis is supposed to provide a lift to any sexual problem.

Upstairs, the small but engaging **Birds' Nest Gallery** casts light on this curious Chinese delicacy. The edible nests, made by swiftlets, are a mixture of saliva, moss and grass, and emerged as a prized supplement among China's royal and noble classes during the Ming dynasty. Today they are still valued for their supposed efficacy in boosting the immune system and curing bronchial ailments. The birds live high up in the limestone

CHINATOWN AND THE FINANCIAL DISTRICT

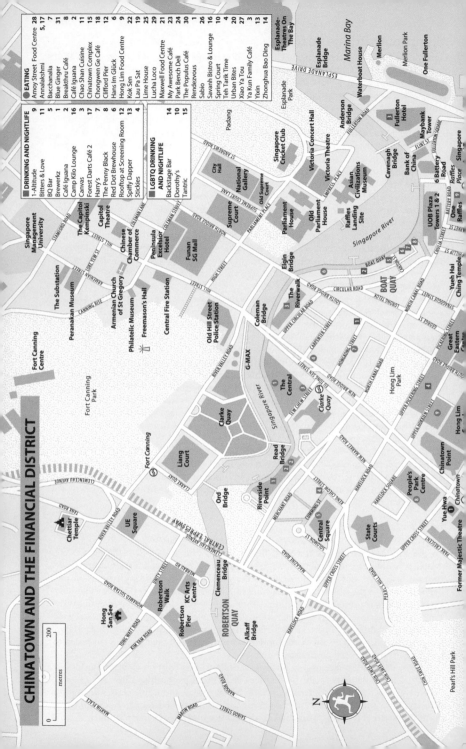

● EATING	
Amoy Street Food Centre	28
Annalakshmi	5, 17
Bacchanalia	7
Blue Ginger	31
Breakthru Café	8
Café Iguana	2
Chao Shan Cuisine	11
Chinatown Complex	15
Chongwen Ge Café	18
Clifford Pier	12
Hans Im Glück	6
Hong Lim Food Centre	9
Kok Sen	22
Lau Pa Sat	19
Lime House	25
Lucha Loco	29
Maxwell Food Centre	21
My Awesome Café	23
Park Bench Deli	24
The Populus Café	30
Rendezvous	1
Sabio	26
Savanh Bistro & Lounge	16
Spring Court	10
Teh Tarik Time	4
Urban Bites	20
Xiao Ya Tou	27
Ya Kun Family Café	3
Yixin	13
Zhonghua Bao Ding	14

■ DRINKING AND NIGHTLIFE	
1-Altitude	9
Bitters & Love	11
BQ Bar	5
Brewerkz	1
Café Iguana	2
Camp Kilo Lounge	16
Canvas	3
Forest Darts Café 2	17
Harry's	7
The Penny Black	8
Red Dot Brewhouse	6
Rooftop at Screening Room	12
Spiffy Dapper	13
Stickies	4

■ LGBTQ DRINKING AND NIGHTLIFE	
Backstage Bar	14
Dorothy's	10
Tantric	15

caves of Southeast Asia, and harvesting them is arduous and sometimes dangerous work, but the nests command such good prices that all over Malaysia, town-centre shophouses are illegally bricked up as "caves" for rearing swiftlets.

The Buddha Tooth Relic Temple

288 South Bridge Rd, just after Sago St • Daily 7am–7pm • Free • ☎ 6220 0220, ⓦ btrts.org.sg • No shorts, vests or non-vegetarian food • Maxwell, Chinatown or Telok Ayer MRT

Right at the end of South Bridge Road is something of an upstart – the imposing **Buddha Tooth Relic Temple**, the most in-your-face addition to Chinatown's shrines in many a year. The place simply clobbers you with its opulence – even the elevators have brocaded walls – and with its thousands upon thousands of Buddhist figurines lining various interior surfaces. It also boasts its own museum and a gallery of Buddhist art.

The temple has its origins in the discovery, in 1980, of what was thought to be a tooth of Buddha inside a collapsed stupa at a Burmese monastery. The monastery's chief abbot visited Singapore in 2002 and decided the island would make a suitable sanctuary for the relic, to be housed in its own new temple. A prime site in Chinatown was duly secured, and the temple opened in 2007.

The main hall

The focus of the **main hall** is **Maitreya**, a Buddha who is yet to appear on Earth. Carved from juniper wood said to be a thousand years old, his statue has a yellow flame-like halo around it. But what really captures the attention are the Buddhas covering the entire side walls. There are a hundred main statuettes, individually crafted, interspersed with thousands more tiny figurines embedded in a vast array of shelving, each with its own serial number displayed. Signage soon makes you aware that figurines and temple fittings can be the object of sponsorship, presumably winning donors good karma while recouping the $62 million construction bill and helping the temple keep up with its outgoings.

Behind the main hall, another large hall centres on the Avalokitesvara Bodhisattva. The **mezzanine** affords great views over proceedings and chanting ceremonies in the main hall, while **level 2** contains the temple's own teahouse.

The Buddhist Culture Museum

Daily 9am–6pm

On **level 3** are some seriously impressive examples of Buddhist statuary in brass, wood and stone, plus other artworks. They're all part of the **Buddhist Culture Museum**, with panels telling the story of Gautama Buddha in the first person. At the back, the relic chamber displays what are said to be the cremated remains of Buddha's nose, brain, liver etc, all looking vaguely like fish roe in different colours.

Sacred Buddha Tooth Relic Stupa

Daily 9am–6pm

On **level 4** you finally encounter what all the fuss is ultimately about – the **Sacred Buddha Tooth Relic Stupa**. Some 3m in diameter and with a gem-encrusted central band, it sits in its own chamber behind glass panels and can't be inspected close up, though there is an accurate scale model at the front. The Maitreya Buddha is depicted at the front of the stupa, guarded by four lions, with a ring of 35 more Buddhas below; floor tiles around the stupa are said to be made of pure gold.

The roof garden

The temple's lovely **roof garden** has walls lined with twelve thousand tiny figurines of the Amitayus Buddha, but its centrepiece is "the largest cloisonné prayer wheel in the world", around 5m tall. Each rotation (clockwise, in case you want to have a go) dings a bell and represents the recitation of one sutra.

West of South Bridge Road

The tight knot of streets between **Pagoda Street** and **Sago Street** is Chinatown at its most touristy, packed with souvenir sellers and foreigner-friendly restaurants. Once, however, this was Chinatown's nucleus, teeming with trishaws and food hawkers, while opium dens and brothels lurked within the shophouses. Until as recently as the 1950s, Sago Street was home to several **death houses** – rudimentary hospices where skeletal citizens saw out their final hours on rattan camp beds. Now its main attraction is the modern **Chinatown Complex**, housing stalls selling clothes, household goods and some religious items. Also here is an open space, behind the Buddha Tooth Relic Temple and Chinatown Visitors Centre (see page 32), where elderly men play Chinese chess on boards printed on tables, and where local residents sometimes indulge in bouts of line dancing. If you're around in the run-up to Chinese New Year, you may find stalls selling festive branches of pussy willow blossom, oranges and so-called waxed ducks, cooked and dried until they become almost flat.

Smith Street

Smith Street is perennially being promoted as "Chinatown Food Street", and there have been several half-cocked attempts to repackage it and Trengganu Street as a hub for street eating – ironically, the very thing Singapore abolished decades ago. The latest of these involves a slew of inauthentically smart hawker "pushcarts" which locals wouldn't be seen dead eating at, much preferring the stalls upstairs at the Chinatown Complex (see above). One of the few traditional businesses left is Nam's Supplies at no. 22, a producer of paper mock-ups of consumer goods – all to be burnt at funerals to ensure that the deceased don't lack creature comforts in the next life.

The Bukit Pasoh conservation area

Outram Park or Maxwell MRT

In the southernmost corner of Chinatown, west of Kreta Ayer Road, is an area packed with restored shophouses, as featured briefly in *Crazy Rich Asians*. The zone is worth a look not only for the beautifully painted facades, some in Art Deco style, but also because it is the evolving new Chinatown in microcosm. **Clan associations** were once the claim to fame of **Bukit Pasoh Road**, but while some cling on, in other cases their premises have morphed into boutique hotels or been rented out; part of the Gan Clan building at number 18/20, for example, is now given over to a restaurant.

A similar tale applies to neighbouring **Keong Saik Road** too, now overflowing with smart restaurants despite being regarded as a red-light area until quite recently (ironically, the tycoon after whom the road was named was a member of the Office for the Protection of Virtue, a group founded in 1888 to help young Chinese women tricked into prostitution). Unmissable at the northern end of the same road is the small **Sri Layan Sithi Vinayagar Temple**, with an unusually gaudy gopura and occasional Chinese worshippers; it's managed by the Hindu association that runs the Chettiar Temple (see page 47).

New Bridge Road and Eu Tong Sen Street

Chinatown's main shopping drag comprises southbound **New Bridge Road** and northbound **Eu Tong Sen Street**. It's worth sampling the *bak kwa* (barbecued pork) sold by shops on or just off New Bridge Road, close to Chinatown MRT. The chewy, flat squares of meat, coated with a sweet red marinade, give off a rich, smoky odour as they cook that is pure Chinatown.

Across on Eu Tong Sen Street are two striking buildings. The Art Deco **Majestic Theatre** was built in 1927 as a Chinese opera house by Eu Tong Sen, the magnate behind the Eu Yan Sang Chinese medicine empire; note the five images of figures from

Chinese opera on its facade. Today it has been sadly reduced to housing a few shops and a betting agency majoring on horseracing at the Turf Club in the north of the island. Just beside it and built a few years later, the **Yue Hwa Chinese Products Emporium** occupies the former *Great Southern Hotel*, in whose fifth-floor nightclub wealthy locals would drink liquor, smoke opium and pay to dance with so-called "taxi girls".

The most worthwhile of the shopping centres here, however, has to be the **People's Park Complex**, a 1970s green-and-yellow concrete slab topped with apartments, plus a separate block behind housing a market. Despite its unprepossessing appearance, the place has benefited from the recent wave of Chinese migrants: ground-level snack stalls sell a bevy of foods that have locals scratching their heads, such as sweet potato buns and seaweed rolls, and you might occasionally encounter a busker singing songs in dialect Chinese on the overhead bridge linking to Pagoda Street.

Ann Siang Hill

Ann Siang Hill is a lane that leads southeast off South Bridge Road up the hill of the same name, where it forks into Club Street on the left and Ann Siang Road, which veers gently right. Despite being only a few paces removed from the hubbub of the main road, the hill is somehow a different realm, a cosy collection of gentrified shophouses with a villagey feel. Packed with swanky restaurants, cafés and bars, plus the occasional boutique, the area typifies the new Chinatown.

Looking now rather out of place at 25 Ann Siang Road is a plain, open-fronted room, bunting and Chinese lanterns dangling from the ceiling; it is in fact the office of a clan association, its name (not signed in English) unusually translating as the **Lee Clan Book Room**, indicating that its focus is on promoting literacy and literature among its members. At the southern end of the road, a short flight of steps leads up to **Ann Siang Hill Park**, a sliver of greenery whose only attraction is that it offers a back route to Amoy Street, to which there's no direct road access from here.

Club Street

The temple-carving specialist shops on Club Street have long since gone, as have most of the clan associations and guilds whose presence gave the street its name remain. Most notable of the survivors is the **Chinese Weekly Entertainment Club** at no. 76, on a side street also called Club Street. Flanked by roaring lion heads, this mansion-like building is actually a private club, constructed in 1891 as a venue for Peranakan tycoons to socialize in.

The Singapore City Gallery

URA Centre, 45 Maxwell Rd • Mon–Sat 9am–5pm • Free • ☎ 6226 3529, ⓦ ura.gov.sg/citygallery • Maxwell, Telok Ayer or Tanjong Pagar MRT

Town planning may not sound the most fascinating premise for a museum, but then again, no nation constantly remodels with such ambition as Singapore. The planners' latest grand designs for the island are mapped and exhibited south of Ann Siang Hill at the surprisingly absorbing **Singapore City Gallery**, within the government's Urban Redevelopment Authority headquarters.

Permanent displays on the first and second floors make all the right noises about the value of the venerable shophouses and other colonial-era properties that still exist. But there can be a "government knows best" attitude to everything, and that conservation here simply means preserving buildings and not the vocations and cultures that went with them. There's also little explanation of how the state is able to plan in the sweeping way it does (reason being that the state is ultimately Singapore's biggest landlord).

By far the most memorable display is the vast and intricate scale model of downtown Singapore, with every row of shophouses, every roof of every building – including some not yet built – fashioned out of plywood. Unfortunately the model-makers' offices aren't open to the public, though you may be able to glimpse them at work through the glass.

Amoy Street

Amoy Street, together with Telok Ayer Street, was designated a Hokkien enclave in the colony's early days (Amoy being the old name of Xiamen city in China's Fujian province). Long terraces of smartly refurbished shophouses flank the street, all featuring characteristic five-foot ways, or covered verandas, so called because they jut five feet out from the house. If you descend here from Ann Siang Hill Park, you'll emerge by the small **Sian Chai Kang Temple** at no. 66. With the customary dragons on the roof, it's dominated by huge urns, full to the brim with ash from untold numbers of burned incense sticks. Two carved stone lions guard the temple; the fancy red ribbons around their necks are said to attract prosperity.

3

Telok Ayer Street

One street removed from Amoy Street is Telok Ayer Street, whose southern end starts near Tanjong Pagar MRT. The name, meaning "Watery Bay" in Malay, recalls the mid-nineteenth century when the street would have run along the shoreline. Nowadays, thanks to land reclamation, it's no closer to a beach than is Beach Road, but some of Singapore's oldest buildings cling on between the modern towers – temples and mosques where newly arrived immigrants and sailors thanked their god(s) for their safe passage.

The first building of note you come to if you walk up from the station is the square 1889 **Chinese Methodist Church**, whose design – portholes and windows adorned with white crosses and capped by a Chinese-temple-style roof – is a pleasing blend of East and West. Just beyond McCallum Street, the blue-and-white **Al-Abrar Mosque** is built on the spot where South Indian worshippers set up a makeshift thatched mosque in 1827.

Thian Hock Keng Temple

158 Telok Ayer St • Daily 7.30am–5.30pm • Free • ☏ 6423 4616, ⓦ thianhockkeng.com.sg • Telok Ayer or Tanjong Pagar MRT

From across the street, the immaculately restored **Thian Hock Keng Temple** looks spectacular: dragons stalk its broad roofs, while the entrance to the compound bristles with ceramic flowers, foliage and figures. Construction began in 1839 using materials imported from China, on the site of a joss house where immigrants made offerings to Ma Zu, the queen of heaven. A statue of the goddess, shipped in from southern China in time for the temple's completion in 1842, stands in the centre of the main hall, flanked by the martial figure of Guan Yu on the right and physician Bao Sheng on the left.

Against the left wall, look out for an altar containing the curious figures of General Fan and General Xie. The two are said to have arranged to meet by a river bridge, but Xie was delayed; Fan waited doggedly in the appointed spot and drowned in a flash flood, which supposedly accounts for his black skin and the grimace on his face. When Xie finally arrived, he was filled with guilt and hanged himself – hence his depiction, with his tongue hanging down to his chest.

Incidentally, the pagoda visible to the left from Telok Ayer Street, called **Chongwen Ge**, formed part of an adjacent school and now hosts a Peranakan café and tile shop (see pages 137 and 163). It's also worth walking round to Amoy Street to see the back-wall **mural** by Yip Yew Chong, an accountant who does street art in his spare time; the eye-catching piece kicks off on the right with a sepia-tinted Chinatown of old

SHOPHOUSES

Though Singapore has no shortage of striking modern buildings, it's the island's rows of traditional **shophouses** that are its most distinctive architectural feature. Once often cramped and unsanitary, many were demolished in the years following independence, but since the 1980s whole streets of them have been declared conservation areas and handsomely restored.

As the name suggests, shophouses were originally a combination of shop and home, with the former occupying the ground floor of a two- or three-storey building; eventually many came to be built purely as townhouses, but the original name stuck. Unusually, the facade is always recessed at ground level, leaving a space here that, combined with adjoining spaces in a row of shophouses, would form a sheltered walkway at the front (the **"five-foot way"**, so named because of its minimum width) – hence the lack of pavements on Singapore's older streets. Another notable feature is that shophouses were built narrow and surprisingly deep. Behind the ground-floor shop or reception hall there might be a small courtyard, open to the sky, then yet another room; this layout can be seen at the Baba House (see page 74) and the Katong Antiques House. Also, shophouses were often built back to back, with tiny **alleyways** separating the rear sections of adjoining rows; it's down one such alleyway that the brothels of Desker Road (see page 55) are tucked away.

The oldest shophouses date from the mid-nineteenth century and are generally no longer standing. Slightly later examples, which still exist on and around Telok Ayer and Arab streets, for example, have shuttered windows and tiled roofs, features that continued to be used for several decades. Otherwise, their **decoration** was limited, say, to simple stuccowork. However, by the turn of the twentieth century, the shophouse had blossomed into a dizzy melange of styles, which both European and local architects enjoyed blending. So-called Neoclassical, Chinese Baroque and Rococo shophouses featured decorative Corinthian columns, mini-pediments, fanlights, curvy gables and multicoloured wall and floor **tiling** – sometimes referred to as Peranakan tiles because wealthy Peranakans often owned smart shophouses, but actually featuring European geometrical designs. Local ornamentations included wooden trelliswork and eaves overhung with a row of fretted fascia boards, both often seen in Malay palaces; Peranakan *pintu pagar*, half-height swing doors like those in Wild West bars; and Chinese touches such as floral and animal motifs with symbolic meanings. You can see fine wedding-cake-like rows of shophouses with various such features on Sam Leong and Petain roads at the northern edge of Little India (see page 55), off Orchard Road on Emerald Hill Road (see page 86), around Joo Chiat Road in Katong (see page 99), and at Spottiswoode Park, close to the Baba House.

By the 1930s, global recession and prevailing artistic trends had caused a swing towards more sober Art Deco and modernist buildings, with plainer geometrical facades, often topped by a central flagpole. Shophouses with so-called Tropical Deco stylings continued to be built in Singapore after World War II, even though Art Deco had become old hat elsewhere; there are quite a few examples in Chinatown, on South Bridge Road for example.

Boxy 1960s shophouses were the form's last hurrah. By the 1980s, shophouses had pretty much fallen out of favour as they were just too small to make efficient use of scarce land.

As with heritage buildings the world over, today's surviving shophouses are often handsomely restored shells concealing insides that have been totally gutted and modernized. Many no longer serve as shops, homes or clan houses, functioning instead as bars, beauty salons or offices.

and ends with a full-colour fantasy in which both existing and demolished towers in the Financial District loom over a river still busy with cargo-filled bumboats.

Yu Huang Gong

150 Telok Ayer St • Daily 8am–6pm, but with closures every ten days or so • ☏ 6295 6112 • Telok Ayer MRT

To the right of Thian Hock Keng but not part of the same compound, despite appearances, is the compact, equally pristine Taoist **Yu Huang Gong**, the **Jade Emperor's Temple**. Like its neighbour, it dates from the 1840s, when it was built as a clan hall, the Keng Teck Association, by a group of Baba merchants with roots in the same part of southeast China. Its beautifully painted door gods and other fine features are the result of an arduous restoration effort that allowed what had been a crumbling shrine to reopen its doors in 2015.

Nagore Durgha Shrine

Museum daily 10am–6pm • Free • Telok Ayer MRT

It's a testament to Singapore's multicultural nature that on the same street as Thian Hock Keng's is the charming brown-and-white **Nagore Durgha Shrine** to the Muslim ascetic, Shahul Hamid of Nagore. It was built by South Indian Muslims, as was the Jamae Mosque (see page 63), so it's no surprise that the buildings appear cut from the same cloth, so to speak; more significantly, the shrine is one of the oldest buildings in Singapore, having been finished in the late 1820s.

Part of the shrine now houses an excellent small **museum** of the history of Telok Ayer Street. The few simple artefacts and photographs also do a good job of unpacking the nuances of Muslim Indian identity in Singapore, a place where Hindu members of the Indian community are referred to by the part of India they emigrated from, whereas their Muslim counterparts have been lumped together under the banner of their faith.

3

Ying Fo Fui Kun

98 Telok Ayer St • Mon–Fri 9am–5pm, Sat 9am–noon • Free • Telok Ayer MRT

The **Ying Fo Fui Kun** is one of the smartest of Chinatown's surviving clan houses, established in 1822 by Hakkas from Guangdong province, and has narrowly avoided being swallowed up by the adjacent Far East Square complex. Recently refurbished, it boasts an immaculate altar with gilt calligraphy and carvings, but it's still hard to imagine that modest shophouses like these were once the social hub of an entire community. Like others of its kind, the clan association that runs it now has to mount occasional membership drives to stop itself decaying into a senior citizens' club, a real danger in a country where provincial dialects – traditionally used as a marker of identity and regional roots among the Chinese – have been on the decline since the 1970s after an often aggressive state-run campaign to make people speak Mandarin.

Far East Square

Telok Ayer MRT

Far East Square is a sort of heritage development that absorbs the northernmost section of Amoy Street into what is otherwise a rather mundane collection of shops, restaurants and offices on Cross Street. Also co-opted into the complex is the **Fuk Tak Chi Street Museum** at 76 Telok Ayer St. This was once Singapore's oldest surviving temple,

---

TAKING CHINESE TEA

At two **Tanjong Pagar teahouses**, visitors can glean something of the intricacies of the deep Chinese connection with tea, not just sampling from their extensive menu (at about $7 a cup) but also by taking part in a tea workshop. These introduce participants to the history of tea cultivation, the different varieties and the rituals of brewing and appreciating the drink. The water, for example, has to reach an optimum temperature that depends on which type of tea is being prepared; experts can tell its heat by the size of the rising bubbles, described variously as "sand eyes", "prawn eyes", "fish eyes", etc. Both venues also stock an extensive range of tea-related accoutrements such as tall "sniffer" cups used to savour the aroma of the brew before it is poured into squat teacups for drinking.

Tea Chapter 9–11 Neil Rd ☎6226 1175, ⓦtea chapter.com. Tea appreciation sessions starting at $48 per head for three blends. Daily 11am–10.30pm. **Yixing Yuan Teahouse** 60 Tanjong Pagar Rd ☎6224 6961, ⓦyixingxuan-teahouse.com. Tea "demonstrations" (Sat 11am) for $30 per head for a group of five, slightly more for smaller groups. Mon–Sat 10am–8pm, Sun 10am–7pm.

having been established by the Hakka and Cantonese communities in 1824; today it actually forms part of the entrance to a hotel, and the altar holds a model junk crewed by sailors in blue shorts. A diorama depicts Telok Ayer Street in its waterfront heyday, with pigtailed labourers taking part in a procession to the temple.

Hong Lim Park

North of Upper Pickering St and sandwiched between New Bridge Rd and South Bridge Rd • Clarke Quay or Chinatown MRT

A few minutes' walk southwest from the Singapore River, **Hong Lim Park** amounts to not much more than a field ringed by trees, but it's of symbolic significance as the home of **Speakers' Corner**, at the park's New Bridge Road end. Citizens are, in theory, able to speak their minds here, just as people do at its famous exemplar in central London. This being Singapore, the reality is more regulated: speakers are required to register beforehand and are banned from discussing religion or anything that could be deemed to provoke racial discontent. Despite this, the site's libertarian leanings have rubbed off on the park itself, which has regained some of its historic role as a site for rallies and also hosts the annual gay pride event, Pink Dot SG.

Boat Quay

Raffles Place MRT

The pedestrianized row of waterfront shophouses known as **Boat Quay**, almost at the old mouth of the Singapore River, is one of the island's notable urban regeneration successes. Derelict in the early 1990s, it's since become a thriving hangout, sporting a huge collection of restaurants and bars. The area's historical significance may be easier to appreciate through its street names – Synagogue Street nearby, for example, was indeed the site of Singapore's first synagogue.

The Yueh Hai Ching Temple

30B Philip St • Daily 8am–6pm • Raffles Place or Telok Ayer MRT

The twin-shrined **Yueh Hai Ching Temple** (also called **Wak Hai Cheng Bio**) feels even more isolated than the Thian Hock Keng, nestling as it does among the towers where Chinatown shades into the Financial District. Completed in the 1850s, it is another of Chinatown's temples built on the old coastline. Hai Ching means "clear sea" and an effigy of Tian Hou or Mazu, the queen of heaven and protector of seafarers, is housed in the right-hand shrine; the temple was a destination for newly arrived migrants. Be sure to look up at the roof, crammed with tiny depictions of scenes from Chinese folklore. Created using the *jiannian* technique, involving multicoloured porcelain shards, the scenes have been hand-painted back to their original glory as part of a recent restoration.

Tanjong Pagar

The district of **Tanjong Pagar,** fanning out south of Chinatown between Neil and Maxwell roads, was once a veritable sewer of brothels and opium dens. Then it was earmarked for regeneration as a conservation area, following which dozens of shophouses were painstakingly restored and converted into bars, restaurants and shops, notably on Neil Road and Duxton Hill just south of it. A grander example of the area's architecture can be found right where South Bridge Road flows into Neil and Tanjong Pagar roads: here you'll easily spot the arches and bricked facade of the **Jinrikisha Building**, constructed at the start of the twentieth century as a terminus

DETAIL OF THE SRI MARIAMMAN TEMPLE

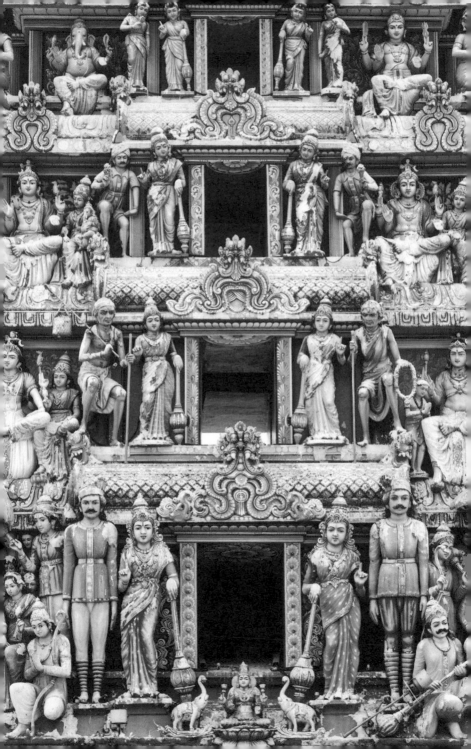

for rickshaws. They were superseded by trishaws after World War II, and today the building serves as office space – with a celebrity landlord, the Hong Kong actor Jackie Chan.

Tanjong Pagar's main sight is the **Baba House**, though as an architectural attention-grabber it's rivalled by the seven interlinked towers of the **Pinnacle@Duxton**, a showpiece public housing development that offers fine views over much of Singapore.

Say Tian Hng Buddha Shop

35 Neil Rd • Daily 10am–9pm • ☎ 6221 1042, ⓦ buddhashop.sg • Optional tours $48 • Maxwell, Chinatown or Tanjong Pagar MRT, or bus #61 or #166 from South Bridge Rd

Close to the start of Neil Road, plain glass cabinets in an ancient-looking shop hold a cornucopia of figurines – Taoist idols, in fact. This is Say Tian Hng, a family-run maker and mender of Taoist deities since 1896, and which plausibly claims to be the last enterprise of its kind in Singapore. The firm is run by the matriarch, now in her late eighties; staff don't mind tourists having a quick look around, but if you really want to learn about the techniques used and the lore behind each idol, sign up for one of their occasional tours, which are more like workshops (2hr 30min; dates online).

The Baba House

157 Neil Rd • Visits Mon–Sat only and must be booked online in advance • Free • ☎ 6227 5731, ⓦ babahouse.nus.edu.sg • Outram Park MRT (Cantonment Rd exit), or bus #174 from Orchard Rd or Bras Basah Rd

The **Baba House** is one of Singapore's most impressive museums, because it is and isn't a museum: what you see is a Peranakan house from the turn of the twentieth century, meticulously restored to its appearance in the late 1920s, a particularly prosperous time in its history.

The house is easily spotted as it's painted a vivid blue. Note the phoenixes and peonies on the eaves above the entrance, signifying longevity and wealth and, together, marital bliss. Even more eye-catching is the *pintu pagar*, the pair of swing doors with beautiful gilt and mother-of-pearl inlays.

The ground floor

Yet more exquisite inlay work is in evidence on the antique chairs in the **main hall**, used for entertaining guests. The altar, among the last of its kind in Singapore, is backed by an exquisitely carved wood screen behind which the women of the household could eavesdrop on proceedings. Behind is the **family hall**, with an air well, open to the sky, in its midst. Note the original tilework depicting roses and tulips, indicating a European influence, and the gilt bats on the walls; the Mandarin term for bats is *bianfu*, and *fu* also happens to be the pronunciation of the Chinese character meaning "good fortune".

The upper floors

Upstairs at the front end of the house, the centrepiece of the **main bedroom** is an ornate wooden four-poster bed with gilt and red lacquer decorations, and bearing carved motifs such as musical instruments and yet more bats. Interestingly, the floor contains a peephole that exploits a small shaft down to the main hall. The third storey, a later addition, is used for temporary exhibitions.

The Pinnacle@Duxton

1 Cantonment Rd • Skybridge (50th floor) daily 9am–9pm, limited to 200 visitors per day • $5 at the management office on the ground floor of Block 1G, the southernmost tower; EZ-Link card required to let visitors through security gate • ☎ 8683 7760, ⓦ pinnacleduxton. com.sg • Outram Park or Tanjong Pagar MRT, or bus #167 from Orchard Rd/the Colonial District to the Maritime House bus stop

It's hard to believe that the **Pinnacle @ Duxton**, comprising seven slab-like towers that form a sickle when viewed from the air, is actually a state housing project – the result of an international design contest and, at fifty storeys high, the tallest in the country. The towers' facades boast an intricate arrangement of windows and balconies that gives them the appearance of a console packed with sliding controls and buttons. Two continuous decks called **Skybridges** link all seven towers. The upper Skybridge, right at the top of the structure, offers fascinating perspectives in all directions: northeast over Chinatown's serried collection of red-roofed shophouse terraces and the Financial District; southwest to the port at Keppel, with Sentosa Island beyond; west to the Southern Ridges and Jurong; and northwest to Bukit Timah.

The Financial District

The area south of the mouth of the Singapore River was swamp until land reclamation in the mid-1820s rendered it fit for building. Within just a few years, Commercial Square here had become the colony's busiest business address, boasting the banks, ships' chandlers and warehouses of a burgeoning trading port. The square was later Singapore's main shopping area until superseded by Orchard Road in the late 1960s; today the square, now called Raffles Place, forms the nucleus of Singapore's **Financial District** (also referred to as the **CBD**, or Central Business District). In 1995, the area unexpectedly hit the headlines because of the antics of rogue trader Nick Leeson, who brought about the **Barings Bank collapse**.

These days the Financial District has lost its tight focus, the banking towers spilling over almost seamlessly on to Marina South, the parcel of reclaimed land that also holds the striking *Marina Bay Sands* hotel and casino. That extension makes it hard to appreciate that for much of the last century, Singapore's proud waterfront was only a stone's throw from Raffles Place, running more or less along Fullerton Road, Collyer Quay, Raffles Quay and Shenton Way. A few examples of gracious colonial architecture lining that route still stand in mute witness to those times.

Raffles Place

Raffles Place makes a good prelude to a stroll along the south bank of the river to Boat Quay (see page 72) or across Cavenagh Bridge (see page 38) to the Colonial District, but the main reason to visit the Financial District itself is to feel like an ant in a canyon of skyscrapers. To see what things look like from the top of that canyon, the best place to head is **One Raffles Place**, the complex to the west of the square, with truly stunning views from its rooftop bar, *1-Altitude* (see page 151).

Battery Road

Heading towards the river from Raffles Place, you come to Battery Road, whose name recalls the days when Fort Fullerton (named after Robert Fullerton, first governor of the Straits Settlements) and its attendant battery of guns used to stand to the east on the site of what is now the Fullerton Building. From here, Cavenagh Bridge is only a couple of minutes' walk away.

The main attraction here, Boat Quay aside, is the elegant **Fullerton Building**, worth viewing from Collyer Quay to the east for its facade fronted by sturdy pillars. This was one of Singapore's tallest buildings when it was constructed in 1928 as the headquarters for the General Post Office – converted in the late 1990s into the luxury

3

Fullerton hotel, which rivals the *Raffles* for character. It's worth setting aside a few minutes to plunge into the Neoclassical and Art Deco splendour of the atrium, with a Y-shaped marbled staircase surmounting a carp-filled fishpond, and enormous columns reminiscent of Egyptian temples. Ask staff to point you to the small **heritage gallery** documenting the building's erstwhile role not just in the island's postal service (note the British-style red postbox on show, and apparently still in use) but also as home to the Ministry of Finance and other government bodies.

The structure jutting upwards from the roof, visible from the Fullerton Road side of the building, was once a lighthouse that guided boats back to Clifford Pier after dark; now it's been remodelled to house a swanky Italian restaurant.

Merlion Park

Fullerton Road • Unrestricted access • Free • Raffles Place MRT

The **Merlion Park** is named for the cement statue of Singapore's national symbol, the **Merlion**: half-lion, half-fish and wholly ugly. Created in 1972, the creature reflects the island's maritime connections and the old tale concerning the derivation of its present name, derived from the Sanskrit "Singapura", meaning "Lion City". Originally it was installed close to **Anderson Bridge** and to **Waterboat House** – another understated Art Deco structure, now a dining venue although once home to offices from where harbour staff monitored the seawater quality. In 2002, however, the statue was nudged east to its present spot after the new Esplanade Bridge obscured views of it from the water.

Clifford Pier and Customs House

Clifford Pier 80 Collyer Quay • **Customs House** 70 Collyer Quay

The Art Deco **Clifford Pier** building, long the departure point for boat trips out to Singapore's southern islands, was rendered defunct by the barrage that seals Marina Bay off from the sea. Now both it and the nearby **Customs House** building – with an octagonal observation tower at its far end, like something you'd see at an airfield – have been transformed into restaurant and leisure complexes, run by the Hong Kong-based conglomerate behind the *Fullerton* hotel. Part of Clifford Pier forms the entrance to the hotel's even-pricier new sibling, the *Fullerton Bay*.

Incidentally, the curious low tower in front of the *Fullerton Bay*, topped by what looks like an outsized slide-projector carousel, is a 1970s project refurbished to form part of a substantial new office development, **OUE Bayfront**. Almost predictably, it, too, houses a number of restaurants.

Lau Pa Sat

18 Raffles Quay • Daily 24hr • Raffles Place, Telok Ayer or Downtown MRT

The best place for refreshments in the Financial District is the charmingly old-world **Lau Pa Sat**, literally "old market", although it's also called **Telok Ayer Market**. An octagonal cast-iron structure, it was built in 1894 as a produce market, and was soon joined by a second market (which became the "new market") on the site of the present *Swissôtel Merchant Court* hotel, facing Clarke Quay. Lau Pa Sat has served as a hawker centre since the 1970s, except for an interregnum in the 1980s when tunnelling for the MRT required the whole thing to be dismantled, then reassembled piece by piece. Now spruced up once again after a recent refit, it includes a central clock tower from which chimes peal out every fifteen minutes. Aficionados of satay should turn up in the evening, when vendors set their barbecues up in a row outside on Boon Tat Street.

SUPERTREE GROVE

Marina Bay

It's hard not to be awed by Marina Bay, the project that has transformed downtown Singapore's seafront over two generations. A hugely ambitious piece of civil engineering, it entailed the creation of three expanses of reclaimed land and a barrage to seal off the basins of the Singapore and Kallang rivers from the sea. The result is a seaside freshwater reservoir, which reduces Singapore's dependence on Malaysian water supplies. The Marina Bay Sands casino resort dominates the area, along with the extravagant Gardens by the Bay. The Esplanade arts complex is worth a detour for its skyline views, and more of the same is available at the Singapore Flyer. For one week in September, at least until 2021, you'll find crash barriers around the Singapore Flyer and the nearby Padang as the roads are transformed into the circuit for the night-time Formula 1 race.

Marina Centre

The large triangle of reclaimed land east of the Padang and the *Raffles Hotel*, robbing Beach Road of its beach, is officially called **Marina Centre**, though locals invariably invoke the names of the **Marina Square** or **Suntec City** malls when referring to it. The transition from the historical neighbourhoods to the west is a jarring one: ordinary amenities such as places of worship and schools are absent, and instead the area is dominated by the Suntec Convention Centre, plush offices and hotels, and the aforementioned malls. At the heart of the Suntec development is one minor sight – the huge, circular **Fountain of Wealth**, where there are free sound-and-light shows nightly between 8 and 9pm or so. The best reason to come, though, is to enjoy **views** of the Singapore cityscape from either the southern end of Marina Centre or the Singapore Flyer – or both.

Esplanade – Theatres on the Bay

1 Esplanade Drive • Daily 10am till late • Optional guided tours Mon–Fri 11am $20/$10 • ☎ 6828 8377, ⊚ esplanade.com • Esplanade MRT, or City Hall MRT then a 10min walk via the underground Citylink Mall

Opinion is split as to whether the two huge, spiked shells that roof the **Esplanade – Theatres on the Bay** project, just east of the Padang and the Esplanade Park, are peerless modernistic architecture or indulgent kitsch. They have variously been compared to kitchen sieves, hedgehogs, giant insect eyes and even durians (the preferred description among locals).

The venue boasts a concert hall, theatres, gallery space, numerous restaurants and, on the third floor, a branch of the National Library specializing in arts-related resources. You can take a behind-the-scenes tour of the facilities, but what lures most casual visitors are the views, particularly fine at dusk, across the bay to the Financial District and *Marina Bay Sands*. It is also worth timing a visit to catch one of the venue's many **free performances** (schedules online).

The Singapore Flyer

30 Raffles Ave, a 10min walk east of Theatres on the Bay • Daily 8.30am–10.30pm; 30min • $33/$21 • ☎ 6333 3311, ⊚ singaporeflyer. com • Promenade MRT

Standing a lofty 165m tall – the same elevation as the summit of Bukit Timah, the island's highest point, and about 30m taller than the London Eye – the **Singapore Flyer** falls slightly flat as an attraction, because it's simply not in the right place. From here the most atmospheric areas of old Singapore, including the remaining rows of shophouses in Chinatown and Little India, are largely obscured by a forest of somewhat interchangeable towers; better views can be had more cheaply from the Pinnacle@ Duxton (see page 75), or from the rooftop bars such as *1-Altitude* (see page 151).

The flight

The dollar-a-minute ride – billed as a **flight** – initially has you looking east over the Kallang district and its Sports Hub stadium complex. In the distance beyond the shipping lanes, Indonesia's Riau archipelago looks so close yet is historically much less connected to Singapore than Malaysia, thanks to the 1824 Anglo-Dutch treaty under which the British let the islands south of Singapore slip into the Dutch sphere of influence. Looking north, it's more exciting to pick out the golden domes of the Sultan Mosque and the shophouses of Arab Street beyond the twin Gateway buildings on Beach Road. As your capsule reaches maximum height, you might just make out the low hump of Bukit Timah, Singapore's tallest hill, topped with a couple of radio transmitters, on the horizon beyond Theatres on the Bay.

The descent affords good views of Marina Bay Sands and the Financial District. Originally the latter was featured on the ascent, but feng shui concerns meant the wheel's direction had to be reversed (apparently having the capsules rise pointing towards the banks' towers was channelling good luck up and away from the area).

MARINA BAY

Gateway • Transnasional Buses • Nicoll Highway

Bras Basah

Singapore Management University

Carlton Hotel
CHIJMES

Raffles Hotel

Capitol Kempinski Hotel

St Andrews Cathedral

Supreme Court

National Gallery

Parliament House

Old Parliament House

Raffles Landing Site

UOB Plaza Towers 1 & 2

One Raffles Place

FINANCIAL DISTRICT

Ocean Building

Lau Pa Sat (Telok Ayer Market)

One Shenton

Shenton Way

Purvis Street

Victoria Street

Seah Street

Beach Road

Stamford Road

Hill Street

North Bridge Road

Fashion St

Raffles City Shopping Centre

City Hall

Citylink Mall

Singapore Recreation Club

Padang

Cenotaph

Esplanade Park

Victoria Concert Hall

Victoria Theatre

Asian Civilizations Museum

Waterboat House

Merlion

Singapore River

Fullerton Hotel

One Fullerton

Singapore Land Tower

Raffles Place

Clifford Pier

The Fullerton Bay Hotel

OUE Bayfront

Customs House

The Sail

Asia Square Tower 1

Downtown

Asia Square Tower 2

Marina One

Marina Bay

Suntec City Mall
Tower 1
Tower 2
Tower 3
Tower 4
Tower 5

Fountain of Wealth

Nicoll Highway

Rochor Flyover

Ophir Flyover

MARINA CENTRE

Esplanade

Millenia Walk

❶ Marina Square Mall

❶ ❶

Esplanade-Theatres on the Bay

❷

Marina Bay Seating Gallery

Esplanade Bridge

Floating Sports Ground

Helix Footbridge

Art Science Museum

Marina Bay

❷ Marina Bay Sands ❸
❷
❸
❸

Lions Bridge

Dragonfly Bridge

Bayfront

❹ Red Dot Design Museum

Marina Bay

Raffles Boulevard

Temasek Boulevard

Raffles Avenue

Republic Boulevard

Formula 1 Race Track

Singapore Flyer

East Coast Parkway

East Coast Parkway

Bayfront Avenue

Sheares Bridge

Flower Dome

Cloud Forest

Far East Organization Children's Garden

Gardens by the Bay South

Gardens by the Bay

Marina Barrage

Marina Reservoir

Sheares Avenue

Marina Gardens Drive

Marina Mall

Marina Grove

Straits Boulevard

Central Boulevard

Marina Boulevard

Commerce St

Park St

MARINA SOUTH

Marina South

Marina South Pier

Marina South Pier

Marina Coastal Expressway

Marina Coastal Drive

Tanjong Pagar Drive

Marina View

Union St

Cross Street

Boon Tat St

Straits Boulevard

Tanjong Rhu Road

MARINA EAST

East Coast Parkway

Nicol Highway

Bayfront Avenue

Bay East Drive

Marina Bay Golf Course

Bay East Garden

Tanjong Rhu MRT station

N

0   200
metres

Marina Bay Cruise Centre

St John's & Kusu Islands

● EATING

Lavo	4
Nostra Cucina	3
Paulaner Bräuhaus	1
TWG Tea Garden	2

■ DRINKING AND NIGHTLIFE

Cé La Vi	3
Orgo	2
Tap Craft Beer Bar	1

■ ACCOMMODATION

Marina Bay Sands	2
Ritz-Carlton Millenia	1
Westin	3

● SHOPPING

Lim's Legacy	1
Red Dot Design Museum	4
The Shoppes at Marina Bay Sands	3
That CD Shop	2

Marina South

Unlike Marina Centre, which began to open for business in the 1990s, **Marina South** seemed to take years to get going. It had its own MRT station, yet few amenities except a middling park (now subsumed into **Gardens by the Bay**), and its main purpose was to serve as a conduit for part of the East Coast Parkway highway. Then came the bombshell of allowing casinos to set up in Singapore, which ultimately led to the building of **Marina Bay Sands**. Marina South is also the site of a thicket of glass towers making up Singapore's new financial district, although visitors may find it hard to distinguish where it starts and the old one ends.

Marina Bay Sands

10 Bayfront Ave • Box office ☎ 6688 8826, ⓦ marinabaysands.com • Bayfront MRT, or bus #106 from Orchard Rd/Bras Basah Rd or #133 from Victoria St

Rarely does a building become an icon quite as instantly as the *Marina Bay Sands* hotel and casino, its three 55-floor towers topped and connected by a vast, curved-surfboard-like deck, the **SkyPark**. The most ambitious undertaking yet by its owners, Las Vegas Sands, it opened in 2010 and quickly replaced the Merlion as the Singapore image of choice in the travel brochures, summing up the country's glitzy fascination with Mammon. Even if you have no interest in the casino – open, naturally, 24/7 – the complex, which includes a convention centre, a shopping mall, concert venues and restaurants, is well worth exploring. The hotel atrium, often so busy with people gawping that it feels like a busy train station concourse, is especially striking, the sides of the building sloping into each other overhead to give the impression of being inside a narrow glassy pyramid.

In the evening, a free laser show, **Spectra** (daily 8pm & 9 pm, Fri & Sat also 10pm; 15min), splays multicoloured beams from atop the hotel's towers onto Marina Bay, with fountains shooting up from below. Visible from around the bay, the display isn't that captivating unless you're at the hotel itself.

4

THE MARINA BAY PROJECT

Marina Bay can be viewed as yet another triumph, perhaps the most impressive, of Singapore's long-term urban planning. However, there is an alternative view, namely that its success was born more out of serendipity than foresight. The original idea had been to create a new downtown area for the tiny island. To that end, **Marina Centre** became the first zone to be reclaimed from the sea, in the 1970s and 1980s. Its malls and hotels were already beginning to open in the early 1990s, and development there was crowned by the opening of Esplanade – Theatres by the Bay in 2002.

But back in 1987, Lee Kuan Yew, fed up with the constant (and still ongoing) bickering over the pricing of the water supplies that Malaysia pipes to Singapore via the Causeway, had floated another idea: what if land reclamation, combined with a dam, could create an enormous coastal **reservoir**? The scheme, together with smaller counterparts elsewhere, would reduce or end this potentially crippling dependency. Still, it wasn't until seventeen years later that the government would invite companies to tender to build the **Marina Barrage**. One year after that came the announcement that Singapore would allow casinos to set up. With the successful launch of *Marina Bay Sands*, **Marina South** finally seemed to have found its *raison d'être*.

The last piece of the jigsaw was the sheer amount of green space built into the area, in the form of gardens, plus a golf course at **Marina East**. On the face of it, this doesn't offer a fantastic return on the huge amount of taxpayers' money pumped into creating Marina Bay. It could be that the reservoir's arrival has curtailed the density of the surrounding buildings – cleanliness of the waters being now paramount – or, more likely, that fallow land will be developed as the need arises.

The SkyPark

Observation deck Mon–Thurs 9.30am–10pm, Fri–Sun 9.30am–11pm • $23/$17, tickets and access via box office on basement 1 of tower 3, at the northern end of the complex

From what would once have been an impossible vantage point, high above the sea before the creation of Marina Bay, the observation deck of the **SkyPark** affords superb views over Singapore's Colonial District on one side and the conservatories of the Gardens by the Bay project on the other. Unfortunately tickets are overpriced, and don't allow you up close to that famous 150m infinity pool. However, you don't need a ticket at all if you treat yourself to a meal or a drink at any SkyPark venue, such as *Cé La Vi* (see page 151).

The ArtScience Museum

At the northern end of the complex, close to the Helix Footbridge that links the area with the Singapore Flyer and Marina Centre • Daily 10am–7pm, last admission 6pm • Prices vary depending on the exhibition

The **ArtScience Museum** is easily spotted: its shape is meant to represent a stylized lotus blossom, though from certain angles it looks more like a stubby-fingered hand. Its remit is to decode the connections between art and science, but the top-drawer travelling exhibitions it puts on may only be tenuously linked to the museum's supposed aim. There's only one permanent gallery, Future World, in which children (and grown-ups) can interact with colourful multimedia installations by, for example, crafting and scanning objects which then pop up in a large-scale animation.

The Red Dot Design Museum

11 Marina Boulevard • Mon–Thurs 10am–8pm, Fri–Sun 10am–11pm • Entry by donation (at least $6.40 for foreign visitors), free during MAAD market • ☎ 6514 0111, ⓦ museum.red-dot.sg • Downtown, Bayfront or Marina Bay MRT

Housed in a low-slung glass structure, the **Red Dot Design Museum** focuses on international product design and the creative use of illustration and multimedia, following the process from conceptualization all the way through to the realized work, be it a sports car or an art installation. It's at its best during the crafts market, **MAAD** (certain weeks Fri 5pm–midnight) when local artists and designers showcase their work. The gift shop is a good place to pick up unusual gadgets and accessories (see page 164).

Gardens by the Bay

18 Marina Gardens Drive • Daily 5am–2am; conservatories 9am–9pm • Free admission; OCBC Skyway $8/$5; conservatories $28/$15; last ticket sales at 8pm • ☎ 6420 6848, ⓦ gardensbythebay.com.sg • Bayfront MRT (enter via the Dragonfly Bridge) or Gardens by the Bay MRT (when open)

From afar, two vast conservatories, roofs arched like the backs of foraging dinosaurs, announce the southern section of **Gardens by the Bay**. The gardens are nominally split into three chunks around Marina Bay, but everyone uses the name to apply to the southern area (formally Bay South Garden), which is by far the largest and practically a second botanical garden for the island.

One conservatory houses Mediterranean and African flora, the highlight being the stands of small, bizarrely shaped **baobab** trees; less impressive are the collections of flowering plants, so tidy that they look like a formal display in a well-kept European park. The neighbouring conservatory nurtures **cloud forest** of the kind found on Southeast Asia's highest peaks, and includes a 35m "mountain" covered in ferns, rhododendrons and insect-eating sundews and butterworts.

The gardens' other big draw is the **Supertree Grove**, an array of towers resembling gigantic golf tees and sheathed in a sort of red trelliswork, from which climbers, ferns and orchids poke out. Bizarrely, the Supertrees had a starring role in the 2015 game *Call of Duty: Black Ops III*, in which players have to blast their way out of a devastated version of the gardens. Although impressive from afar, the towers don't look quite so alluring close up; more exciting is to walk the long, slightly wobbly **OCBC Skyway**, arcing between the tallest two Supertrees high up and offering good 360° views. At night, though, the

Supertrees come into their own when built-in solar cells illuminate them in myriad colours, and they take centre stage in free **sound and light shows** (7.45pm & 8.45pm).

Singapore Maritime Gallery

Upstairs at Marina South Pier, 31 Marina Coastal Drive • Tues–Sun 9am–6pm • Free • ☎ 6325 5707, Ⓦ maritimegallery.sg • Marina South Pier MRT, or a 10min walk from the southern end of Gardens by the Bay

One of the country's most low-profile museums, tucked away in the boat terminal for Singapore's southern islands (see page 113), turns out to be a little gem. The **Singapore Maritime Gallery** takes only half an hour to see and boasts no pretty pictures, but it offers serious insights into how the little island became one of the world's busiest ports. Panels explain how Singapore has kept its nose in front over the years by, for example, being an early adopter of containerization and constantly developing facilities in new locations. There's also a worthy discussion of how fuel changes might mitigate the hugely underappreciated problem of shipping emissions, but the most fun exhibit is a **simulated bridge** where you attempt to steer your vessel through a violent storm playing out on a five-panel display.

The Marina Barrage

8 Marina Gardens Drive • Unrestricted access to barrage and grounds; Singapore Sustainability Gallery Wed–Mon 9am–6pm • Free • ☎ 6514 5959, Ⓦ pub.gov.sg/marinabarrage • Gardens by the Bay MRT (when open), or Tanjong Pagar MRT, then bus #400 (from Anson Rd; 3 hourly), or a 20min walk from Marina South Pier MRT

As a feat of engineering, the **barrage** at the southeastern corner of Marina Bay is undoubtedly impressive, but it's underwhelming to walk along the top of the dam, a straight, 330m-long concrete structure. The barrage's modus operandi is simple: it only allows water to flow seaward, driven either by pumps or, when the tide is low or Marina Bay is swollen by rains, simply under gravity. As a result, the salinity of Marina Bay fell inexorably once the dam commenced operations in 2008, to the point that it is now a freshwater reservoir.

West of the dam is the barrage's control complex, whose enormous **green roof** – planted with grass and surrounding an oval-shaped central atrium – is the key attraction for many locals. It's popular as a spot to picnic and fly kites in the cool of the evening, with great vistas back towards the Singapore Flyer and the glittering skyline of the Financial District and Marina Centre.

The Singapore Sustainability Gallery

Part of the space beneath the green roof is taken up by the **Singapore Sustainability Gallery**, a museum that tries its best to talk up the island's eco-friendly ambitions. Although it makes all the right noise on the importance of cutting greenhouse emissions, the profusion of environmental targets it sets for Singapore give a sense that the island is trying to play green catch-up to similarly wealthy nations in the West, most notably in promoting recycling and exploiting its obvious solar-power potential. Ultimately, this is still a nation that profits nicely from hosting one of the world's largest oil refineries, at Jurong.

Bay East Garden

Western shore of Marina East • Daily 24hr (south entrance from Marina Barrage 7am–7pm) • Tanjong Rhu MRT (when open), or bus #158 southbound from Aljunied or Mountbatten MRT to the north gate at Rhu Cross, or walk from Marina Barrage to the south gate

The sole attraction in **Marina East** – the third "jaw" of Marina Bay – is **Bay East Garden**, the east wing of Gardens by the Bay, and a plain Jane compared to its southern neighbour. After much talk of themed gardens and other ideas, it seems the site has finally found its proper purpose: from 2021, a "founders' memorial" will be built here to commemorate prominent leaders from the era of decolonization in the Fifties and Sixties. For now, come here to chill out, stroll and enjoy more views of the jagged skyline.

UNESCO LISTED BOTANIC GARDENS

Orchard Road and the Botanic Gardens

It would be hard to conjure an image more at odds with the present reality of Orchard Road than historian Mary Turnbull's depiction of a colonial-era "country lane lined with bamboo hedges and shrubbery, with trees meeting overhead". A hundred years ago, merchants would have strolled past rows of nutmeg trees, followed at a discreet distance by their manservants. Today, Orchard Road is lined with symbols of consumption: huge, glitzy shopping malls and fancy restaurants and bars, either in the malls themselves or housed in top-flight hotels. However, the bucolic allure of the plantation avenue of old survives 1500m west of its start, where you'll find the area's one true sight, the marvellous Botanic Gardens.

5

Orchard Road channels eastbound traffic from Tanglin Road all the way to Bras Basah and Selegie roads, 3km away near the Colonial District; all **buses** along Orchard Road return west along Penang Road, Somerset Road, Grange Road and Orchard Boulevard.

Orchard Road

Although the parade of designer names on **Orchard Road** – often with multiple outlets for each brand – is impressive, the area has not been totally untouched by the malaise afflicting central shopping precincts the world over, losing trade to malls in the suburbs. The most striking of the malls, **Ion Orchard**, right above Orchard MRT, has a bulgy glass frontage vaguely reminiscent of Theatres on the Bay, and is topped by a tower of luxury apartments. If you shop here, it's possible to access their 56th-floor viewing gallery and multimedia experience, **Ion Sky**; $20 worth of receipts will earn you one ticket.

Just about the only building complex of significant age – though now highly modernized – remaining on Orchard Road itself can be glimpsed west of Scotts Road, where the **Thai embassy** has its origins in the purchase of a mansion here by the Siamese king in the late nineteenth century.

Dhoby Ghaut

The **Dhoby Ghaut** area, at the eastern tip of Orchard Road, is where Indian *dhobies* (laundrymen) used to wash clothes in the Stamford Canal, which once ran along Orchard and Stamford roads.

ORCHARD ROAD

Cathay building

Cathay Gallery: Level 2, the Cathay building, 2 Handy Rd • Mon–Sat 11am–7pm • Free • Dhoby Ghaut or Bencoolen MRT

5

While the days of the *dhobies* are long gone, something of the past survives in the **Cathay building**, home to the company behind one of Singapore's oldest cinema chains. Behind the 1939 Art Deco facade is a small mall, a multiplex cinema (naturally) and the **Cathay Gallery**, displaying memorabilia of the Cathay Organization's eight decades in the movie business, including its heyday in the 1950s and 1960s, when the company made its own Chinese- and Malay-language films.

The Istana

Open on five public holidays a year • $2 grounds admission fee, plus $2 to enter the Istana • Opening days listed at ⓦ istana.gov.sg • Dhoby Ghaut MRT

A three-minute walk west along Orchard Road from Dhoby Ghaut MRT takes you past the Plaza Singapura mall, beyond which stern-looking soldiers guard the main gate of Singapore's **Istana** (Malay for "palace"), completed in 1869 as a replacement for Government House at Fort Canning. With ornate cornices, elegant louvred shutters and a high mansard roof, this Neoclassically styled building was the official residence of Singapore's British governors; now it's home to Singapore's president, a ceremonial role for which elections are nonetheless contested. Also within the grounds is **Sri Temasek**, a much less grand two-storey house that was the official residence of the colonial secretary. At the main gate, the first Sunday of the month (except July & Aug) sees a changing-of-the-guard ceremony at 5.45pm.

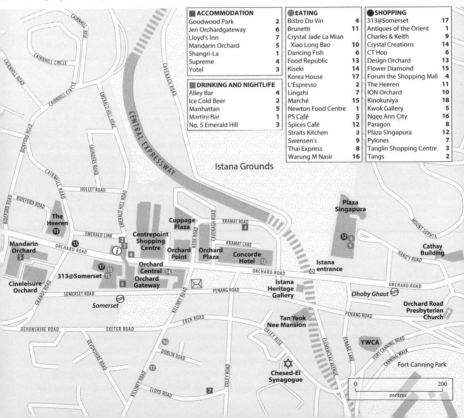

5

Istana Heritage Gallery

35 Orchard Rd (opposite the Istana main gate) • Thurs–Tues 10am–6pm • Free • ☎ 6904 4289

Although you'd have to be lucky to be in town just when the Istana happens to be open, you can pop into the **Istana Heritage Gallery** any time. This mini-museum houses few artefacts, mostly refined gifts given to the president by foreign dignitaries, and mainly relies on photos of colonial-era balls and so forth to give a sense of the Istana's evolution over its many decades of existence.

Tan Yeok Nee Mansion

101 Penang Rd • Not open to the public • Dhoby Ghaut MRT

Across Orchard Road from the Istana is a little architectural curiosity, the **Tan Yeok Nee Mansion**, built in the 1880s in traditional southern Chinese style for a wealthy Teochew merchant who dealt in pepper and gambier, a resin used in tanning. Featuring ornate roofs and massive granite pillars, this courtyard house served as headquarters to the Singapore Salvation Army from 1940 until 1991, and hosted the Asian offshoot of the University of Chicago's business school until 2015. Today it is occupied by a centre for traditional Chinese medicine.

Emerald Hill

Somerset MRT

Not ten minutes' walk west of the Istana, a number of architecturally notable houses have survived the bulldozers at **Emerald Hill**, behind the Centrepoint mall. The hill was granted to Englishman William Cuppage in 1845 and was for some years afterwards the site of a large nutmeg plantation. After his death in 1872, the land was subdivided and sold off. Walk up Emerald Hill Road today and you'll see some exquisite early twentieth-century houses in the so-called Chinese Baroque style, typified by the use of coloured ceramic tiles, carved swing doors, shuttered windows and pastel-shaded walls with fine plaster mouldings. Unsurprisingly, quite a few now host trendy restaurants and bars.

The Goodwood Park Hotel

22 Scotts Rd • Orchard MRT

Malls line the initial stretch of Scotts Road, leading north from Orchard MRT towards Newton Circus, before giving way to the impressive **Goodwood Park Hotel**, with gleaming walls and a distinctive squat, steeple-like tower. Having started out in 1900 as the Teutonia Club for German expats, it was commandeered by the British Custodian of Enemy Property with the outbreak of war across Europe in 1914, and didn't open again until 1918, after which it served for several years as a function hall. In 1929, it became a hotel, though by 1942 Japanese officers were billeted here and at the *Raffles* (designed by the same architect, incidentally); perhaps fittingly, the *Goodwood Park* was later used for war-crimes trials. Today the hotel remains one of the classiest in town and is a well-regarded venue for a British-style tea.

The Botanic Gardens

1 Cluny Rd • Daily 5am–midnight (certain sections open by day only) • Free • ☎ 6471 7300, ⓦ sbg.org.sg • Tanglin gate: Napier MRT (once open) or Farrer Road MRT; bus #7 from Arab St area or #174 from Chinatown, both via Penang Rd/Somerset Rd. Bukit Timah Rd entrance: Botanic Gardens MRT

Singapore has long made green space an integral part of the island's landscape, but none of its parks comes close to matching the refinement of the **Singapore Botanic Gardens** – aptly anointed as the island's sole UNESCO World Heritage Site. Founded in 1859, the gardens were where the Brazilian seeds that gave rise to the great rubber plantations of Malaya were first nurtured in 1877. Henry Ridley, named the gardens' director the following year, recognized the financial potential of rubber and spent the next twenty years persuading Malayan plantation-owners to convert to this new crop, an obsession that earned him the nickname "Mad" Ridley. In later years the gardens became a centre for the breeding of new orchid hybrids.

These days the park extends all the way north to Bukit Timah Road, where the Botanic Gardens MRT station gives access to newer, less interesting parts of the gardens; the itinerary that follows assumes the classic approach up Tanglin and Napier roads to the **Tanglin gate** at the start of Cluny Road. If you're feeling peckish while visiting, you can either take advantage of restaurants and cafés within the gardens or, more interestingly, nearby at **Dempsey Hill** (see page 143) or **Holland Village** (see page 146).

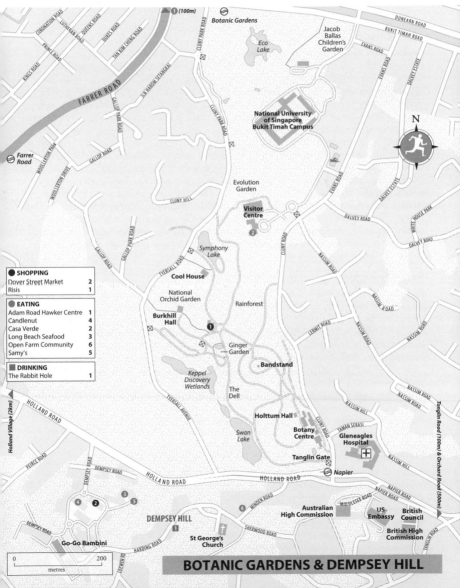

BOTANIC GARDENS & DEMPSEY HILL

5

Into the gardens

Once through the Tanglin gate, you can take a sharp right up the slope to the **Botany Centre** just ahead, a research centre where you can pick up free garden maps from the information desk. Alternatively, continue straight down the path from the gate, lined with frangipanis, casuarinas and the odd majestic banyan tree, for five minutes to reach the tranquil Swan Lake, nearly as old as the gardens themselves. To the left of the path is the new **SPH Walk of Giants** – a walkway at treetop height – and, beyond it, another new section on wetland plants; both are very much still bedding in. Stay on the path, however, and at the lake's far end you can wander through a tiny tract of surviving rainforest to the **ginger garden**, packed with flowering gingers as exotic and gaudy as anything you could hope to see in the tropics.

The National Orchid Garden

Daily 8.30am–7pm, last admission 6pm • $5/free

A feast of blooms of almost every hue is on show at the **National Orchid Garden.** There's an entire section of orchids named after dignitaries and celebrities who have visited; *Dendrobium Margaret Thatcher* turns out to be a severe pink with two of its petals looking like twisted ribbons, while *Vandaenopsis Nelson Mandela* is a reassuring warm yellowy-brown. Looking slightly out of place is the black-and-white **Burkill Hall**, exemplifying the so-called Tropical Tudor style, few examples of which now survive in Singapore; the gardens' director once lived here.

Be sure to visit the **Cool House**, which is due to reopen at the end of 2019 after a two-year refit. It mimics the misty conditions at the tops of equatorial mountains, and its previous incarnation housed some stunning slipper orchids, their petals forming a pouch below, as well as insectivorous pitcher plants. Finally, at the exit, the gift shop stocks an incredible range of orchid paraphernalia, including blossoms encased in glass.

Beyond the orchid garden, head up the boardwalk to enter a second patch of **rainforest** with a trail past numbered highlights, including another fine banyan tree. The trail and forest end above **Symphony Lake**, where occasional concerts are staged.

From Symphony Lake back to Tanglin gate

By now you've seen the best of what the gardens have to offer, and there's not that much to be gained by continuing north. If you head back to Tanglin gate, look out for one of the park's most stunning trees, a 47m *jelawai*, on the edge of the rainforest tract; this and several other exceptionally tall trees are fitted with lightning conductors. Close by, to the right, is one of the loveliest spots in the whole of Singapore, a grassy area centred on a 1930s **bandstand**, encircled by eighteen rain trees for shade.

Heading straight on from here, you should arrive back at the Botany Centre via **Holttum Hall**, a 1920s house that hosts a museum of the gardens' history (daily 9am–6pm). Its most striking exhibit is a chandelier made entirely of test tubes and lab flasks – celebrating the gardens' role in plant research. Alternatively, head downhill through the **sundial garden** to end up back at Swan Lake.

From Symphony Lake north to Bukit Timah Road

Beyond Symphony Lake is yet another colonial house, once home to the gardens' deputy director, and, marooned in the middle of the gardens, the **Visitor Centre**, with its own gift shop and café. Continuing on, bear gradually right to reach the **Ethnobotany Garden**, which focuses on plants used by Southeast Asia's indigenous people. With children in tow, you might want to plough on to the **Jacob Ballas garden** (see page 169), or else it's several minutes' walk through the bamboo garden at the northern end of the park to reach the MRT station. For inexpensive stomach-fillers, follow the overhead footbridge from the station to cross to the far side of the canal, where you'll find the **Adam Road hawker centre** (see page 143).

Northern Singapore

North of downtown, it's still possible to glimpse Singapore's wilder side. True, satellite new towns and suburbs shadow the major thoroughfares, but the island's core remains dominated by thirty square kilometres of rainforest and reservoirs, forming a central nature reserve. Jungle hikes, notably at Bukit Timah, are not too taxing. Points of interest include the Former Ford Factory – actually a museum of wartime – and Bukit Brown, one of Singapore's last remaining historic cemeteries. Two sights lurk southeast of Bukit Brown: the slick Lian Shan Shuang Lin Buddhist complex, and the Sun Yat Sen Nanyang Memorial Hall. But it is up in the far north of the island that you'll find the area's main lure, Singapore's highly regarded zoo (and its Night Safari and River Safari spin-offs), as well as the Sungei Buloh Wetland Reserve.

The Sun Yat Sen Nanyang Memorial Hall

11 Tai Gin Rd • Tues–Sun 10am–5pm • $4/$2 • ☎ 6256 7377, ⓦ sysnmh.org.sg • Bus #139 from Serangoon Rd in Little India stops close by; alternatively bus #131 from Farrer Park MRT (exit A) to Zhongshan Mall, from where it's a 5min walk north to the museum • To walk from here to Lian Shan Shuang Lin Monastery (see below), 15min away, head east along Ah Hood Rd and Jalan Rajah to the apartment block numbered 108, where bridges over the canal and highway will leave you just west of the temples

Sun Yat Sen was the first leader of republican China, and it was during the final years of imperial rule that he visited Southeast Asia to drum up support for his revolutionary movement. The villa where he lodged in Singapore is now a museum, the **Sun Yat Sen Nanyang Memorial Hall**. There are panels about Sun's activities, of course, and portraits of the great and the good of Singapore society who backed him, but the unifying theme is really the modern evolution of Chinese identity. More interesting for non-historians are displays about the ending of the hideous practice of foot-binding in women, and men ceasing to sport pigtails. In the section on literacy and education, look out for the antique **printing press** with movable type for thousands of Chinese characters.

There are also two fantastical recent **paintings** to gawp at. Taking up an entire wall is Li Shu Ji's *Overseas Chinese as the Mother of the Revolution*, showing Sun in some Malayan jungle idyll, thronged by Chinese settlers; his three-fingered gesture isn't a selfie attempt with a non-existent phone, but symbolizes democracy, nationalism and welfare. Just as weird is *Sun Yat Sen and Chinatown*, our hero standing amid a motley crew of street characters, with what could well be the Sri Mariamman Temple in the distance.

Lian Shan Shuang Lin Monastery

184 Jalan Toa Payoh, just north of the Pan-Island Expressway • Mon–Fri 8am–5pm, Sat 9am–1pm • ☎ 6259 6924, ⓦ shuanglin.sg • Free • Bus #8 from Toa Payoh MRT stops a 5min walk beyond the complex • To walk from here to the Sun Yat Sen Nanyang Memorial Hall (see above), use the bridges just west of the Cheng Huang Temple to get across the highway and canal, then head west along Jalan Rajah and Ah Hood Rd (15min)

The **Lian Shan Shuang Lin Monastery** (an older name, the **Siong Lim Temple**, is also used) revels in a spacious compound that makes Chinatown's shrines seem boxy by comparison. The complex has its roots in an endowment of land by one of Singapore's many migrants-made-good, allowing it to be built in the 1900s.

Arriving by bus, you enter the complex from the east, close to its impressive seven-storey **pagoda**, a small gold Buddha set into one of its eight sides. To the north (right) is the **Guan Yin Dian**, holding a multi-armed and -eyed bronze representation of the Bodhisattva Guan Yin. Northwest of the pagoda, the **Gong De Tang** contains serried ranks of what look like small wooden trophies, some bearing people's photographs: these are **ancestral tablets**, representing the departed.

You'll know you've reached the main courtyard by the two **granite pillars** in its southern corners. On the north side is the lavish **Hall of Celestial Kings**, holding a quartet of deities, one depicted with a pipa (Chinese lute) to offer musical guidance, another wielding a magical umbrella. Less impressive but of greater spiritual significance is the **Mahavira Hall** beyond, housing three Buddhas.

Set slightly apart in the far west of the site is the substantial but comparatively drab **Cheng Huang Temple**, last overhauled in the 1970s (everything else was more fancily restored in the 1990s). What look like two toy ponies mysteriously placed here may be covered in four-digit numbers – scribbled by devotees hoping for a lottery win.

Bukit Timah

Making up the western fringes of the central nature reserve, **Bukit Timah** is Singapore's highest hill and the ideal place to tackle Singapore's remaining pocket of primary rainforest. The roots of its name, Malay for "hill [of] tin", are a mystery: the only mineral resource here is granite, as two quarry lakes within this part of the reserve attest. Locals often refer to the peak as "Bukit Timah Hill", a deliberate tautology to distinguish it from the surrounding Bukit Timah suburb.

NORTHERN SINGAPORE

MALAYSIA

Straits of Johor

MALAYSIA
Johor Bahru

0 2
kilometres

N

PUNGGOL
Punggol
Sengkang
Buangkok
Hougang
Kovan
Serangoon
Woodleigh
Bartley
Tai Seng
Ubi
Macpherson
Potong Pasir
Mattar
Kaki Bukit

Seletar Airport

Lower Seletar Reservoir

Yishun
Khatib
Canberra (opens 2019)

SEMBAWANG
Sembawang
Admiralty
Woodlands North

WOODLANDS
Woodlands South
Woodlands
Woodlands Checkpoint
JB Sentral Train Station
Woodlands Train Station
CAUSEWAY
Marsiling

KRANJI
Kranji
Kranji War Cemetery & Memorial
Singapore Turf Club

Kranji Reservoir

SUNGEI BULOH WETLAND RESERVE

LIM CHU KANG

Yew Tee
Choa Chu Kang
Bukit Gombak
Bukit Batok

JURONG
Boon Lay
Lakeside
Jurong Lake
Chinese Garden
Jurong East
Science Centre Singapore
Pioneer
Joo Koon

Springleaf
Lentor
Upper Seletar Reservoir

Zoo, Night Safari & River Safari

Dairy Farm Nature Park

Upper Peirce Reservoir
Lower Peirce Reservoir

CENTRAL NATURE RESERVE
Tree Top Walk

Yio Chu Kang
Ang Mo Kio
Mayflower
Bright Hill
Upper Thomson
Mary-mount
Caldecott

Lorong Chuan
Bishan
Braddell
Toa Payoh

Lian Shan Shuang Lin Monastery
Sun Yat Sen Nanyang Memorial Hall

MacRitchie Reservoir Park
MacRitchie Reservoir

Bukit Brown Cemetery
Mount Pleasant
Adam Road Hawker Centre

BUKIT TIMAH
BUKIT TIMAH NATURE RESERVE
Bukit Timah (164m)

Tan Kah Kee
Sixth Avenue
King Albert
Beauty World

Bukit Panjang
Cashew
Hillview
Former Ford Factory
Bukit Batok

Bukit Timah Nature Reserve

Hindhede Drive • Daily 7am–7pm; visitor centre daily 8am–5.30pm • ⓦ nparks.gov.sg • Free • Beauty World MRT (exit B), then walk 10min north on the same side of the road to the Courts furniture store, where an overhead bridge connects to Hindhede Rd; access also possible via surrounding parks such as Dairy Hill Nature Park (see page 93) and even from MacRitchie Reservoir Park (see page 93)

The nature reserve at Bukit Timah was established in 1883 by Nathaniel Cantley, then superintendent of the Botanic Gardens. Wildlife abounded in this part of Singapore in the mid-nineteenth century, when the natural historian **Alfred Russel Wallace** came here to do fieldwork; he later observed that "in all my subsequent travels in the East I rarely if ever met with so productive a spot". Wallace also noted the presence of tiger traps, but by the 1930s Singapore's tigers had met their end.

Long-tailed macaques are relatively easy to spot; you may be luckiest in the early morning or late afternoon. Other possible wildlife sightings include the elusive pangolin and pit vipers (seldom dangerous, unless startled or provoked). Otherwise, what really impresses is the dipterocarp forest itself, with its towering **emergents** – trees that have reached the top of the jungle canopy as a result of a lucky break, such as a fallen tree allowing enough light through to the forest floor to nurture saplings to maturity.

Exploring the reserve

Anything genuinely wild seems to be anathema to Singapore's park authorities, so don't expect a full-blown jungle-trekking experience. All four **trails**, colour-coded on maps, consist largely of family-friendly boardwalks, steps and stretches of proper road. Most people tackle the red trail (30min), which is the road up to the summit at a paltry 164m; a flight of narrow steps halfway along – the Summit Path – offers a shortcut to the top.

Former Ford Factory

351 Upper Bukit Timah Rd, 1km northwest of Bukit Timah • Tues–Sun 9am–5.30pm • $3 • ⓦ nas.gov.sg/formerfordfactory • Beauty World MRT, then bus #67, #170, #171 or #961 three stops north to Bukit Batok Nature Park, followed by a 5min walk north

Bukit Timah's old Ford car factory was the first plant of its type in Southeast Asia when it opened in October 1941. Within a few weeks, Japanese troops would land on the Malay Peninsula, and on February 15, 1942, Lt Gen Percival, head of the Allied forces in Singapore, surrendered to Japan's General Yamashita in the factory's boardroom. Today the worthwhile **Former Ford Factory** museum recreates the scene among its displays.

LONG-TAILED MACAQUES

Encounters with **long-tailed macaques** are common enough as to be unremarkable in Singapore's central nature reserve; one estimate puts their numbers island-wide at 1500. While sightings are never guaranteed, the animals have a habit of popping up when you least expect it, perhaps in trees fringing roads or strolling along the roads themselves.

The macaques have red-tinged brown fur and grow to lengths of some 40 centimetres (minus tail); males are larger and heavier. As social animals, they live in small troops bonded around related females; sexually mature males in the group are unrelated and have their own hierarchy.

Although the animals will consume animal matter, by far the most important component of their diet is **fruit**. Should you encounter them, note that **feeding macaques is prohibited** to stop them becoming more reliant on humans (it is not uncommon for the creatures to pick through people's bins). Official advice also warns against disturbing or provoking the animals, so don't allow children to chase or yell at them.

If you don't see any, console yourself with the thought that one reason for the monkeys to venture out is hunger, so their absence may mean they are content to forage deeper in the reserve, in part thanks to a green corridor built over the Bukit Timah Expressway to counter the dissection of the jungle by new roadways. You can learn more about Singapore's macaques and other primates by signing up for a free guided **monkey walk** with the Jane Goodall Institute (most weekends; ⓦ janegoodall.org.sg).

In some detail, the museum focuses on the build-up to war, the occupation and, less successfully, its messy aftermath – including the communist insurgency in Malaya – and the beginnings of decolonization. Run by Singapore's National Archives service, it ergo leans heavily on documents and ephemera – everything from Japanese textbooks imposed on schools and the notorious wartime "banana money" (bananas were depicted on one Japanese-issued banknote) to sketches by POWs at Changi and watercolours commissioned by the occupying administration. Not least among the privations of occupation were food shortages, as recalled by a display outside on wartime crops.

6

Dairy Farm Nature Park

Dairy Farm Rd • Daily 7am–7pm • Free • Ⓦ nparks.gov.sg • Hillview MRT

Dairy Farm Nature Park is a grand name for what is simply the northern fringe of the Bukit Timah nature reserve, but is one of three parks meant to serve as "buffers" for the reserve itself, cushioning it against human impacts. The main reason to come is to tackle an alternative route up Bukit Timah, the **Dairy Farm loop**, beginning at a long, low building called the **Wallace Education Centre** along Dairy Farm Road. As displays meant for visiting school groups explain, the centre was once a cowshed at, bizarrely, the area's now defunct dairy farm.

Steps close by are the start of the loop, which forks after just a few minutes; both branches eventually join the yellow trail marked on Bukit Timah maps and will get you to the summit in 30 to 45 minutes. If you turn right where the trail forks, you can later ascend via a branch trail called the **Seraya loop**, which can boast good views over a quarry lake if the vegetation at the vantage point has recently been hacked back.

MacRitchie Reservoir Park

Main entrance at the eastern end of Lornie Rd • No formal hours • Free • Ⓦ nparks.gov.sg • Caldecott MRT, then a 5min walk west along Toa Payoh Rise and up Thomson Rd, or bus #166 from Little India MRT (exit A), or bus #167 from Newton MRT (exit A)

In the southeastern corner of the central reserve, **MacRitchie Reservoir** is one of the oldest of Singapore's reservoirs – it was created in the 1860s – and the closest to downtown, Marina Bay excepted. The manicured gardens surrounding the entrance on Lornie Road don't set the right note for a nature park, but it's easy enough to get away from them on flattish trails that skirt the glassy waters and then take you into the jungle (allow three hours for the longest loop). Much more relaxed are the water's-edge boardwalks a short walk to the west and east of the car park.

The Treetop Walk

Close to the western end of Island Club Rd • Tues–Sat 9am–5pm, Sun 8.30am–5pm • Free • To hike there from the reservoir entrance, turn right and use the trails that begin at the eastern edge of the water (1hr 30min one-way); alternatively catch bus #166 or #167 to the start of Island Club Rd, then walk in (45min)

In the jungle on the far side of the reservoir, some 2.5km from the Lornie Road entrance as the crow flies, is the **Treetop Walk**, a 250m circular trail suspended above ground, giving a monkey's-eye view of the forest. It is a bit of a hassle to reach, but as long as there are no noisy school parties bustling across, you've a decent chance of spotting some birdlife.

Kayaking

Rental hours daily 9–10.30am & 2–4.30pm via Paddle Lodge • From $15/hr • ☎ 6258 0057, Ⓦ scf.org.sg

You can get out on MacRitchie's waters in a **kayak**, but the experience is a mixed bag. Only those with a locally recognized kayaking certificate can venture along half the reservoir's length, using monotonous lanes; unqualified kayakers must stick to

6

BIRTH AND SLOW DEATH OF A CEMETERY

Bukit Brown is named after **G.H. Brown**, a British businessman who lived in the vicinity in the mid-nineteenth century. The land was subsequently bought by three Hokkien businessmen, and then in the 1910s, the colonial government acquired part of it to create a sort of official cemetery for all Chinese subgroups; that section would become the Bukit Brown of today. In the 1970s the cemetery was deemed full, since when it has been more or less abandoned (and since when **cremation** has become largely standard practice in Singapore, given the lack of land).

Bukit Brown's present significance stems not merely from the importance of some personages buried there, but also from its sheer size – it stretches 2km east to Thomson Road – and location fairly close to downtown. Despite the site's potential for redevelopment, it seemed immune to the fate of many of Singapore's other old cemeteries, which were uprooted without much outcry. Despite pushback at the announcement to build a highway right through Bukit Brown, that road – Lornie Highway – is now open, slicing through the northwest corner of the cemetery.

designated areas around the reservoir's edges. To find out more, talk to Paddle Lodge in the green building a short walk east of the entrance and car park.

Bukit Brown cemetery

Main entrance opposite the golf course at the western end of Lornie Rd; walk in via Kheam Hock Rd and then left down Lorong Halwa • Any westbound bus from Lornie Rd opposite the MacRitchie Reservoir entrance, or #157 from Toa Payoh MRT

Only 2km west of the entrance to MacRitchie Reservoir Park, the Chinese cemetery at **Bukit Brown** captures something of the ongoing evolution of Singapore society and customs. The site, threatened with redevelopment, has been the focus of a concerted campaign to save it. As a part of this campaign, activists have created cemetery maps marked with the graves of various notables, as well as diagrams of the different tomb types. These materials form part of their free, illustrated guide to the site (download the Bukit Brown Wayfinder at ⓦsingaporeheritage.org). Even so, the cemetery remains confusing to navigate, and the best way to get a proper insight into the place is to come on one of the free volunteer-led half-day walking **tours** (book on ⓦpeatix.com/group/16067). They unpack the symbolism of the tomb designs and inscriptions, and give you the low-down on the lives of the great and the good interred here; one tour is, unsurprisingly, titled Crazy Rich Asians (as it happens, the great-grandfather of author Kevin Kwan was a banking tycoon and is buried here). On a practical note, be sure to bring sunscreen and mosquito repellent.

The site

The cemetery gates are just five minutes' walk from Lornie Road, beyond which the graves are clustered across many low mounds. It's a good site to wander for an hour or so: the grounds are lush, there's the chance to spot birdlife and the tomb designs are fascinating. One of the few times of year when Bukit Brown gets busy is during April's **Qing Ming** festival, when people leave offerings of food and paper money at their ancestors' tombs.

There is a pecking order to the layout: the wealthier residents are buried higher up the slopes. Most tombs have a bench-like gravestone, flanked by figurines that may depict protective deities or mythological characters; a handful even have statues of turbaned Sikh sentinels (burly Sikhs were in demand among wealthy Chinese as security guards).

The most striking tombs slope upwards from front to back, with a horseshoe-shaped wall behind and a groove within the wall for drainage. Most of these tombs are no more than a couple of metres in length, but the largest, that of the tycoon **Ong Sam Leong** (after whom Sam Leong Road, next to the Mustafa Centre in Little India, is named), takes up an entire slope and has its own forecourt that two dozen people could comfortably mingle on.

LIAN SHAN SHUANG LIN MONASTERY

Singapore Zoo

80 Mandai Lake Rd • ☎ 6269 3411, ⓦ wrs.com.sg • About 1hr from downtown: Ang Mo Kio MRT, then bus #138; or Choa Chu Kang MRT, then #927; or Khatib MRT then the special Mandai shuttle bus (daily 8am–10.20pm; at least 3 hourly; $1 by ez-Link card only) • Slightly faster private bus transfers hourly from/to downtown run by SAEx (various departure points; ☎ 6753 0506, ⓦ saex.com.sg) and Safari Gate (hourly from #01-330 Suntec City Mall, Marina Centre, near Promenade MRT; ☎ 6338 6877, ⓦ safarigate.com)

On a promontory jutting into Seletar Reservoir are the **Singapore zoo** and its offshoots, the **Night Safari** and **River Safari** (due to be joined in the early 2020s by the **Bird Park**, relocated from Jurong, and a new rainforest park and resort). All are consistent crowd-pleasers, which is partly down to their more "open" philosophy: many animals are confined in spacious, naturalistic enclosures behind moats, though creatures such as big cats still have to be caged. It's a thoughtful, humane approach that may well please even those who don't generally care for zoos.

The zoo

Daily 8.30am–6pm • $35/$23; see website for details of combination tickets

Home to more than three hundred species, the zoo could easily occupy you for half a day if not longer. A tram ($5) does a one-way circuit of the grounds but as it won't always be going your way be prepared for a lot of legwork.

Highlights include the **Fragile Forest** biodome, a magical zone where you can actually walk among ring-tailed lemurs, sloths and fruit bats; and the **white tigers** – not actually white, they resemble Siamese cats in the colour of their hair and eyes. **Primates** are also something of a strong point: orang-utans swing through the trees overhead close to the entrance, and at the **Great Rift Valley** zone you can see the communal life of a hundred Hamadryas baboons, including some rather unchivalrous behaviour on the part of males, who bite females to rein them in.

Animal shows and feeding sessions take place throughout the day, including the excellent **Splash Safari**, featuring penguins, manatees and sea lions.

Night Safari

Daily 7.15pm–midnight, with shops/restaurants open from 5.30pm and last admission at 11.15pm • $47/$31; see website for details of combination tickets

Many animals are nocturnal, so why not present an opportunity to see them at night? The **Night Safari** section of the zoo addresses this question so convincingly that you wonder why similar establishments aren't more common. There can be long queues for the free tram tours (with commentary; 40min), but this is just a niggle at what is the most popular strand of the zoo. The trams take in around two-thirds of the site. You can forgo them altogether and simply walk around the leafy grounds, an atmospheric experience in the muted lighting, but that way you miss out on several zones, notably those for large mammals such as elephants and hippos. Areas only visitable on foot include the **Fishing Cat Trail**, featuring the Indian gharial – a kind of crocodile, the binturong, sometimes called the bearcat; and the **Leopard Trail**, where you will strain to spot the clouded leopard and slow loris. It's worth catching the **Creatures of the Night** show (hourly 7.30–9.30pm, plus Fri & Sat 10.30pm; included in ticket), an educational affair touching on the importance of conservation and recycling, and starring otters, racoons, owls and wolves, among others.

River Safari

Daily 10am–7pm • $32/$21; Amazon River Quest $5/$3, see website for details of combination tickets

The zoo's **River Safari** enterprise is in some ways the most ambitious of the lot: spanning the divide between aquarium and zoo, it tries to do justice to the fauna of seven of the world's great rivers, and the lands they flow through.

There are too many tanks for comfort at the start, presenting badgers, various alligators and crocs, catfish and other creatures of the Congo, Mississippi, Ganges, Nile and Mekong. Much better is the hangar-like **Giant Panda Forest**, housing two giant pandas – certainly the stars of River Safari – as well as two unexpectedly cute red pandas. The second half of the park is given over almost entirely to what's billed as Amazonia, and much of that is taken up by one ten-minute ride, the so-so **Amazon River Quest**, in which your "boat" is carried along a sluiceway past scarlet ibis and spider monkeys, among others. Seats are limited, so book your River Safari and ride tickets online or you may face a long wait. Saved for last is the hugest tank of all: the **Amazon Flooded Forest**, home to manatees, giant arapaima fish, otters and piranhas.

A proper boat ride is also on offer: the **River Safari Cruise** out on the Seletar reservoir and around the back of the zoo (20min; bookings not needed). Passengers can glimpse giraffes and white rhinos, and perhaps native animals such as monitor lizards and sea eagles.

Kranji and Sungei Buloh

Close to the Causeway, the district of **Kranji** still has a relatively open feel compared to most parts of Singapore, and is also the last refuge of the island's farms – small-scale traditional and hydroponic affairs or high-tech vertical ones. For visitors, two attractions make it worth considering coming this far from town: the **Kranji War Memorial** and, 4km to the west, the wetland reserve at **Sungei Buloh**.

The Kranji War Memorial and Cemetery

9 Woodlands Rd, across from the Turf Club • Daily 7am–6.30pm • Free • Ⓦ cwgc.org • Bus #170 or #961 from Bukit Panjang MRT, or walk west and south from Kranji MRT (10min), or bus #927 from the zoo to the junction of Woodlands and Mandai Rd, then a 15min walk north

The **Kranji War Memorial and Cemetery** is the resting place of the many Allied troops who died in the defence of Singapore. Row upon row of uniform headstones slope up the manicured hill, some identified only as "known unto God". Beyond the simple stone cross that stands over the cemetery is the memorial, around which are recorded the names of more than twenty thousand soldiers (including personnel from the UK, Canada, Australia, New Zealand, Malaya and South Asia) who died in this region during World War II. Two unassuming tombs stand on the wide lawns below the cemetery, belonging to Yusof bin Ishak and Dr B.H. Sheares, independent Singapore's first two presidents.

Sungei Buloh Wetland Reserve

301 Neo Tiew Crescent • Daily 7am–7pm; guided tours Sat 9.30am (booking required via website) • Free • Ⓣ 6794 1401, Ⓦ nparks.gov. sg • Bus #925 from Kranji or Choa Chu Kang MRT to the Kranji reservoir car park, then cross the road to the visitor centre; on Sun the bus becomes #925C from Kranji MRT only and detours slightly further north to the main entrance

The western arm of Kranji is dominated by a coastal reservoir, beyond which is one of Singapore's most rural corners, where something of the island's agricultural past clings on by way of the odd prawn farm or hydroponic vegetable farm. This is also the site of the **Sungei Buloh Wetland Reserve**, the island's only wetland nature park. Its embanked trails and walkways lead through expanses of mangrove and mud flats, with views across the strait to the southern Malaysian city of Johor Bahru. **Birdlife** is the main reason to come. You've a reasonable chance of spotting sandpipers, egrets and kingfishers, and between September and March, migratory birds from around Asia roost and feed here, especially in the early morning. Several hides dot the landscape, and you can get an elevated view over the reserve from the tallest of them, the oversized-treehouse-like **Aerie**. It's worth gazing down at the creeks and mud flats, too, harbouring mudskippers, banded archerfish – which clobber insect prey with water squirted from their mouths – and even the occasional saltwater crocodile.

PERANAKAN SHOPHOUSE, KOON SENG ROAD

Eastern Singapore

In the 1970s, eastern Singapore still had a rural feel, its ribbons of middle-class suburbs interspersed with Malay kampongs (villages). Inevitably, the area hasn't escaped the mushrooming of high-rise new towns, and much of the southeast coast has been radically altered by land reclamation to create the East Coast Park, a mundane strip of leisure and watersports facilities. The closest point of interest to downtown is Geylang, which has retained some of its old identity; neighbouring Katong has traces of its historical Peranakan character. Go east for Changi, where the Japanese interned Allied troops and civilians during World War II, commemorated at the Changi Museum. The Singapore of old clings on at Pulau Ubin, an island visitable by boat from Changi, and to a lesser extent at the curiously named Coney Island, linked by bridges to the mainland at Punggol.

Geylang and Katong

Beyond the Kallang River, marking the eastern edge of downtown, Malay culture has held sway in and around the adjoining suburbs of Geylang and Katong since the mid-nineteenth century, when Malays and Indonesians arrived to work first in the local *copra* (dried coconut) factory and later on its *serai* (lemon grass) farms. The eastern part of **Geylang** retains quite a strong Malay feel, and although Singaporeans regard the whole district as rather seedy, its shophouses exude something of the street life of the Chinatown of old. As for **Katong**, the wealthy, including many of Peranakan descent, built their villas here in prewar times, when it was a beachfront suburb. That heritage lives on to some degree and provides the main lure for visitors, although there's also a distinctive Sri Lankan Hindu temple.

Geylang Road

Kallang, Aljunied or Paya Lebar MRT; or buses to Sims Ave: #2 from Kallang MRT, or #7 from Dhoby Ghaut MRT (exit C), or #67 from Little India

Geylang's main thoroughfare is **Geylang Road**, carrying westbound traffic into town (eastbound cars and buses use Sims Avenue to the north). Lined by shophouses, the 2.5km road is punctuated by more than three dozen numbered *lorongs* (lanes; odd numbers to the north), each packed with more shophouses, some impressively restored; brothels may lurk in a few, while others are tenanted by Buddhist and Taoist organizations. There are some old religious sites, such as the cream-coloured Khadijah Mosque at no. 583, dating from the 1910s, but the overall feel is one of a vibrant, multicultural neighbourhood, peppered with *kopitiams* (coffee shops), roadside tropical-fruit vendors and little shops.

Geylang Serai

Paya Lebar MRT, then a short walk south and east, or buses to Sims Ave: #2 from Kallang MRT, or #7 from Dhoby Ghaut MRT (exit C), or #67 from Little India

At Geylang's eastern edge is the **Geylang Serai** district, its market the focus of the area's Malay life. A two-storey complex, the market is easily spotted on the north side of Sims Avenue, with sloping roofs reminiscent of certain styles of a traditional kampong house. The stalls are predominantly Malay, selling textiles, *kuih* (sweetmeats) and snacks such as *rempeyek*, delicious fried flour rounds encrusted with spices and peanuts. The hawker centre upstairs does an unusually good range of Indonesian rice dishes. Incidentally, the brand new complex just to the west is **Wisma Geylang Serai**, a Malay community event space that had yet to hit its stride at the time of writing.

The Joo Chiat Complex

Geylang Road becomes Changi Road at the northern end of Joo Chiat Road, opposite the Geylang Serai market. The **Joo Chiat Complex** here is worth a look, though it appears to be nothing more than a drab suburban mall from the outside. Inside it feels more like a market, again with a notable Malay/Islamic feel; shops sell batik, a few Malay music CDs and DVDs and – becoming hard to spot – *jamu*, traditional herbal remedies.

Joo Chiat Road

Bus #33 from Bugis, Lavender, Kallang or Dakota MRT to Tembeling Rd, one street away, or #16 from Dakota MRT, or walk from Paya Lebar or Marine Parade MRT

Laidback **Joo Chiat Road** is where Geylang shades into Katong, the latter now a middle-class residential area with plenty of eating and drinking options. The 1.5km stroll south into Katong proper at East Coast Road is hardly a chore thanks to several distractions, including some traditional businesses amid the increasingly fancy shops.

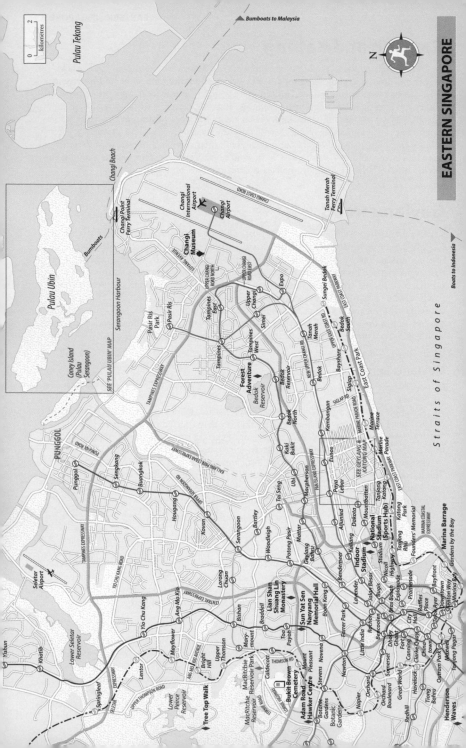

At no. 95, look out for **Kway Guan Huat**, making spring-roll wrappers. At no. 252, one of several restored shophouses is home to **Chiang Pow Joss Paper Trading**, producing funerary paraphernalia, while **Nam San** at no. 263 makes *otah*, a kind of flattish seafood dumpling that's wrapped up in leaves to be cooked.

The immaculate Peranakan shophouses on **Koon Seng Road** (on the left) are the architectural highlight, with restored multicoloured facades, French windows, eaves and mouldings. Back on Joo Chiat Road, at no. 369, **Teong Theng** sells interesting rattan furniture and accessories, standard items in Singapore homes a couple of generations ago, but now almost totally out of favour.

The Intan

69 Joo Chiat Terrace • Tours must be booked in advance; $60 with snacks and tea • ☎ 6440 1148, ⓦ the-intan.com

Just around the corner is **The Intan** (*intan* means "diamond" in Malay), the 1950s mid-terrace home of Peranakan antique collector Alvin Yapp. The place is packed to the gills downstairs with altars, sideboards, inlaid chairs and so on, neatly arranged to feel like everyday furnishings rather than valuable period pieces. Cabinets upstairs display Alvin's hoard of pottery, jewellery and some two hundred pairs of beaded slippers. While Alvin does give guests a basic run-down of Peranakan history and culture, he is at his best when fielding questions about what he has amassed over the past thirty years.

7

East Coast Road

Bus #12 from Clarke Quay, Bugis or Lavender MRT, or #14 from Orchard Rd; both call at Mountbatten MRT en route

Sprawling Katong centres on **East Coast Road** (the name hints at the area's former beach, long obliterated by land reclamation) and its western continuation, Mountbatten Road. It's less colourful than Geylang Road, but worth visiting for a pocket of outlets celebrating its Peranakan history. One of these, Rumah Bebe (see page 164), is on the

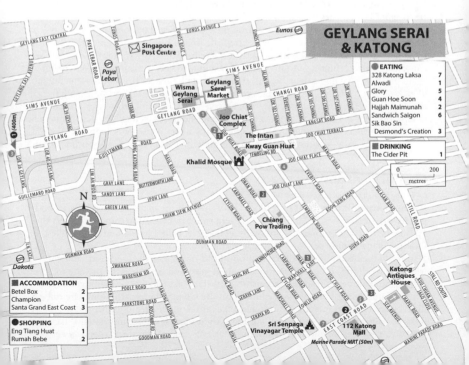

right (west) if you arrive from the northern stretch of Joo Chiat Road. There are also restaurants where you can sample the area's speciality, Katong *laksa* (see page 143).

The Sri Senpaga Vinayagar Temple

19 Ceylon Rd, just off East Coast Rd • Daily 6am–11pm • ☎ 6345 8176, ⓦ www.senpaga.org.sg

In the mid-nineteenth century, a statue of Vinayagar (Lord Ganesh) was apparently unearthed in this area, leading to the building of a temple by the Ceylonese Tamil community. The present-day **Sri Senpaga Vinayagar Temple**, one street west of Joo Chiat Road, has several unusual features, beginning with the gopura – not the multicoloured affair you may have seen elsewhere, but in cream, the deities picked out in a pinky brown.

Inside, the four main columns feature eight sculptures each, depicting all 32 forms of Ganesh, and all murals and deities are conveniently labelled in English as well as Tamil. Most prominent is the striking flagpole-shaped mast, plated in gold and representing the connection between man and the divine.

7

Changi

In Singaporean popular consciousness, the **Changi** district has long embodied a beachside idyll, though it's no great shakes. Most tourists who head this far east come to see the wartime Changi Museum, which is some way before the beach.

Changi Museum

1000 Upper Changi Rd North • Reopens late 2020 after a major overhaul • ⓦ changimuseum.sg • Bus #2 east from Tanah Merah MRT (20min) or Upper Changi MRT (10min)

The infamous Changi Prison was the site of a World War II POW camp in which Japanese jailers subjected Allied prisoners, both military and civilian, to the harshest of treatment. Those brutalities are movingly remembered in the **Changi Museum**. It was once within the prison itself – where drug offenders are still periodically executed – but was moved wholesale just up the road when the prison was extended in 2001.

Novelist James Clavell drew on his experience of Changi in *King Rat*: "the stench was nauseating…stench from a generation of confined human bodies", he wrote. No museum could possibly bring home those horrors, though this one has hitherto done a reasonable job of picking over the facts of the Japanese occupation and the conditions prisoners endured. The museum is closed for renovations, but set to reopen late 2020. It is likely to give pride of place to reproductions of Stanley Warren's so-called **Changi Murals**, depicting New Testament scenes (the originals are housed within an army camp nearby where Warren was interned). It will also retain its predecessor's wooden **chapel**, typical of those erected in Singapore's wartime camps.

Changi Point and the beach

Bus #2 from Tanah MRT (30min) or Upper Changi MRT (20min)

Beyond Changi Prison, the tower blocks thin out and the landscape becomes an odd patchwork of factories, fields and colonial-era military bases. Ten minutes on, via the #2 bus, is the coast at **Changi Point**, with a cluster of eating places and shops called **Changi Village** mainly serving the beach-going public.

To reach the **beach** from the bus terminus, head north past the food court and you will see a footbridge over an inlet to a stretch of grass and trees. It is the prelude to a strip of brownish sand fronting greenish-blue water – actually not uninviting, and the aircraft rumbling in low every few minutes on the Changi flight path soon cease to be a distraction. Facilities include showers and **bike rental** outlets (from $8/hr; you may have to leave your passport as a deposit). For **food**, there's ample choice in Changi Village – the food court is excellent and the restaurants offer everything from steak to *murtabak*.

Pulau Ubin

Downloadable map at ⓦ www.nparks.gov.sg/pulau-ubin • Tanah Merah MRT, then a 30min ride on bus #2 to the Changi Point ferry terminal, left of the footbridge to Changi beach • Boats leave when full (daily roughly 6am–9pm; $3, plus $2 for a bicycle)

Few of Singapore's offshore islands are of any significant size, and those that exist tend to be industrial or military sites (Sentosa being the extravagant exception). Not so **PULAU UBIN**. Covering ten square kilometres, it harks back to the rural Singapore of half a century ago, and warrants a half-day visit for its wetland site, **Chek Jawa**, and its quaint wooden houses – though the scenery may underwhelm if you've been to kampongs in Malaysia or Indonesia. Note that Ubin is the one part of Singapore where **tap water** is deemed not safe to drink.

Ubin village

Bumboats like those used for Singapore River trips, only pleasingly basic, make the 2km crossing from Changi. Beyond Ubin's jetty is a cluster of houses that passes for a **village**, home to simple seafood restaurants, a bright red temple to Tua Pek Kong (sometimes styled as the god of prosperity), a stage where evening Chinese opera performances are put on during the Hungry Ghost festival (see page 159), and small outlets renting **bikes** in various states of repair (from $6 for the day). At the right-hand edge of the village is a **nature gallery** with displays on the island's flora and fauna, while a **volunteer hub** at the opposite end serves as an information point.

7

Around the island

Vehicles are scarce on Ubin, and while a van owner or two in the village may advertise a "taxi" service, cycling is by far the best way to get around; the areas that can be visited stretch some 3km west, north and east of the jetty. Roads are mostly sealed, though there are some undulating stony tracks (heed signs to dismount).

Ubin's landscape is defined by a scattering of old wooden **houses**, some built on stilts, with gardens of allamanda, hibiscus and bougainvillea. It's a classic formula, still common in rural Malaysia and one that gets older Singaporeans feeling nostalgic. The biggest buildings you may happen across are the two storey blocks of the failed *Celestial Resort*, which have been turned into a field laboratory.

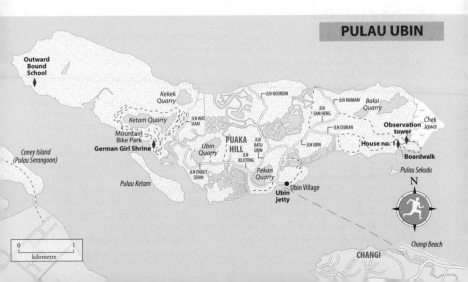

KAYAKING AT UBIN

Ubin is the best place in Singapore for a spot of **kayaking**, and there are a few guided itineraries to choose from, suitable for all ability levels. The **mangrove kayak** trip (4hr; $80/$60) is the simplest and concentrates on the island's small patches of mangroves. Then there's the **Ubin bisect** (6hr; $95), so-named because it takes in Ubin's northern and southern shores and uses creeks and ponds that make it possible to cut right across the island. Both trips use two-person kayaks. For details and booking, contact Asian Detours (☎6733 2282, ⓦadventures.asiandetours.com).

Otherwise, the island has a **mountain-biking** area and several **quarry lakes** (*ubin* is Malay for "granite") that can be scenic, though swimming isn't allowed. If you head west towards the mountain-bike park, look out for the recently expanded shack that is the *Ah Ma Drink Stall* (on the main path near Puaka Hill; no fixed hours) and the **German Girl Shrine**. The latter, a partly wooden affair signed Berlin Heiligtum, commemorates a teenage girl whose family lived on Ubin during the 1910s; unlike the rest of her family, she escaped British arrest during World War I, only to die on the island. As for wildlife, this is one of the best places in Singapore to try to spot a distinctive Southeast Asian bird, the **oriental pied hornbill**, with black-and-white plumage and a bulge called a casque on its upper beak.

Chek Jawa

Daily 8.30am–6pm

For natural interest, the best spot is undoubtedly **Chek Jawa**, at Ubin's eastern end. You're required to leave bikes just a short way from the site and walk to an information kiosk and nature exhibits, inside the restored **House no. 1**. Built in the 1930s, it's a sort of cross between a Tudor cottage and an alpine chalet, complete with fireplace.

Chek Jawa's claim to fame is its intertidal habitat. **Sea grasses** are revealed when the tide is out (ⓦnparks.gov.sg has tide tables), and there are boardwalks for you to scrutinize the coastal **mangroves**; if you're lucky, you might spot horseshoe crabs or mudskippers. There's also a 20m-high observation tower from which you can sometimes see **wild pigs** rooting around in the mud beneath, and which offers vistas north to low peaks in Malaysia.

Coney Island

Daily 7am–7pm • Free • Bus #84 from Punggol MRT to the seafront at Punggol Point, then a 10min walk south for the bridge to the northern end of the island • Bike rental from kiosk at Punggol waterfront, en route to the island: Mon–Fri noon–9pm, Sat & Sun 8am–9pm; $8/2hr Mon–Fri, $8/hr Sat & Sun

Northwest of Changi and inland of Pulau Ubin is one of Singapore's newest green attractions, **Coney Island**, a 2.2km-long sliver of casuarina trees. The story of how it got its English name (Malays call it **Pulau Serangoon**) is confused; "Coney Island" appears in the Singapore press as early as the 1840s, but this refers to a place far to the southwest, and the renaming of Pulau Serangoon may in fact date from a failed attempt to develop it in the 1950s. Until it opened as a nature park in 2015, the island's main claim to fame was that it was once owned by the Aw brothers, who built Haw Par Villa (see page 108).

Most people arrive via the new town of **Punggol** using a dam-cum-bridge to the islet's northern end (the bridge, together with a similar structure at its southern end, hems in the waters of one of Singapore's many coastal reservoirs). The slender **beaches** on the northern shore aren't up to much, although they do offer views across to Pulau Ubin. **Wildlife** includes resident otters, lizards, butterflies and woodpeckers. You may also chance upon the remains of the Aw brothers' prewar house, now unsafe to enter.

With a **bike**, it's easy to explore not just Coney Island but also Punggol's coastal path, mirroring the length of the island and extending some way west of Punggol Point.

FLAMINGOES AT JURONG BIRD PARK

Western Singapore

Hilly and green, the western part of the island is home to one of Singapore's oldest purpose-built suburbs, Tiong Bahru, and the National University of Singapore at Kent Ridge. The latter lies at the end of a 9km series of ridges and peaks collectively labelled the Southern Ridges, stretching southeast to Mount Faber. Several minor attractions nestle along the route, along with a major one – the university's fine natural history museum – but a large part of the ridges' appeal is the chance to walk from one lush hill to another using a network of bridges. Further west is the industrial new town of Jurong, where the prize attraction is the Jurong Bird Park (although this is due to move north in the next few years). In between here and downtown is the suburb of Holland Village, boasting restaurants and bars popular with foreigners.

WESTERN SINGAPORE

MALAYSIA

N

0   2
kilometres

Springleaf

Upper Seletar Reservoir

Zoo, Night Safari & River Safari

Lower Peirce Reservoir

Upper Peirce Reservoir

MacRitchie Reservoir

Tree Top Walk

CENTRAL NATURE RESERVE

Bukit Brown Cemetery

Adam Road Hawker Centre

Stevens

Napier

Vivo City

Henderson Waves

Mount Faber

HarbourFront

Fort Siloso

Keppel Island

Reflections at Keppel Bay

Labrador Park

Tiong Bahru

Redhill

Orchard Boulevard

Botanic Gardens

Farrer Road

Tan Kah Kee

Botanic Gardens

HOLLAND VILLAGE

DEMPSEY HILL

Queenstown

Commonwealth

Holland Village

Sixth Avenue

King Albert

Bukit Batok

Former Ford Factory

Beauty World

Bukit Timah (164m)

BUKIT TIMAH NATURE RESERVE

BUKIT TIMAH

Bukit Panjang

Cashew

Hillview

UPPER BUKIT TIMAH ROAD

BUKIT TIMAH EXPRESSWAY

Dairy Farm Nature Park

Yew Tee

Choa Chu Kang

KRANJI EXPRESSWAY

Bukit Gombak

Bukit Batok

BUKIT BATOK ROAD

PAN ISLAND EXPRESSWAY

Jurong East

Dover

Clementi

CLEMENTI ROAD

Chinese Garden

Jurong Lake

Lakeside

Boon Lay

JLN BAHAR

Pioneer

CORPORATION ROAD

JLN BOON LAY

Science Centre Singapore

Pandan Reservoir

PENJURU ROAD

AYER RAJAH EXPRESSWAY

JALAN BUROH

Buona Vista

one-north

National University of Singapore

Kent Ridge

NUS Museums

Pasir Panjang

PASIR PANJANG

Haw Par Villa

Port facilities

Southern Ridges

Reflections at Bukit Chandu

Labrador Park

Blangah

Telok Blangah

Southern Hill Park

Alexandra Arch

Joo Koon

Port facilities

JURONG ISLAND HIGHWAY

Jurong Bird Park

JURONG

Jurong Island

Gul Circle

Tuas Crescent

AYER RAJAH EXPRESSWAY

Tiger Brewery

PIONEER ROAD

TUAS

Tuas West Road

Tuas Link

Tuas Checkpoint

SECOND LINK

LIM CHU KANG ROAD

KRANJI EXPRESSWAY

Poyan Reservoir

TUAS SOUTH AVENUE

SELETAR EXPRESSWAY

UPPER THOMSON ROAD

LORNIE ROAD

ISLAND CLUB ROAD

Tiong Bahru

Tiong Bahru MRT, then head east along Tiong Bahru road and south along Kim Pong Rd; alternatively Havelock MRT (once open), then a short walk south to Tiong Bahru Rd and Seng Poh Rd

Even if you don't set foot in many of the island's new towns, chances are you will glimpse the uniform blocks of Singapore's public housing projects – in Little India, say (Tekka Market is part of one such development). **Tiong Bahru** is utterly different: a low-rise modernist suburb, to which the residents of nearby Chinatown's slums once aspired to relocate if they made enough money. It is now a conservation area and gentrifying, its neighbourhood shops giving way to boutiques and even pet-grooming services. The main reason to visit is to take in not just its architecture but also some excellent eating options (see page 146).

The neighbourhood's Art Deco/Bauhaus stylings are immediately evident at Kim Pong Road, southeast of Tiong Bahru MRT. Besides characteristically curvy stairwells and contours, the postwar buildings east of the road boast leafy back lanes, giving this the feel of a model estate. Continue south to reach the area's 1930s core, at Moh Guan Terrace and Seng Poh Road; note the **five-foot ways** adapted from shophouse architecture (see page 70).

The only formal attractions as such are the **Qi Tian Gong** or **Monkey God Temple** at 44 Eng Hoon Street (no fixed hours), where the saluting, stick-wielding figure of the Monkey King stands to the right of the altar; and the **Tiong Bahru Market**, celebrated for its venerable food stalls. The market's curves blend in well, disguising the fact that this is actually a 2006 replacement of a 1950s building.

The Southern Ridges and Pasir Panjang

Along Singapore's southwest coast is **Pasir Panjang**, a district whose name means "long sands" in Malay, though its beach and attendant sleepy villages have long since gone. It's

TIONG BAHRU
● SHOPPING
Books Actually — 2
Curated Records — 1
● EATING
40 Hands — 4
Bakalaki — 1
Loo's Hainanese Curry Rice — 2
Tiong Bahru Market — 3

home to one worthy sight, the delightful Buddhist theme park that is **Haw Par Villa** – also a reasonable starting point for exploring the **Southern Ridges** just inland, where you can take in the wartime museum **Reflections at Bukit Chandu** and views from **Mount Faber**.

The account below takes the Southern Ridges walk in an easterly direction, ending at HarbourFront MRT beneath Mount Faber – a sensible choice as this avoids a steep climb up the hill and allows you to finish at the massive **VivoCity** mall, where you can assuage any appetite and thirst worked up along the way (or even continue to Sentosa). An optional extra is Labrador Park, close to Mount Faber, with a few British-era military relics. Note that the links between parks on the walk often offer little shade, so be assiduous about **sun protection** and bring a reasonable supply of water.

Haw Par Villa

262 Pasir Panjang Rd • Daily 9am–7pm; Ten Courts of Hell closes 6pm • Free • ☎ 6773 0103, ⓦ hawparvilla.sg • Haw Par Villa MRT or bus #51 from Upper Cross St, Chinatown

Featuring a gaudy parade of statues of people and creatures from Chinese myth and legend, **Haw Par Villa** started out as the estate of the Aw brothers, Boon Haw and Boon Par, who made a fortune early last century selling Tiger Balm – a cure-all ointment their father devised. Within the grounds was a private zoo, but British red tape caused the brothers to ditch it for statuary; subsequently the park acquired a new title, a mishmash of the brothers' names. Today the place delights with its surreality and refreshing lack of modernization.

The main path curls up and around a hill past one hilariously kitsch tableau after another. One of the best shows titanic combat as the **Eight Immortals** of Taoist mythology attack the Dragon King's undersea palace. Elsewhere, look out for a pool of Chinese-faced mermaids and a curious scene in which a deer and a goat, the latter talking into a bakelite telephone, take tea with a rabbit and a rat, who are newlyweds.

Haw Par Villa's centrepiece is the **Ten Courts of Hell**, a concrete tunnel housing gory depictions of punishments meted out to deceased sinners. Prostitutes are drowned in the "filthy blood pool", tax dodgers and late rent payers "pounded with a stone mallet", to name two. Finally, the dead have their memories wiped by drinking a cup of "magic tea" prior to reincarnation.

Reflections at Bukit Chandu

31K Pepys Rd • Reopens early 2021 after a refit • ⓦ nhb.gov.sg • Pasir Panjang MRT, then a 10min walk north uphill

The Malay Regiment's defence of Pasir Panjang during World War II is remembered at the tiny **Reflections at Bukit Chandu** museum. Near the midpoint of the Southern Ridges trail, it's a ten-minute walk up from Pasir Panjang MRT: head north up Pepys Road until you see a lone surviving colonial house, built as officers' accommodation. It was here that "C" company of the Malay Regiment's 2nd Battalion made a brave stand against the Japanese on February 13, 1942 – two days before the British capitulation – and sustained heavy casualties in the process.

Set to reopen in 2021 after a refit, the previous museum lacked interesting artefacts, although the displays did convey the human toll of the conflict as well as the British ambivalence about working with the Malays. The Malay Regiment was only begun as an experiment in what is now Malaysia to see "how the Malays would react to military discipline", and it was only when they proved themselves that some troops received further training in Singapore. Such apparent slighting is used to justify Malaysia's positive discrimination policies in favour of Malays, which would have been hard for Singapore to swallow had it stayed part of Malaysia.

The canopy walk and Hort Park

After you leave the museum, bear left along the ridge for your first taste of the Southern Ridges trail – and a wonderful introduction it is too, for this is where the elevated

canopy walk begins. Soaring above the actual trail, the walkway takes you east through the treetops, with signage pointing out common Singapore trees, and views north across rolling grassy landscapes. After just a few minutes, the walkway rejoins the trail leading downhill to some mundane nurseries and the west gate of **Hort Park** (daily 6am–11pm; free). A hybrid of garden and gardening resource centre, it's sadly dull; if you do linger in the area, it's better to head along **Hyderabad Road** on the north side of the park, to see some surviving examples of black-and-white colonial villas in the "Tropical Tudor" style.

Alexandra Arch to Mount Faber

For Alexandra Arch, bus #166 from HarbourFront MRT or Dover MRT, or #51 from Upper Cross St, Chinatown

It's possible to start a Southern Ridges walk at the Alexandra Road end of Hort Park, very close to one of the huge, purpose-built footbridges on the trail, the white **Alexandra Arch**. Meant to resemble a leaf, it looks more like the Singapore River's Elgin Bridge on steroids.

On the east side of Alexandra Arch, a long, elevated metal walkway zigzags off into the distance; it's called the **forest walk** though it passes through nothing denser than mature woodland. The walkway zigzags even more severely as it rises steeply to the top of **Telok Blangah Hill** (you can save time by using the steps before the last few bends), whose park offers views of the usual public housing tower blocks to the north and east, and of Mount Faber and Sentosa to the southeast.

Proceed downhill and east, following signage for **Henderson Waves**, and after 700m or so you come to a vast footbridge of wooden slats over metal. Way up in the air over wide Henderson Road, the bridge has high undulating parapets – Henderson Waves indeed – featuring built-in shelters against the sun and rain.

8

Mount Faber

Mount Faber Rd · Free · ☎ 6377 9688, ⦿ onefabergroup.com · HarbourFront MRT, then a stiff walk, or use the cable car from Sentosa (see page 119)

On the far (east) side of the Henderson Waves Bridge is the road to the top of leafy **Mount Faber**, named in 1845 after government engineer Captain Charles Edward Faber. In bygone years this was a favourite recreation spot for its superb views over downtown, but these days you may well have to look out for breaks in the trees to see vistas over Bukit Merah new town to Chinatown and the Financial District, or else head to the hilltop restaurants which enjoy a slightly more elevated view.

To descend from Mount Faber, follow signs for the **Marang Trail**, which eventually leads down a flight of steps on the south side of the hill to VivoCity. If you do want to try the hike up from VivoCity, note that it only takes ten minutes but is steep in places.

VivoCity and HarbourFront Centre

Telok Blangah Rd · HarbourFront MRT

The most interesting thing at the foot of Mount Faber is the **VivoCity** mall, with a curious fretted white facade that looks like it was cut out of a set of huge false teeth, and housing good food courts (in particular *Food Republic* on level 3), a slew of restaurants, a cinema and other amenities; it's also the main gateway to Sentosa. The red-brick box of a building with the huge chimney to the east (on the left if you're descending the hill) of the mall is **St James Power Station**, a power plant converted into a lacklustre nightlife venue. Further east, some 3km of the coast is off-limits until Tanjong Pagar as it's taken up by the Keppel harbour port facilities.

In the other direction on Telok Blangah Road is the **HarbourFront Centre**, a glorified ferry terminal serving Indonesia's Riau archipelago, as well as a stop for cable cars between Mount Faber and Sentosa.

Labrador Park

Port Rd • Unrestricted access • Free • Ⓦ nparks.gov.sg • Labrador Park MRT, then a 15min walk south

Labrador Park is a mundane patch of coastal greenery, once genuinely a bit wild – this was one place to find insectivorous pitcher plants, scarcely present at all today, thanks to a family-friendly makeover. From the seafront, you'll spot the pointy glass towers of **Reflections at Keppel Bay**, a housing development for the super-rich, with its own marina.

A shabby machine-gun emplacement behind the children's swings at the back of the park hints at the site's history as **Fort Pasir Panjang**, built in the 1880s as one of a number of British coastal defences. Climb the wooded hillock behind the park to view the remains of yet more emplacements, forming the **Labrador Battery**, along with a tunnel that gave access to an ammunitions store.

If you head roughly back the way you arrived but hug the seafront rather than using the road, you eventually arrive at the **Bukit Chermin boardwalk**, which passes the hill of that name en route to Reflections at Keppel Bay. The finest sight here is the black-and-white colonial mansion on the hillside, 30 Bukit Chermin Road.

The museums at NUS

For the museums: Kent Ridge MRT and then free campus bus #A2 or #D2, or bus #151 from King Albert Park MRT

The **National University of Singapore** (NUS) scores well on international league tables for its research and teaching. It's a frustrating place for visitors, though, with no obvious hub and confusingly numbered buildings. Thankfully its art and science **museums** are practically side by side and easy to reach.

The NUS Museum

University Cultural Centre, 50 Kent Ridge Crescent • Tues–Sat 10am–6pm • Free • ☎ 6516 8817, Ⓦ museum.nus.edu.sg

Complementing the National Gallery and Singapore Art Museum, the **NUS Museum** has its own take on Asian art, with temporary exhibitions of new work and semi-permanent displays (revised every few years) covering classical Chinese art and modern South and Southeast Asian art and sculpture. Best of all, on the top floor, are the rippled homunculi and other sculptures by one of the most distinctive personages of twentieth-century Singapore art, **Ng Eng Teng**, his figures sometimes contorted, other times smooth and rotund, and at once both angst-ridden yet somehow serene.

The Lee Kong Chian Natural History Museum

2 Conservatory Drive • Tues–Sun 10am–7pm (last entry 5.30pm) • $21/$13 • ☎ 6601 3333, Ⓦ lkcnhm.nus.edu.sg

The **Lee Kong Chian Museum of Natural History** is not just Singapore's most underrated museum, but also arguably its best and most academically rigorous. Benefiting from a new purpose-built home, it dazzles with the sheer volume of biological specimens it inherited in the 1970s when the National Museum narrowed its focus to history.

The **ground floor** is given over to a sprawling collection of zoological specimens. It's a place to admire the matchless diversity of form in nature: five-, six- and eight-pointed sea stars; swifts, sunbirds and parrots in every hue; tricoloured moths and stripy weevils – row upon row of astonishing creatures neatly pinned up or pickled in jars. The centrepiece is a set of three enormous fossilized sauropod **dinosaurs**, the largest 27m long, unearthed in Wyoming in the 2000s; twice an hour, they are the focus of a hopeless sound-and-light show, the place's one bum note.

The upstairs gallery recaps the collections' chequered history, highlighting the formative role played by colonial-era figures such as Raffles, Farquhar and, of course, the great naturalist Alfred Russel Wallace. Just as crucial are panels on Singapore's geology and ecology, offering seldom-heard insights into the impact of land reclamation and development on wildlife.

Holland Village

Holland Village MRT or bus #7 or #77 from Orchard Rd or the Botanic Gardens

Only a short bus ride from downtown, **Holland Village** is a residential district that housed some of the Singapore-based British troops a few decades ago, and today foreigners still home in on its restaurants (see page 146) and bars (see page 152).

Jurong and Tuas

The new town of **Jurong** was created out of swampy terrain in the 1960s, amid great scepticism about its chances of success. Today it and neighbouring **Tuas** boast diverse industries including pharmaceuticals, Google data centres, and oil refining – in which Singapore is a world leader despite having nary a drop of black gold – and Tuas will also hold next-generation port facilities in the 2020s. Jurong's centre is now being redeveloped, partly to house the terminus of the planned high-speed rail link with Kuala Lumpur, although following the surprise election of a new Malaysian government in 2017 the whole project was up in the air over cost issues. **Jurong Bird Park** is the only must-see in the area, though the **Singapore Science Centre** is ahead of the curve for science museums. For grown-ups, there are tours of the **Tiger Brewery**.

Jurong Bird Park

2 Jurong Hill (due to move close to the zoo in the early 2020s) • Daily 8.30am–6pm • $30/$20 • See website for prices of combination tickets including the zoo, Night Safari, River Safari • ☎ 6265 0022, ⓦ wrs.com.sg • Boon Lay MRT, then bus #194 (heading back, you can catch the bus from the stop where you arrived, rather than attempting to cross the Ayer Rajah Expressway)

Lining Jalan Ahmad Ibrahim, the **Jurong Bird Park** is home to one of the world's biggest bird collections, with four hundred species. You'll need at least a couple of hours to have a good look around, though you can save a little time using the park's tram rides ($5/$3).

Besides four huge **walk-in aviaries**, the park has a number of worthwhile smaller enclosures, such as the popular **Penguin Coast** (feeding times 10.30am & 3.30pm), its

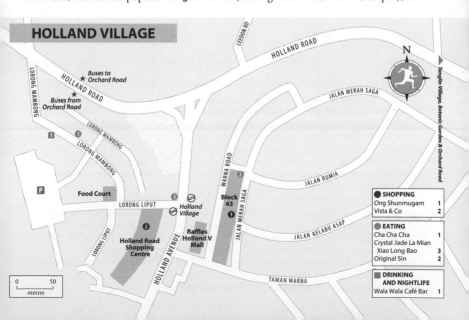

HOLLAND VILLAGE

HOLLAND ROAD
LEEDON RD
JALAN MERAH SAGA
Buses to Orchard Road
Buses from Orchard Road
LORONG MAMBONG
HOLLAND ROAD
LORONG MAMBONG
LORONG MAMBONG
Tanglin Village, Botanic Garden & Orchard Road
WARNA ROAD
JALAN RUMIA
P
Food Court
LORONG LIPUT
Holland Village
Block 43
JALAN MERAH SAGA
JALAN KELABU ASAP
LORONG LIPUT
Holland Road Shopping Centre
Raffles Holland V Mall
HOLLAND AVENUE
TAMAN WARNA

● **SHOPPING**
Ong Shunmugam   1
Vista & Co   2

● **EATING**
Cha Cha Cha   1
Crystal Jade La Mian
  Xiao Long Bao   3
Original Sin   2

■ **DRINKING AND NIGHTLIFE**
Wala Wala Café Bar   1

0   50
metres

mock Portuguese galleon meant to evoke the sighting of penguins by explorers such as Vasco da Gama. Another must-see is **Parrot Paradise** and its incredibly precious blue macaws, most fabulously a Spix's macaw. The critically endangered bird, thought to be extinct in its native Brazil, had a starring role in the Angry Birds Rio game and associated movie *Rio*; the 150 or so known specimens are being cared for in captivity worldwide in the hope of an eventual release back into the wild.

The park also puts on various bird shows, the most exciting of which is **Kings of the Skies** (daily 10am & 4pm), in which eagles, hawks, falcons and owls show off their predatory skills. Another crowd-pleaser is **High Flyers** (daily 11am & 3pm), a sort of park's greatest hits featuring parrot stunts, swooping hornbills and a flamingo invasion.

The walk-in aviaries

The **Wings of Asia** section showcases some birds you may have fleetingly glimpsed around Singapore, as well as species from the surrounding region, including fairy bluebirds, black-naped orioles and the winsome Luzon bleeding-heart dove, with a carmine blotch on its breast. Close by are **Jungle Jewels**, featuring South American birdlife, and the **Lory Loft**, populated by dozens of multicoloured lories and lorikeets, which have no qualms about perching on your arm. At the far end of the park from the main entrance is the **Waterfall Aviary**, long the park's pride. It boasts a 30m-high waterfall and six hundred winged denizens, including crested guinea fowls and hoopoes.

Science Centre Singapore

8

15 Science Centre Rd (check online for details of its impending new address) • Tues–Sun 10am–6pm; also open Mon during school breaks and public holidays • $12/$8, special exhibitions may be ticketed separately • ☎ 6425 2500, ⓦ science.edu.sg • Jurong East MRT, then a 10min walk west or bus #66 or #335

Interactivity is the watchword at **Science Centre Singapore**, on the eastern edge of the artificial Jurong Lake. Galleries hold hundreds of hands-on displays focusing on genetics, space and other subjects, allowing you to calculate your carbon footprint, test your high-frequency hearing and grasp the biology of ageing. With kids in tow, you might want to extend your visit to the winter-themed Snow City (see page 169) or stick with science at the Omni-Theatre.

Omni-Theatre

21 Jurong Town Hall Rd • Tues–Fri 10am–6pm (also Mon during school breaks and public holidays), Sat & Sun 10am–7pm; observatory Fri 7.45–10pm • $14; observatory free • ⓦ science.edu.sg

Just north of the Science Centre, the **Omni-Theatre** shows hourly IMAX movies about space and the natural world. It also has an observatory that does **stargazing** sessions on Fridays. Being almost on the equator, Singapore enjoys views of both the northern and southern skies, though light pollution and clouds put a big dampener on things.

Tiger Brewery

459 Jalan Ahmad Ibrahim • Tours Tues–Sun hourly 1–5pm (children welcome but must be accompanied by adults) • $18/$12; book in advance • ☎ 6860 3005, ⓦ tigerbrewerytour.com.sg • Joo Koon MRT, then bus #182/#182M

Tiger is undoubtedly one of Singapore's best-known brands internationally, brewed here since 1931 as a joint venture between Heineken and a local drinks manufacturer. The German giants Beck's soon set up a brewery to produce a rival, Anchor, but Tiger's parent company acquired the upstart. In 1990 the firm became Asia Pacific Breweries and moved into its present plant in Tuas, where it makes Tiger, Anchor as well as Guinness and other brands. **Tours** of the brewery take in a mini-museum and let you see the space-age brewing, canning and bottling halls, before you indulge in some free quaffing in the sizeable bar, done out like an old-fashioned pub.

UNIVERSAL STUDIOS, SENTOSA

Sentosa and the southern isles

Though only just off the south coast of the main island of Singapore and linked to it by a bridge, Sentosa still has something of an out-of-town feel to it, and locals treat it as a kind of resort for full-day trips or weekend breaks. Don't expect a quiet, unspoilt deserted isle, though – this is effectively one giant theme park with a plethora of hotels, three fairly ordinary beaches and, to boot, exclusive apartment blocks for the uber-rich at its eastern end. Still, if you have kids in tow you'll find plenty to keep them entertained for hours. Other, much smaller, islands lie further south within Singapore's territorial waters, including St John's and Kusu. They are easy enough to reach by ferry and are almost too pristine, being somewhat manicured in true Singapore style.

9 Sentosa

Nominal $1 admission fee • ☎ 1 800 7368672, ⓦ sentosa.com.sg • HarbourFront MRT, then a 10min walk using the Sentosa Boardwalk footbridge from the VivoCity mall (see page 109)

Sentosa was briefly in the world's gaze in June 2018 as it was here, specifically at the *Capella* hotel, that US President Donald Trump met North Korea's Kim Jong-un. Such a choice of venue would have been unimaginable thirty years ago, before the rampant construction and investment that transformed Sentosa into the most developed of Singapore's southern islands. It's ironic that its name actually means "tranquil" in Malay; back in colonial times, when it was home to a British military base, it had the rather less heartwarming name Pulau Blakang Mati, or the "Island of Death Behind".

Contrived but enjoyable in parts, the Sentosa of today is promoted for its rides, passable beaches, hotels and massive casino/entertainment complex, *Resorts World Sentosa*, on the northern shore. Besides the much-hyped Universal Studios theme park, *Resorts World* boasts half a dozen hotels, a couple of museums and the fabulous S.E.A. Aquarium.

It's best to visit Sentosa on a weekday outside the school holidays (see page 31), unless you don't mind the place being positively overrun. Almost all **transport** around the island is free (see page 118).

Resorts World Sentosa

Close to Waterfront station on the island's north shore • In addition to single-attraction tickets, some combination tickets and discounts may be available online • ☎ 6577 8888, ⓦ rwsentosa.com

The *Resorts World* development is visually plastic, like something out of a Silicon Valley corporate headquarters, but it does boast some of Sentosa's biggest attractions. Booking online for Universal Studios or the aquarium is a good idea, not only to save queuing (though be prepared to queue for rides at the former), but also because tickets may sell out in advance on certain days.

Universal Studios Singapore

Resorts World Sentosa • Daily 10am–6pm at least; days with extended hours listed online • $76/$56; many rides have minimum height requirements and may not be suitable for young children

The ersatz character of *Resorts World* becomes rather entertaining at the **Universal Studios** theme park, where fairy-tale castles and American cityscapes rear bizarrely into view in the sultry heat. The park is divided into seven themed zones, encompassing everything from ancient Egypt – the least convincing of the lot – to DreamWorks' animated hit *Madagascar*. Standard tickets offer unlimited rides, but there's much more to do than get flung around on cutting-edge roller coasters or, in the case of the *Jurassic Park* Rapids Adventure, on a circular yellow raft: museum-type exhibits unwrap the world of film production, and you can watch musical spectaculars in a recreation of Hollywood's Pantages theatre.

The Maritime Experiential Museum

Turn right from the Sentosa Boardwalk where it reaches the island • Daily 10am–7pm or later • $16/$10, with S.E.A. Aquarium $45/$33

Highlighting the historical trade links between the Indian Ocean and South China Sea, the **Maritime Experiential** is merely so-so, with unconvincing mock-ups of old bazaars and the odd model junk. Amusingly, one panel on Indian Ocean traders lists a vast range of their wares, including frankincense, pearls, ebony and cotton, whereas a corresponding panel on European traders lists just two contributions: religion and colonization.

The most impressive exhibit is the **Jewel of Muscat**, an Arab dhow built to resemble the one that yielded the ninth-century hoard on display at the Asian Civilizations Museum (see page 38). Constructed without nails – coconut fibre binds the timbers – it was a gift to Singapore from the Omani government in 2010. Delivery took 68 days, under sail, of course. Also worth seeing is the **Typhoon Theatre**, where videos show Chinese actors with American accents enacting the events leading up to

SENTOSA

Riau Archipelago (Indonesia)

Sentosa Cove

Pulau Brani

ELLENBROOKE ROAD

Tanjong Beach

5

2

Capella Hotel

St James Power Station

HarbourFront

VivoCity

HarbourFront Centre

Cruise Centre

Boardwalk Footbridge

Crane Dance

Trickeye Museum

Mount Faber

Cable car

Keppel Island

Waterfront Station

UNIVERSAL STUDIOS

S.E.A. Aquarium and Maritime Museum

Adventure Cove Waterpark

RESORTS WORLD CASINO & HOTELS

Imbiah Lookout

Imbiah Station

ARTILLERY AVENUE

Kidzania

SILOSO ROAD

Cable car

Sentosa Luge

Merlion Replica

Beach Station

Palawan Beach

MegaZip (Mega Adventure Park)

WaveHouse

Images of Singapore Live & Madame Tussauds

Siloso Beach

Wings of Time

Fort Siloso

1

3

Capella Hotel

ACCOMMODATION
Hotel Michael	2
Le Méridien Sentosa	4
Rasa Sentosa Resort	1
Siloso Beach Resort	3
Sofitel Sentosa Resort and Spa	5

● SHOPPING
VivoCity	1

■ EATING
Food Republic	1
Slappy Cakes	3
Soup	2
Trapizza	4

■ DRINKING AND NIGHTLIFE
Ola Beach Bar	1
Tanjong Beach Club	2

N

0   500
metres

9

a shipwreck – evoked with thunder and lightning, sprays of water across the audience and a final capsize that does something unexpected to the entire room.

The S.E.A. Aquarium

In the basement of the Maritime Experiential Museum • Daily 10am–6pm or later • $39/$29, with Maritime Museum $45/$33 • Interactions with marine life possible with an Adventure Cove Waterpark ticket

Awe-inspiring in its ambition and scale, the **S.E.A. Aquarium** has tanks covering ten habitats, arranged in a long loop which is meant to be taken clockwise. The aquarium used to focus on precisely the waters covered by the Maritime Experiential Museum, but now has specimens from the Americas as well, oddly including poisonous, brightly coloured rainforest frogs.

Highlights include an 8m-tall cylindrical **coral garden** and, right at the end, a magnificent evocation of a **shipwreck** swarming with schools of Southeast Asian fish, including mottled honeycomb stingrays. Both these tanks pale in comparison, however, with the monster **Ocean Gallery** halfway through. Some 36m long, with walls 70cm thick, it's so vast that a restaurant and several hotel suites have their own vistas on to part of it. Here you can watch mindboggling shoals of small silvery fish moving in unison, while giant manta rays, goliath groupers and sharks sweep through. Elsewhere, look out for the fabulous collection of **jellyfish**, some glowing as if inside a very exotic lava lamp thanks to coloured lighting.

Adventure Cove Waterpark

A 2min walk west beyond the Maritime Experiential Museum • Daily 10am–6pm • Day ticket $38/$30; diving or other interactions with marine life cost extra (see website for details)

The **Adventure Cove Waterpark** is justifiably the priciest of several water-themed play parks in Singapore, and by no means just for kids. The magic ingredient is the presence of actual sea life: **Rainbow Reef** lets you snorkel in the presence of thousands of fish, while at **Adventure River** you float down a long channel past surreal marine-themed statues, eventually ending up inside a watery glass tunnel within an aquarium tank, where the fish gawp at you drifting by. You can also pay extra to be lowered inside a glass enclosure into the shark tank or wade in a pool filled with rays. Of the rides and slides, the star is undoubtedly the **Riptide Rocket**, a sort of roller coaster that uses magnets to hoist riders' dinghies on the upward legs; the lines for it get ever longer as the day wears on, so it's best tackled early.

Trick Eye Museum

Just right (west) of the Sentosa Boardwalk for visitors arriving on foot • Daily 10am–9pm • $25/20

If you're the sort of person who likes sticking your head into life-size fairground figures with the faces cut out, then the **Trick Eye Museum** is practically made for you. Here you can insert your head or, in some cases, all of yourself into giant tableaux, and pull faces or poses within famous Impressionist paintings or any number of surreal rooms. It's a fad that has swept East Asia, where the museum is the tenth member of its franchise, the crowds drawn by the prospect of silly selfies and associated Facebook likes.

Crane Dance

Close to the Maritime Museum and Waterfront station • Daily 9pm (maintenance closures listed on website); 10min • Free

Sentosa isn't much of a night-time destination, but if you linger after sunset, you may want to catch either *Wings of Time* (see page 118) or **Crane Dance**. The latter was commissioned by *Resorts World* to be "the world's largest animatronic performance", featuring the computer-manipulated courtship of two enormous mechanical birds. If you're not sure about sticking around for the lighting and water effects, you could preview the whole shebang on YouTube.

Other Sentosa attractions

Just about every patch of Sentosa that isn't a beach, hotel or golf course is packed with rides or other diversions, ranging from a Merlion replica whose insides you can tour to a vertical wind tunnel that replicates the sensation of skydiving by keeping a person aloft on a continuous upward blast of air. The selection here covers a few of the more interesting and sensibly priced offerings.

Madame Tussauds and Images of Singapore LIVE

Imbiah Lookout • Mon–Fri 10am–6pm, Sat & Sun 10am–7.30pm • $42/$32 (online discounts available) • ☎ 6715 4000, ⓦ madametussauds.com/singapore • Imbiah station

Inevitably, the **Madame Tussauds** waxwork franchise has fetched up in Singapore, its seventh opening in Asia, and oddly enough it's packaged together with **Images of Singapore LIVE**, a journey through Singapore's history using a mixture of life-sized dioramas, glossy multimedia effects and costumed actors. Along the way you can meet characters such as a nineteenth-century lamplighter in Commercial Square – as Raffles Place was then known – and be at the *Raffles Hotel* during a Japanese air raid in 1941. It culminates in **Spirit of Singapore**, an illuminated boat ride down a fake river, past miniaturized historic streetscapes and vistas of Marina Bay, on to Madame Tussauds, where there's a deliberate sprinkling of local and East Asian figures, including Malaysian actress Michelle Yeoh, who played the hostile matriarch in *Crazy Rich Asians*. Otherwise you get the expected cast of celebrities from the worlds of showbiz and sport, including a doll-like Taylor Swift and an unconvincing Lewis Hamilton, hard to place without a racing car alongside. Finally there's **Marvel 4D**, a "multisensory cinema" devoid of waxworks; instead, you watch an animated short of Marvel comics characters set in Singapore, with the chance to make yourself extra-Instagrammable by posing amid the action or donning the Iron Man suit.

Luge and Skyride

Daily 10am–9.30pm • $23.50 for two circuits • ☎ 6274 0472, ⓦ skylineluge.com • Beach Station for Skyride, Imbiah station for Luge

Unexpectedly fun, the **Skyride**, akin to a ski lift, takes you up a leafy slope at the start of Siloso beach, after which you ride your **Luge** (rhymes with "huge") – like a small unmotorized go-kart – and coast down either of two long, curving tracks back to your starting point.

Mega Adventure Park

A 5min walk west of Imbiah station • Daily 11am–7pm • ☎ 3163 4398, ⓦ sg.megaadventure.com

Megazip is a flying-fox setup where you slide, suspended from a steel cable, from a hilltop down to an islet beyond Siloso Beach ($50). Other possibilities here are a mini-bungy jump ($25) and an obstacle course that's all ropes and netting ($45).

A J Hackett

A 5min walk west of Beach station • Mon–Thurs & Sun 11.30am–7pm, Fri & Sat 11.30am–9pm • $200 for bungy jump • ☎ 6911 3070, ⓦ ajhackett.com/sentosa • Siloso Beach

New Zealand bungy pioneer **A J Hackett** has arrived in Singapore with a 50m-high bungy tower – actually two towers linked by a narrow bridge, meant as a challenge for people with a fear of heights. That and the jump itself aside, there's also a massive swing experience to choose from.

Fort Siloso

At the northwest tip of the island, beyond Siloso Beach • Daily 10am–6pm • Free ☎ 6736 8672 • Beach tram or Sentosa bus #A, or a short steep walk up from Siloso Beach, or take the lift up to the Sentosa Skywalk, an elevated bridge leading to the top end of the site

Sentosa's one bona fide historical attraction is the sprawling **Fort Siloso**, some of its observation posts, gun emplacements and tunnels staffed by uniformed mannequins; like the much smaller fort at Labrador Park on the mainland opposite (see page 110), it guarded Singapore's western approaches from the 1880s onwards. The **Surrender Chambers** are considered the main attraction, re-enacting the British and Japanese surrenders of 1942 and 1945, respectively, using waxwork figures and commentary, but the site is rewarding even if you don't pay to see this. Other chambers offer a deeper analysis of British military failings in the region than anything at the National

9

Museum, although the history can be confused: some panels spin the old story that Singapore's guns were pointing the wrong way as they were meant to deter a naval attack from the south, while others stick to the revisionist idea (also presented at Labrador Park) that the guns could turn to fire northwards and did so, but were ineffective due to various shortcomings. Curiously, Japanese labelling is almost ubiquitous, as if sending a none-too-subtle "don't try that again" message.

Kidzania

Behind Palawan beach • Daily 10am–6pm • $58 for kids, $35 adults • ☎ 1800 653 6888, ⓦ kidzania.com.sg

Although pricey, the international Kidzania franchise does provide children with terrific role-playing opportunities. Their Singapore set-up is a mini-town in which kids can try "working" in pukka simulations of well-known banks and restaurants, or guiding guests around the "Peranakan Museum", among others. There's also a "job information centre" – ironically, something that doesn't exist on the island in real life.

Wings of Time

Close to Beach Station • Daily 7.40pm & 8.40pm; 20min • $18 • ⓦ wingsoftime.com.sg

The minority of visitors who hang around Sentosa after dusk are either heading to one of the beach bars (see page 152) or to **Wings of Time**, a kids' fable cast as a lavish sound- and-light show, featuring pyrotechnicv s, lasers and live actors. Most of the action takes place on a series of offshore platforms, as well as aerial screens of water and mist, with seating right at the beach.

Beaches

The best that can be said about Sentosa's three **beaches**, created with vast quantities of imported beige sand, is that they're decent enough, with bluey-green waters and the odd lagoon. For tranquillity, however, you may do better at Changi (see page 102), because at Sentosa you have to deal with not only crowds but also the view of one of the world's busiest shipping lanes. **Siloso Beach**, which extends 1500m northwest of Beach Station, is the busiest of the three, with well-established resorts and facilities, including good restaurants. Also here is the **Ola Beach Club** (☎ 6265 5966, ⓦ olabeachclub.com), offering everything from kayaking ($25/hr) to a water-based jetpac that allows you to hover several metres above the sea ($200/45min). **Palawan Beach**, just southeast of Beach Station, features a suspension bridge leading out to an islet billed as the "Southernmost Point of Continental Asia" – though a sign concedes that this is so only by virtue of three man-made links, namely the suspension bridge itself, the bridge from HarbourFront to Sentosa, and the Causeway. Beyond Palawan, **Tanjong Beach** tends to be quieter than the other two as it starts a full kilometre from Beach Station.

ARRIVAL AND DEPARTURE   SENTOSA

The most sensible way to get to Sentosa is on foot: from HarbourFront MRT, head up through the VivoCity mall and out along the Sentosa Boardwalk (10min), where you pay the $1 admission fee as you reach the island.

By light rail The Sentosa Express (daily 7am–midnight; $4 including Sentosa admission; EZ-link cards accepted) leaves from level 3 of the VivoCity mall. See page 109.

By cable car The most stylish way to reach Sentosa is via the recently revamped cable-car system from Mount Faber

(see box opposite).

By bus Bus #123 runs all the way from Orchard Rd to Beach station. *Resorts World* operates its own #RWS8 service between HarbourFront/VivoCity and its casino ($2). At the weekend night buses #NR1 and #NR6 run between *Resorts World* and downtown (Fri & Sat 11.30pm–2am; $4.50).

By taxi It's straightforward to get a taxi to the island, though note that trips incur a surcharge of several dollars.

GETTING AROUND

All transport services within Sentosa are free with the exception of the cable car service.

By light rail Sentosa Express trains call at Waterfront station on Sentosa's northern shore for *Resorts World*, then at the central Imbiah Station, and finally at Beach Station on

SENTOSA'S CABLE CARS

Eight-seater cable cars, each with glittering lighting inside and out, shuttle between **Mount Faber** (see page 109) and **Imbiah Lookout** on Sentosa (daily 8.45am–10pm; two-way $33/$22; ⓦonefabergroup.com), calling at the HarbourFront Centre en route. The best time for views is at dusk, when you see Singapore lighting up from Jurong in the west to the Financial District to the northeast. The service has recently been complemented by a **branch line** within Sentosa, from near the Imbiah station to Siloso Point (for Fort Siloso; same times; two-way $15/$10). Two-way rides on both lines cost $35/$25 (after 6pm, adults and children both pay $25 per ticket).

the southern shore (for the beaches). Note that you do not need a ticket to ride the train back to VivoCity.

By bus The island has three colour-coded internal buses #A, #B and #C, that run on loop routes, plus a so-called beach tram running the length of the southern beaches; all call at Beach station. routes are explained on the map available at the Sentosa Express terminal and at the information point at the southern end of the Sentosa Boardwalk.

By bike You can rent a bicycle from Gogreen on Siloso Beach for a hefty $15/hr (daily 10am–7.30pm).

Maps It is worth picking up a copy of the official Sentosa map at the Sentosa Boardwalk or Sentosa Express terminal; it has the latest times and prices for each sight and shows any new attractions/facilities. To download it, head to ⓦsentosa.com.sg/Plan-Your-Visit/Find-Fun.

The southern isles

Scheduled ferries depart from the Marina South Pier, next to Marina South Pier MRT • Return fares $18/$12 • ⓦsla.gov.sg/islands • Ferry operators: Singapore Island Cruise ☎6534 9339, ⓦislandcruise.com.sg; Marina South Ferries ☎6423 0272, ⓦmarinasouthferries.com

Beyond Sentosa are what might be termed Singapore's southern isles. A handful are of minor interest to visitors: from west to east, Sisters' Islands, St John's Island, Lazarus Island and Kusu. All lie around 6km south of the "mainland"; some are good for strolling, swimming and a picnic, but bring your own as there's nowhere to buy food.

Kusu

Singapore Island Cruise boats generally follow a circular route, calling at St John's, then Kusu, before returning (during the pilgrimage season ferries serve St John's and Kusu separately); check with Marina South Ferries on their latest routes • Ferries: Mon–Fri 4 daily, Sat 9 daily, Sun 10 daily; 45min

Kusu, also known as **Turtle Island**, is by far the most interesting of the southern isles. Local legend tells of a Chinese and a Malay sailor who were saved from drowning by a turtle that transformed itself into an island; today the island is home to a major **temple**, complete with turtle statues, and three Malay *keramat*s (shrines). Once a year during the ninth lunar month (mid-Oct to mid-Nov), tens of thousands of local pilgrims descend upon Kusu's temple to pray for prosperity.

St John's Island and Lazarus Island

Ferries to St John's: Mon–Fri 4 daily, Sat 9 daily, Sun 10 daily; 30min

Around 2km long, **St John's Island** has some grassy spaces and a lagoon for swimming, and it can be of interest to birdwatchers as the brahminy kite, a raptor, is commonly seen overhead. The island also hosts the **Sisters' Islands Marine Park Public Gallery** (Mon–Fri 10am–2.30pm, Sat 10am–3.30pm, Sun 10am–5.30pm; free), with exhibits about Singapore's first marine park. The park itself holds eight artificial reef scaffolds for its corals, some of which were relocated from the seas around Jurong, and an underwater "trail" is being developed for experienced divers; see ⓦnparks.gov.sg for details. A causeway, a few minutes' walk east of the jetty, takes you to neighbouring **Lazarus Island**, retaining somewhat more forest cover than any of its neighbours. The island's best feature, however, is a wide lagoon on its eastern shore with a crescent beach.

INFINITY POOL AT MARINA BAY SANDS

Accommodation

While prices may disappoint, the range of accommodation in Singapore will not. The island has a plethora of luxury hotels – including a handful that exude colonial splendour, notably the Raffles and the Fullerton – plus competently run, no-frills and mid-range establishments (note that the cheapest rooms may be windowless). There are also plenty of upstart boutique hotels, the best of which have an unorthodox design aesthetic. Numerous hostels and guesthouses (the distinction between them is blurry) exist, too, offering affordable dorm beds and some private rooms. Many are in refurbished shophouses and practically all offer air-conditioning, a comfy communal lounge and breakfast; the very slickest have bespoke bunk or capsule beds. Airbnb is restricted, barring homeowners from letting out properties for less than six months (in theory, at least).

ACCOMMODATION PRICES

If there's one thing that might leave a nasty taste in the mouth in Singapore, it's the **cost** of accommodation. Although you generally get good value for money, room rates are the steepest in the region. Not many **mid-range hotels** downtown now charge less than $150 a night for a double; in **guesthouses** and **backpacker hostels**, private rooms start at $50 a night, dorms at $20 a night, though you can pay double or treble these prices to stay at the fanciest places.

One quirk is that many hotels and even a few hostels are **priced dynamically**, altering their rates from day to day and week to week depending on how many vacancies they have. Although it is generally cheaper to book as early as possible, there can be excellent last-minute **promotional discounts** at many establishments. **High season**, when good deals are harder to come by, covers June to the end of August, the Formula 1 Grand Prix (mid- to late September), Christmas and New Year, plus, to a lesser extent, the CommunicAsia regional media trade show (June).

The rates quoted in our reviews represent typical starting prices for twin/double rooms if you book early, and include the ten percent **service charge** levied by most accommodation (except budget places and the cheaper mid-range establishments) plus seven percent **GST** on top; read the fine print on any online deals to check whether these surcharges have been included. For high season, reckon paying twenty percent more on average. At **weekends**, guesthouses and cheaper hotels may bump up prices by ten percent.

ESSENTIALS

Breakfast Hostels and guesthouses almost always provide a simple, self-service breakfast of toast and cereal plus coffee and tea, the more expensive places throwing in eggs and fruit as well. Cheaper hotels may well include breakfast in the rate if they have a café; at expensive hotels it's almost always a paid extra unless you're staying on a package deal that includes it.

Check-in/check-out The earliest time you can check into a hotel room is usually 2pm. You have to be checked out by noon or pay for another day's stay.

Children's beds The majority of mid-range and upmarket hotels in Singapore make no charge for children under 12, and beds may well be large enough that kids can easily snuggle up beside parents. If you do need to have an extra bed put in the room, it may incur a surcharge of $50 or so.

Hourly rates If a hotel has hourly or "transit" rates, it often means that locals use them for discreet hanky-panky, which may involve prostitution. Normally only cheap hotels offer such rates; sll establishments reviewed here should be free of this.

Internet access Wi-fi is practically de rigueur at accommodation, whatever the category, and is seldom a chargeable extra.

Reservations It's a good idea to book, especially if you're considering one of the more popular guesthouses, and not just for peace of mind: many of the best rates are only available online. Besides contacting establishments directly, you can try ⓦ agoda.com for a good selection of hotel deals, while ⓦ hostelworld.com lists most guesthouses in town.

THE COLONIAL DISTRICT

The Capitol Kempinski 15 Stamford Rd ☏ 6368 8888, ⓦ kempinski.com; City Hall MRT; map p.36. Occupying two period buildings, the Capitol and Stamford House, this new 150-room hotel prides itself on being both luxurious and intimate. Everything is suitably plush, with tasteful dark wood and marble. Facilities include a small rooftop pool where built-in recesses serve as jacuzzis, plus a gym and spa. The "classic" rooms are cheapest, and should be open by the time you read this; deluxe rooms **$550**

Fort Canning 11 Canning Walk, northern side of Fort Canning Hill ☏ 6559 6770, ⓦ hfcsingapore.com; Dhoby Ghaut or Fort Canning MRT; map p.36. Hotel facades don't come much more imposing than that of the former British military HQ that houses this plush boutique hotel. Little colonial atmosphere survives inside, however, and it is an uphill trek for either nearby station. Rooms are spacious, immaculately decorated, and boast a bathtub that's curiously often either smack in the middle of the room or out towards the window, with blinds for privacy. Pools on two levels and lush gardens, too. **$360**

Peninsula Excelsior 5 Coleman St ☏ 6337 2200, ⓦ ytchotels.com.sg; City Hall MRT; map p.36. Really two hotels fused together – as hinted at by the presence of two swimming pools at either end, one of which abuts the current lobby – and nicely modernized, unlike the 1970s shopping arcades below. **$220**

Robertson Quay Hotel 15 Merbau Rd ☏ 6735 3333, ⓦ robertsonquayhotel.com.sg; Fort Canning or Clarke Quay MRT; map p.36. A circular riverside tower with great views of the river, a cute round pool and a gym. Rooms are on the small side and the place can be a little disorganized, but at their prices, you can probably put up with all that. **$120**

10

10

TOP 5 MONEY NO OBJECT

The Fullerton See page 125
Raffles See page 123
Shangri-La See page 126
Sofitel So See page 126
The South Beach See page 122

Swissôtel The Stamford 2 Stamford Rd ☎ 6338 8585, ⓦ swissotel.com/singapore-stamford; City Hall or Esplanade MRT; map p.36. Upper-floor rooms – and the restaurants and bars on the 70th to 72nd floors – aren't

for those with vertigo, though the views are as splendid as you'd expect from one of the tallest hotels in the world, with over a thousand rooms. Perhaps even more impressive is having an MRT station (City Hall) in the basement, and a big sports facility with two pools and several tennis courts. **$400**

YMCA 1 Orchard Rd ☎ 6336 6000, ⓦ ymcaih.com. sg; Dhoby Ghaut or Bencoolen MRT; map p.36. It's predictably staid and the rooms are plain, but hardly anywhere downtown will you get amenities like a pool and gym at the prices charged here (except, as it happens, at the *YWCA* nearby). **$140**

BRAS BASAH ROAD TO ROCHOR ROAD

The grid of streets between Bras Basah Road and Rochor Road (and a bit beyond, uphill from Selegie Road) has been rendered a bit sterile by redevelopment, but remains a good choice as it's within walking distance of the Singapore River, Little India and the eastern end of Orchard Road. Hotels here tend to be either upmarket or, especially around Bencoolen St, budget affairs.

GUESTHOUSES

G4 Station 11 Mackenzie Rd ☎ 6334 5644, ⓦ g4station. com; map p.50. An unexciting but well-located hostel with a roof terrace. Each resident gets a big locker to themselves plus use of wi-fi. All bathrooms are shared. Dorms **$30**, doubles **$80**

Hangout @ Mount Emily 10A Upper Wilkie Rd ☎ 6438 5588, ⓦ hangouthotels.com; Little India MRT; map p.50. Owned by the company behind the historic Cathay cinema at the foot of Mount Emily, the *Hangout* is an impressive designer guesthouse with a breezy rooftop terrace that's great for chilling out in the evening. The only drawback is that it's short walk uphill from Selegie Rd and Little India MRT. Book online, both because the place is popular, and for discounts. Dorms **$40**, doubles **$140**

HOTELS

Carlton 76 Bras Basah Rd ☎ 6338 8333, ⓦ carltonhotel. sg; City Hall or Bras Basah MRT; map p.50. With a lobby dominated by a spidery glass artwork suspended from the ceiling, this towering four-star hotel has elegant rooms in two wings, a pool and gym – and keen rates for what's on offer. **$320**

Ibis 170 Bencoolen St ☎ 6593 2888, ⓦ ibis.accorhotels. com; Rochor or Bencoolen MRT; map p.50. If you've stayed in other hotels run by this no-frills chain, you'd probably describe them as functional and modern – a perfect match for Singapore, then. **$200**

InterContinental 80 Middle Rd ☎ 6338 7600, ⓦ inter continental.com; Bugis MRT; map p.50. Like the adjoining Bugis Junction mall, the *InterContinental* incorporates some of the area's shophouse terraces, a fact

marked by the "heritage" rooms with Chinoiserie-style decor; other rooms are smart and contemporary. Weekend discounts often available. **$425**

★ **Hotel G** 200 Middle Rd ☎ 6809 7988, ⓦ hotel gsingapore.com; Bencoolen or Rochor MRT; map p.50. This hotel occupies a converted office building, which is perhaps why they went for a bit of post-industrial chic for the ground-floor restaurants, all artfully exposed ducting and pipes. The rooms, functional and not over-decorated, are designated "good" (boxy), "great" or "greater" (more spacious); all are snug, soundproofed and feature pale wood floors and furniture. **$175**

Hotel Mi 41 Bencoolen St ☎ 6251 8822, ⓦ hotelmi. com; Bencoolen or Bras Basah MRT; map p.50. Decent enough budget hotel with formulaic rooms, each with an abstract wall design above the bed, and the bonus of a small pool and gym. **$135**

★ **Marriott South Beach** 30 Beach Rd ☎ 6818 1888, ⓦ marriott.com; Esplanade or City Hall MRT; map p.50. One of the most architecturally arresting entrants to Singapore's hotel scene in recent years, this is both a prestige commercial development and a conservation project (see page 60). The lobby – all individually styled chill-out spaces, some featuring the work of local artists – certainly makes a statement, as do the 650-plus über-chic rooms, the work of French designer Philippe Starck. One of the two pools has glorious views out over the "Chopsticks" war memorial and the Padang. **$450**

Marrison 103 Beach Rd ☎ 6333 9928, ⓦ marrisonhotel. com; Bugis MRT; map p.50. This hotel is surprisingly comfortable, the rooms done out in neutral hues. A good deal, given the location and that breakfast at a nearby restaurant is included. **$130**

Naumi 41 Seah St ☎ 6403 6000, ⓦ naumihotel.com; Esplanade or Bugis MRT; map p.50. The slate-grey exterior, with what look like vines crawling up behind netting, doesn't inspire, but inside is a fine boutique hotel where rooms are kitted out like a luxury apartment. Rooms on one floor are reserved for women only, and there's a rooftop pool overlooking the *Raffles*. **$360**

Raffles 1 Beach Rd ☎6337 1886, ⓦraffles.com/ singapore; City Hall or Esplanade MRT; map p.50. With 115 suites, the *Raffles* remains refreshingly low-rise and still has colonial-era charm in spades, especially evident in the opulent lobby and the courtyards fringed by frangipani trees and palms. Amenities include ten restaurants and bars, a rooftop pool and a spa. There's a round-the-clock butler service, too. $800

South East Asia 190 Waterloo St ☎6338 2394, ⓦseahotel.com.sg; Rochor or Bugis MRT; map p.50. Behind the yellow and white 1950s facade is a cheapie with surprisingly serviceable rooms, although the decor looks about 25 years old. Breakfast – included – is either Chinese vegetarian (they have their own veggie restaurant) or Western continental. Cash only. $100

10

LITTLE INDIA, ARAB STREET AND LAVENDER STREET

Accommodation in **Little India** and nearby tends to be slightly cheaper than elsewhere. The hotels can be uninspired, but there's a good selection of guesthouses in Little India in the zone from Rochor Road up to **Lavender Street**, and with an excellent public swimming pool not far away (see page 32). The area around **Arab Street** also has a few good places to stay.

HOSTELS AND GUESTHOUSES

Bunc@Radius 15 Upper Weld Rd ☎6262 2862, ⓦbunchostel.com; Rochor or Jalan Besar MRT; map p.50. *Bunc* is a sprawling "flashpacker" hostel with an expansive lobby and a warren of dorms featuring individual lighting fixtures and sockets for each bed (some of the beds are even built for two). Dorms $25

Cube Boutique Capsule Hotel 54–56 Bussorah St ☎6291 1696, ⓦcubestay.sg; Bugis MRT; map p.50. If you really must be in thick of humming Bussorah St, then there is where to stay, with unusually fancy capsules boasting built-in TVs and security panels for locking away valuables. The impressive blue and cream facade conceals a plethora of dorms and private rooms, some with two double capsules, as well as an official tourist office and a cosy pantry for meals. Dorms $50, two-capsule rooms (women-only) $120

★**Dream Lodge** 172 Tyrwhitt Rd ☎6816 1036, ⓦdreamlodge.sg; map p.50. This comfy, superbly run hostel boasts plush capsule beds with privacy drapes and lockers beneath. There's a cosy lounge with a quirky wall drawing of Singapore landmarks by a young student, and bike rental is on offer. Before you leave, you can opt to have your photo turned into a badge and stuck on their wall adorned with the faces of previous guests. Dorms $40, double capsules $75

Gap Year 322 Lavender St ☎8356 7600; Bendemeer or Boon Keng MRT; map p.50. Not the most thrilling of hostels but decently run, with knowledgeable staff. Choose from standard dorms or slightly fancier family rooms. Dorms $20, four-bed family room $130

★**Fisher BnB** 127 Tyrwhitt Rd ☎6297 8258, ⓦfisherbnb.com; Bendemeer or Lavender MRT; map p.50. Unexpectedly smart shophouse-based guesthouse with a twelve-bed women's dorm, a sixteen-bed mixed dorm and a four-bed family room. The bathroom decor is bang up to date – the management is especially proud of the Japanese-built bidets. Dorms $35, family room $150

★**The InnCrowd** 73 Dunlop St ☎6296 9169, ⓦthe-inncrowd.com; Rochor or Jalan Besar MRT; map p.50. Perennially excellent hostel with dorms and a range of rooms, each with TV. Shared showers and toilets are kept spotless, and there's a comfy lounge, cheap beer and free internet access. They run tours too, including a scooter-powered trip around the old quarters and Gardens by the Bay. Dorms $20, doubles $60

The Little Red Dot 125 Lavender St ☎6294 7098; Bendemeer or Lavender MRT; map p.50. A competently run, cosy hostel where you can take your pick from ordinary dorm beds or capsule-style ones, though the latter cost more. There's a pleasant first-floor communal terrace to while away downtime. Dorms $20, four-bed rooms $130

★**The Pod** 289 Beach Rd ☎6298 8505, ⓦthepod capsulehotel.com; Bugis or Nicoll Highway MRT; map p.50. Ultra-slick designer place where you check yourself in using an electronic kiosk. Their slogan is "pay for the stay, everything else is free" – and that includes use of their laundry and laptops, plus a cooked breakfast. As the name suggests, all beds are capsule-style, and there are even "suites", rooms with one or two solitary pods. Prices rise by a fifth at weekends. Weekdays: dorms $40, double-pod room $90

Rucksack Inn 280 Lavender St ☎6295 2495, ⓦrucksackinn.com; Bendemeer or Farrer Park MRT; map p.50. This hostel has friendly and informed staff and offers mixed dorms (one with pod-type beds), a female dorm and a handful of private rooms in various sizes. Dorms $26, doubles $90

Traveller@SG 1st floor, 111H King George's Ave ☎6683 2674; Lavender or Bendemeer MRT; map p.50. Exceptionally plain hostel, bar a few colourful murals, occupying part of a low-rise residential block. A decent choice if you want a quiet stay and aren't fussed about slickness or a buzzy vibe. Note that staff may split their time between here and their sister hostel at no. 111J. Dorms $20

HOTELS

Andaz Singapore 5 Fraser St ☎6408 1234, ⓦsingapore.andaz.hyatt.com; Bugis MRT; map p.50.

10

> ### TOP 5 HOSTELS
> **Dream Lodge** See page 123
> **Fisher BnB** See page 123
> **The InnCrowd** See page 123
> **The Pod** See page 123
> **Wink** See page 125

Hyatt's premium *Andaz* does away with the international business hotel formula, instead aiming to craft boutique hotels with the odd local touch. Rooms here are plush with lots of warm tones, perhaps meant to harmonize with the domes of the Sultan Mosque visible below. Views are definitely a strong point, considering that the hotel starts on level 25 of its section of the Duo development; restaurants, bars and the pool all take advantage of that elevation with yet more panoramas. **$620**

Asphodel Inn 380 Race Course Rd ☎ 6296 9298, ⓦ asph.com.sg; Farrer Park MRT; map p.50. A recent refit has really lifted this once very humdrum budget hotel; rooms are still simply furnished but all have windows, and bathrooms boast modern fittings. **$100**

The Daulat 16 Madras St ☎ 6408 5555, ⓦ thedaulat.com; Rochor or Jalan Besar MRT; map p.50. This tiny hotel has an equally tiny rooftop pool, a mere 10m sliver of water. Rooms can be boxy, but some have unusual touches, including upstairs beds in the suites. Rates include breakfast. **$200**

Destination 700 Beach Rd ☎ 6679 2000, ⓦ your destinationhotel.com; map p.50. A decent mid-range option with bland but nicely soundproofed rooms, in a modern tower. The rooftop pool has good views out towards Marina Bay. **$200**

Fragrance Imperial 28 Penhas Rd ☎ 6297 8888, ⓦ fragrancehotel.com; Bendemeer or Lavender MRT; map p.50. Despite the drab yellow exterior, this is a cut above fellow members of the budget chain, with slick if smallish rooms, a café and rooftop swimming pool. Rates include breakfast. **$150**

The Great Madras 28 Madras St ☎ 6914 1515, ⓦ thegreatmadras.com; Rochor or Jalan Besar MRT; map p.50. Housed in a snazzily done-up old building, *The Great Madras* valiantly straddles the hotel/hostel divide. Most of the rooms are standard en-suite affairs, but they also offer "hostel rooms" with double beds, sliding doors and shared bathrooms. Facilities include an in-house barber and, like its sister hotel *The Daulat* a few doors down, a

rooftop pool. Simple self-service breakfast included. Hostel rooms **$150**, ordinary rooms **$210**

Haising 37 Jalan Besar ☎ 6298 1223, ⓦ haising.com. sg; Jalan Besar or Rochor MRT; map p.50. Friendly, secure Chinese-run cheapie offering simple, a/c en-suite rooms with TV, rather boxy but not bad for the price. Small surcharges apply at the weekend. Singles **$55**, doubles **$65**

Hilton Garden Inn 3 Belilios Rd ☎ 6491 0500, ⓦ hilton gardeninn3.hilton.com; Little India MRT; map p.50. Towering over Little India, this *Hilton* mid-range post offers understated contemporary decor, a small outdoor pool and some great vistas out over the surrounding shophouses from the higher rooms. Good value. **$225**

★ **Mayo Inn** 9 Jalan Besar ☎ 6295 6631, ⓦ mayoinn. com; Jalan Besar or Rochor MRT; map p.50. A partial refurbishment has given a new lease of life to the two dozen rooms at this simple, good-value hotel, which feature modern bathrooms and, in some cases, what's billed as a neat Japanese-style "bed" – a wooden dais with a mattress on top. Small breakfast included. **$120**

Moon 23 23 Dickson Rd ☎ 6827 6666, ⓦ moon.com.sg; Jalan Besar or Rochor MRT; map p.50. Aiming to offer a boutique-hotel experience without straining your wallet, the *Moon 23* has stylishly kitted-out rooms with snazzy wallpaper and strategically placed drapes – to help take your mind off the fact that many are actually windowless. Rates include breakfast. **$200**

One Farrer 1 Farrer Park Station Rd ☎ 6363 0101, ⓦ onefarrer.com; Farrer Park MRT; map p.50. The classiest place to stay in the area and, together with the hospital next door, part of a huge new development. The hotel offers a wide range of rooms, the best of which have access to exclusive lounge and gym facilities (less elevated guests have to make do with the glorious 50m pool). **$350**

The Sultan 101 Jalan Sultan ☎ 6723 7101, ⓦ thesultan. com.sg; Lavender MRT; map p.50. A pleasant, low-key boutique hotel based in a series of refurbished shophouses. Rooms include a handful of cosy singles plus so-called attic rooms on the top floor. Breakfast included. Singles **$140**, doubles **$150**

Wanderlust 2 Dickson Rd ☎ 6396 3322, ⓦ wanderlust hotel.com; Jalan Besar or Rochor MRT; map p.50. There's a touch of modern-art wackiness at *Wanderlust*: the "industrial glam" lobby includes barber's chairs and many rooms are colour-themed, some with multicoloured lighting whose hues you can control. **$250**

CHINATOWN AND BOAT QUAY

When it comes to guesthouses, Little India's main competitor is **Chinatown**, which also boasts a good selection of boutique hotels. **Boat Quay**, on the south bank of the Singapore River, is dominated by restaurants and bars, but has one spectacularly worthwhile place to stay, the *Fullerton* hotel.

HOSTELS AND GUESTHOUSES

★ **Adler** 259/265 South Bridge Rd ☎ 6226 0173, ⓦ adlerhostel.com; Chinatown or Maxwell MRT; map p.64. What looks like a fancy furniture store from the street is really the lounge at one of the swankiest hostels in town. Its "suite dorms" boast purpose-built capsule beds (including doubles) and the hostel serves an above-average breakfast. There's also a recently opened café/bar. Dorms $55, double beds $100

Beary Best! 16 Upper Cross St ☎6422 4957, ⊛bearybesthostel.com; Chinatown MRT; map p.64. A spick-and-span hostel done out in bright colours and, as the name suggests, bears – ursine stuffed toys litter the place. Beds come with individual reading lights, there's a self-service laundry, and the management offers bike rental and free tours of downtown's old quarters. If you prefer pod beds, try their new pod hostel next door. Dorms $30, rooms $90

★ **Bohemian Chic** 40 Mosque St ☎8380 0500; Chinatown MRT: map p.64. Not truly Bohemian but appealingly quirky, with glittery masks like something from a Baroque-era ball lining one wall in the lounge. No dorm has more than eight beds (choose from capsules or cheaper double-deckers), and breakfast includes sandwiches in additional to the self-service basics. Dorms $35, capsule beds $55

★ **Met A Space Pod** 51A/B Boat Quay ☎6635 2694, ⊛metaspacepod.com.sg; Clarke Quay or Raffles Place MRT; map p.64. This hostel has high-tech capsule beds that can give you the impression of climbing into a washing machine drum, if not your own personal cylinder on a spaceship. Each bed has a built-in control panel, TV and safe. The kitchen, bathrooms and breakfasts are much more down to earth. Dorms $40

Royal Lodge 66A Pagoda St ☎6816 0288, ⊛royal hostel.com.sg; Chinatown MRT; map p.64. An unexciting but competently run place with a ten-bed women's dorm, slightly larger mixed dorms and lots of pastel colours, just footsteps from the MRT station. Guests get breakfast vouchers to use at nearby café chains. Good value for Chinatown. Dorms $30

Tribe Theory 39 Ann Siang Rd ☎6423 0237, ⊛tribe theory.com.sg; Chinatown or Maxwell MRT; map p.64. You don't have to be an entrepreneur to stay here, but it probably helps. Besides revelling in a good location on chichi Ann Siang Hill, this designer hostel with pod-style beds makes a pitch for people who run start-ups, or would like to. The loft space, packed with multicoloured pouffes, serves as a coworking/networking space and a venue for guest speakers to talk tech. Dorms $50, double capsules $75

★ **Wink** 8A Mosque St ☎6222 2940, ⊛winkhostel. com; Chinatown MRT; map p.64. Deservedly popular for several years now, this hostel was one of the first with hi-tech capsule beds (including some doubles). Facilities include an upstairs kitchen and lounge, modern bathrooms, a library and kitchenette. Dorms $30, double capsules $95

HOTELS

Amoy 76 Telok Ayer St ☎6580 2888, ⊛stayfareast.com; map p.64. Entered via the Fuk TaK Chi Museum, this hotel manages to squeeze the best out of every nook and cranny of its

shophouse conversion. Rooms are on the small side but feature the odd unusual touch such as slatted bathroom floors. $325

Clover 5 Hongkong St ☎6653 8888, ⊛hotelclover.com; Clarke Quay MRT; map p.64. Functional, contemporary rooms in a six-storey building crowned by a small rooftop pool. Good value, with breakfast included. Their sister hotel, round the corner, offers slightly bigger rooms with cool murals and access to the same pool, for about ten percent extra. $180

★ **The Fullerton** 1 Fullerton Square ☎6733 8388, ⊛fullertonhotels.com; Raffles Place MRT; map p.64. Nearly as impressive as the *Raffles*, with a stunning atrium (see page 75); rooms and bathrooms are spacious and feature contemporary styling rather than the Art Deco touches of the original building. Amenities include a gym, spa and pool. $550

★ **Hotel 1929** 50 Keong Saik Rd ☎6347 1929, ⊛hotel1929.com; Outram Park MRT; map p.64. This shophouse hotel looks genuinely 1929 on the outside; inside, the retro-chic rooms take you back four or five decades. Rooms, including a few singles, feature attractive mosaic-tiled bathrooms and mattresses on platforms for beds. Pay a little extra for one with a balcony if you fancy a good view out over the street. Rates include a small buffet breakfast. $150

The Inn at Temple Street 36 Temple St ☎6221 5333, ⊛theinn.com.sg; Chinatown MRT; map p.64. Packed with old-fangled furniture for that period feel, but the rooms are boxy and there's no breakfast. Still, you can't argue with their prices. $125

Parkroyal on Pickering 3 Upper Pickering St ☎6809 8888, ⊛parkroyalhotels.com; Clarke Quay or Chinatown MRT; map p.64. Looming over Hong Lim Park, this sleek hotel is one of the most architecturally striking buildings to have been built in Singapore since *Marina Bay Sands*. It has three towers, linked by curvy-sided rice-terrace-like structures overflowing with vegetation. The use of wood and glass throughout allows plenty of sunlight in, emphasizing the nature theme. Another garden crops up at the open-sided central tier that serves as a "wellness floor", home to the infinity pool, spa and gym. $425

Porcelain 48 Mosque St ☎6645 3131, ⊛porcelainhotel. com; Chinatown MRT; map p.64. Browns and beiges are the default colours of most Singapore hotels, but *Porcelain* is all blue and white a la Ming pottery, giving the smallish rooms a calming quality. $150

Six Senses Duxton 83 Duxton Rd ☎6914 1428, ⊛sixsenses.com; Maxwell or Tanjong Pagar MRT; map p.64. Multiple shophouses have been knocked together to create this new hotel that evokes both opulence – think lashings of black and gold – and calming wellness, with complimentary yoga sessions and Buddhist singing bowls in the rooms and lobby (some large enough to stand in). Guests can use the rooftop pool, spa and gym at their sister property just a 5min walk away. $420

10

10

TANJONG PAGAR AND THE FINANCIAL DISTRICT

With just a sprinkling of hotels, neither **Tanjong Pagar** nor the **Financial District** are all that interesting as places to stay, although proximity to Chinatown makes them worth considering.

Oasia Downtown 100 Peck Seah St ☎ 6812 6900, ⓦstayfareast.com; Tanjong Pagar MRT; map p.64. This is what a Gardens by the Bay Supertree would like if it were magically recast as a hotel: 27 storeys of rooms behind a red-clad facade, with trailing creepers growing up it. Some rooms retain great views, others less so, but the place has two rooftop pools by way of compensation. $375

★ **Sofitel So** 35 Robinson Rd ☎ 6701 6800, ⓦsofitel. com; Telok Ayer or Raffles Place MRT; map p.64. Almost lost amid the staid bank buildings, this is a super-cool, Karl Lagerfeld-influenced conversion of two narrow office blocks into a stylish whole. The "heritage wing" has decor like a French palace; across the atrium from it is the quirky, eclectic "hip wing", where you might find Russian dolls on the tables or wall-mounted plastic hands for hanging clothes. $475

MARINA BAY

Marina Bay is the blandest part of downtown to stay in, but is worth considering if you're after four- and five-star comforts – best epitomized by *Marina Bay Sands*, of course.

Marina Bay Sands 10 Bayfront Ave, Marina South ☎ 6688 8888, ⓦmarinabaysands.com; Bayfront MRT; map p.79. Not just one of the island's most famous buildings but also the largest hotel in Singapore, with an astonishing 2500 rooms. Frankly they're no better than those in other five-star hotels, unless you can afford, say, one of the Straits suites, with two en-suite bedrooms, a baby grand piano and butler service – for at least $5000 a night. Otherwise, stay here for the architecture and that amazing infinity pool. $500

Ritz-Carlton Millenia 7 Raffles Ave ☎ 6337 8888, ⓦritzcarlton.com; Promenade MRT; map p.79. Arguably king of the pricey hotels in Marina Centre, with magnificent views across to the Financial District, even from the bathrooms, where butlers will fill the bath for you. $575

Westin 12 Marina View ☎ 6922 6888, ⓦmarriott. com; Downtown or Shenton Way MRT; map p.79. You're guaranteed a fabulous view from one of the tallest towers in the Marina South financial district – the lobby is on the 33rd floor and the sleek contemporary rooms, infinity pool and other amenities extend upwards from there. $600

ORCHARD ROAD

You generally pay a small premium to stay on or around **Orchard Road**, even though its malls have lost some of their shine. Most of the area's hotels are luxury affairs, with a couple of more reasonably priced options.

Goodwood Park 22 Scotts Rd ☎ 6737 7411, ⓦgoodwood parkhotel.com; Orchard MRT; map p.84. Set on a leafy hillock, designed by the architect responsible for the *Raffles*, and likewise a genuine landmark in a cityscape characterized by transience. It still oozes the refinements of a bygone era, too, and boasts a variety of rooms and suites, plus several highly rated restaurants and two pools. Not as pricey as you might assume. $350

Jen Orchardgateway 277 Orchard Rd ☎ 6708 8888, ⓦhoteljen.com; Somerset MRT; map p.84. A fine debutant right on Orchard Rd, occupying the tenth floor and up of the Orchard Gateway mall. Rooms are spacious and swish, but the best feature is the rooftop pool, with great views of the spires of the Financial District. $325

★ **Lloyd's Inn** 2 Lloyd Rd ☎ 6737 7309, ⓦlloydsinn. com; Somerset MRT; map p.84. Less than a 10min walk from Orchard Rd, what was once a motel-like ugly duckling has been transformed into a sleek establishment where beds are raised on platforms with storage space underneath, and some bathrooms are open to the outside air (there's a privacy curtain, of course). There's also a water

feature, intended for foot-dipping, taking up much of the garden. Breakfast included, at a nearby café. $220

Mandarin Orchard 333 Orchard Rd ☎ 6737 4411, ⓦmeritus-hotels.com; Somerset MRT; map p.84. Female staff at this old favourite wear kitsch quasi-oriental uniforms, but don't let that put you off; this old favourite has kept at the top of its game – luxurious to a fault, well placed right in the middle of Orchard Rd, and with its own high-end mini-mall. $425

★ **Shangri-La** 22 Orange Grove Rd ☎ 6737 3644, ⓦshangri-la.com; Orchard MRT; map p.84. A 10min walk west of Orchard Rd, the oldest member of what is now a global chain still epitomizes elegance, with 750 rooms set in oodles of landscaped greenery. Facilities include tennis courts and a spa. $500

Supreme 15 Kramat Rd ☎ 6737 8333, ⓦsupremeh.com. sg; Dhoby Ghaut MRT; map p.84. This 1970s concrete box has predictably dated rooms, though they're not too cramped; rates are a steal and include breakfast. $125

★ **Yotel** 366 Orchard Rd ☎ 6336 6000, ⓦyotel.com; Orchard MRT; map p.84. This upstart international chain wants to make the hotel experience rather like flying: you can largely check in by yourself, mattresses are custom-made foldable affairs so you can have the bed flat or partially reclined, like an airliner seat, and clothes hangers and a desk surface slot out of the walls like a food tray. All rooms ("cabins") have lovely floor-to-ceiling windows, and there's a decent pool plus a room service robot that trundles around delivering bottles of water and other small items. **$225**

GEYLANG AND KATONG

With such a huge range of accommodation available downtown, there are few compelling reasons to stay in the suburbs except to save a little money. **Katong**, with its Peranakan heritage and good restaurants, is as good as place to do this as any, though some of the seediness of **Geylang** can spill over into Joo Chiat Road after dark.

★**Betel Box** 200 Joo Chiat Rd ☎6247 7340, ⓦbetelbox.com; Paya Lebar MRT; map p.101. Styling itself Singapore's socially committed hostel, *Betel Box* tries to highlight the island's cultural heritage by running trips to interesting neighbourhoods. A 15min walk from Paya Lebar MRT, or bus #33 from Bedok or Kallang MRT. Dorms **$20**, doubles **$80**

Champion 60 Joo Chiat Rd ☎6342 0988, ⓦchampionhotel.com.sg; Paya Lebar MRT; map p.101. As dull as its shophouse neighbours on the outside, this suburban hotel punches above its weight on the inside, borrowing just enough chic touches from much pricier offerings in Chinatown. A 10min walk from Paya Lebar MRT. No breakfast. **$110**

Santa Grand East Coast 171 East Coast Rd ☎6344 6866, ⓦsantagrandhotels.com; map p.101. One of the nicer offerings from this budget chain, partly housed in a conservation building. Rooms are more than adequate, and the secluded rooftop pool is a bonus. Rates include breakfast. **$170**

SENTOSA

Staying on **Sentosa** is more feasible than ever thanks to improved transport links (see page 118); even so returning to your hotel for a short break from sightseeing downtown can still be a bit of a drag. Besides the places listed here, note that new "staycation" hotels targeted at locals are opening up; for more details see ⓦstayfareast.com.

Hotel Michael ☎6577 8888, ⓦrwsentosa.com; map p.115. The main reason to stay at *Resorts World* is to take advantage of packages that offer free or discounted admission to Universal Studios and the like. *Hotel Michael* is more interesting than the rest, thanks to fittings and decor by the American architect and designer Michael Graves. **$425**

Le Méridien Sentosa 23 Beach View, near Imbiah station ☎6818 3388, ⓦmarriott.com; map p.115. A splendid hotel, housed partly in a former British barracks dating from 1940. All rooms feature elegant contemporary fittings, but the most impressive are the pricey *onsen* suites with their own large outdoor Japanese hot tub. **$375**

Rasa Sentosa Resort Western end of Siloso Beach ☎6275 0100, ⓦshangri-la.com; map p.115. One of the best pre-casino-era hotels, in leafy grounds at the far end of Siloso Beach. Family-friendly, it boasts a large freeform pool with water slides, a "Toots Club" with purpose-built play areas and activities, plus a spa. **$400**

Siloso Beach Resort 51 Imbiah Walk ☎6722 3333, ⓦsilosobeachresort.com; map p.115. The central swimming pool is a stunner, its curvy fringes planted with lush vegetation and featuring a waterfall and slides; it far outshines the somewhat tired rooms. Still, the resort is tranquil enough (the music from the nearby beach bars stops around 10pm) and rates include breakfast. **$250**

Sofitel Sentosa Resort & Spa 2 Bukit Manis Rd ☎6708 8310, ⓦsofitel-singapore-sentosa.com; map p.115. One of Sentosa's swankiest hotels, in secluded grounds above Tanjong Beach, with a spa featuring outdoor pools and imported Moroccan clay said to have detoxifying powers. The rooms are overflowing with contemporary fittings, including a minibar styled like a hatbox. **$400**

10

DIM SUM STALL, FOOD REPUBLIC

Eating

Singapore is nothing if not a foodie nation: along with shopping, eating is a mass pastime here, and a mind-boggling number of food outlets on just about every road cater to this obsession. One of the joys of the eating scene is its distinctive and affordable street food, featuring local Chinese and Indian dishes you won't find in China or India, served up in myriad hawker centres and food courts, as is great Malay and Indonesian food. Also worth discovering is Nonya cooking, a hybrid of Chinese and Malay cooking styles developed by the Peranakan community. Western food of all kinds is plentiful too, though it tends to be pricier than other cuisines from Asia, which are equally available. Quite a few of the more run-of-the-mill restaurants swing both ways by offering Western and Asian dishes, and there's no shortage of upmarket places serving a fusion of the two.

On the whole, proper restaurants are the places you go if you want a bit of comfort and the chance to savour more specialist local food or the best international cuisine. Note that for local food, restaurants aren't necessarily better than *kopitiams* or, indeed, food courts – they just charge quite a bit extra for posh surroundings and (sometimes indifferent) service. For a blowout, look out for buffet and high-tea offers (see page 137).

Singapore also has any number of outlets serving Western-style coffee (as opposed to the versions at hawker centres and food courts, which normally come with sweetened condensed milk), plus venues specializing in Asian desserts or ice cream (see page 131).

Note that restaurants are often caught up in a game of musical chairs, pressured into shifting every few years because of short leases and rising rents, especially for much-prized shophouses and other street-level venues. If a place reviewed appears to have vanished, websites or Facebook pages should tell you if it has closed or simply moved.

ESSENTIALS

Costs Unlike many other things in Singapore, food is very good value. If you eat at hawker centres, food courts or *kopitiams*, a meal of rice with toppings, or a serving of noodles, will cost $5–8 including a soft fizzy drink or juice. There are lots of affordable restaurants too, plus any number of swanky places charging as much as their counterparts in the West. East Asian or Indian cuisine is generally best value; anything else tends to be pricey for what it is, though you can mitigate this by taking advantage of the two- or three-course set lunches many restaurants have on weekdays. If a stall's signboard or a restaurant menu lists more than one price next to a dish, it indicates that different portion sizes are available. Finally, note that restaurants may sell seafood by weight; make sure staff give you a clear idea of how those innocent-looking prices translate into platters of crab or prawn, as it's possible to get carried away when ordering and then have to swallow a much bigger bill than you expected. All price indications in our reviews include any tax and service charge that may apply.

Deliveries It's possible to have restaurant food sent to your accommodation using Deliveroo or ⓦfoodpanda.sg (app available), although do ensure first that your hostel or hotel will accept such deliveries.

Dress code The Singapore restaurant scene is by and large remarkably casual, and even fairly pricey venues don't require much by way of dressing up for the occasion. That said, it doesn't hurt to call ahead to check whether attire has to be "smart casual".

Hawker centres and food courts Street food is alive and well in Singapore – just not on the street. Regulations have long consigned hawkers to purpose-built hawker centres, essentially indoor markets with alternating rows of tables and stalls. The oldest places often feature some of the best food, but their age also means they can be cramped, stuffy and thus hot. Food courts are essentially updated versions of these hawker centres, more spacious and, in the case of those in malls, with air-conditioning. Some have become chains, notably *Food Republic*, *Food Junction* and *Kopitiam*.

Incidentally, don't assume that such places only serve local food – a minority of stalls offer other East Asian cuisines and some specialize in simple Western dishes, from steak to burgers with chips. Many food courts are self-service, in which case you pay when you order; where a stall prepares dishes to order, tell the vendor roughly where you intend to be seated (better still, quote the number on the table if there is one) and pay when the food arrives.

Kopitiams *Kopitiam* is a Hokkien Chinese term that literally means "coffee shop" – but don't go to one expecting croissants and cappuccinos. A *kopitiam* is like a mini version of a hawker centre, though of a much older provenance: the quintessential local diner, it usually takes up the ground floor of a shophouse and contains perhaps a dozen tables with four or five "stalls" serving a handful of standard dishes, though more elaborate places may have a range of *zichar* (see page 136) offerings from a kitchen at the back. Unfortunately *kopitiams* are increasingly vanishing from downtown, though they are worth seeking out wherever shophouses survive.

Opening hours Only formal restaurants and Western-style cafés keep set hours, typically noon–2pm and 6–10.30pm in the case of restaurants. Because hawker centres and food courts are basically food markets, they seldom have precise opening times. As a rule food courts in shopping malls keep the same hours as the malls, while hawker centres are open from dawn until at least 10pm, though individual stalls will open as they please, meaning that you may find fewer trading outside meal times or late in the evening. To the extent that *kopitiams* have set opening times, they may likewise be prone to vary.

Ordering Chinese, Malay and, to a lesser extent, Indian restaurant meals tend to be shared affairs, where everyone tucks in to a common set of dishes with their own portion of rice as an accompaniment, so it's customary to order collectively. It's worth scanning the menu reader (see page 144) to familiarize yourself with the most common dishes and terms. While English menus are always available

11

11

at proper restaurants, note that some staff are migrant workers and may not be good at fielding anything but routine queries.

Reservations Only formal restaurants take bookings; hawker centres, food courts and *kopitiams* do not (and often do not have phone numbers, though we have given details where available). It is worth booking ahead for many restaurants, particularly for Friday or Saturday evening, or lunchtime on Sunday, when they are at their busiest. One popular way to reserve tables is using the Chope app, which may offer discounts on some meals.

Special diets Several Chinese and Indian restaurants and a few hawker stalls specialize in vegetarian food; the Chinese-run ones are often vegan, though they also tend to use mock meats made of gluten or soya that may be unappealing to some. If you're strict about your food being cooked separately from non-vegetarian items, you should stick to these outlets. Even if you're not so strict, when ordering elsewhere you may find that vegetable-based dishes may routinely include bits of meat or seafood, or be flavoured with meat stock, *hae ko* or *belachan*, the last two being pungent shrimp pastes; when ordering, make clear what you want to avoid. Halal food is predictably easy to find: most hawker centres have a row of stalls serving halal Indian or Malay food, and many international as well as local fast-food chains, plus some hotel restaurants, serve halal meat.

Table manners Local dishes are generally eaten with fork and spoon – never a knife as the food is usually sliced up enough that one is unnecessary – and it's the spoon you eat off, with the fork used to help to pick up and move morsels of food, plus rice, on to the spoon. Of course you have the option of using chopsticks with Chinese food, but don't make the mistake of trying to consume rice off a plate with them, as this is once again where the spoon comes into play. If you have a rice bowl, however, then hold it right to your mouth and snaffle the rice using the chopsticks as a shovel. More familiarly, they also serve as tongs: one chopstick is laid between thumb and forefinger, and supported by your fourth and little fingers, while the second chopstick is held between thumb, forefinger and second finger, and manipulated to form a pincer. Indian and Malay food is traditionally eaten using the right hand as a scoop and the right thumb to flick food into your mouth, and there are always sinks near the tables for washing before and after the meal.

Tipping It is not customary to tip hawkers or when eating in food courts, *kopitiam*s or cheap restaurants, and all upmarket and most mid-range restaurants add a ten percent service charge (plus the state's 7.7 percent GST on top of that) to your bill in any case. That leaves the lower end of mid-range as a grey area: here you may wish to offer a tip, though it's by no means expected.

THE COLONIAL DISTRICT

Some of the genteel edifices of the Colonial District now house interesting, generally pricey, restaurants, though on the whole the area is not the most exciting for food.

★**Cedele** #03-28A Raffles City Shopping Centre ☎6337 8017, ⓦcedelegroup.com; City Hall MRT; map p.36. A café/bakery chain, *Cedele* serves up some of the best sandwiches in Singapore ($10) – think, say, pulled pork with peperonata and avocado – and sells a vast variety of specialist breads and rich cakes. Some branches, like this one, also have a restaurant with soups, pies and inventive light meals such as the beetroot burger ($18), which even non-veggies love. Mon–Fri noon–10pm, Sun noon–9pm.

Coriander Leaf #02-01 CHIJMES, 30 Victoria St ☎6837 0142, ⓦcorianderleaf.com; City Hall or Esplanade MRT;

map p.36. Pan-Asian and Mediterranean food in elegant upstairs premises, encompassing everything from Lebanese meze to Thai mango salad. The lunch sets offer a choice of four cuisines ($40), while at dinner a mix-and-match menu of smaller plates takes over. They serve an impressive range of Asian liqueurs and whiskies, too. Mon–Fri noon–2.30pm & 6–10.30pm, Sat 6–10.30pm.

The English House 28 Mohamed Sultan Rd ☎6545 4055, ⓦtheenglishhouse.com; Fort Canning MRT; map p.36. This bold new venture of UK celeb restaurateur Marco Pierre White is an ultra-posh guesthouse, located in two restored shophouses, with a restaurant and bar below. Decor features *kopitiam*-style marble tables and posters of Seventies UK entertainment icons, and the food

MARKETS AND SUPERMARKETS

The most interesting places for you to buy fresh produce and ingredients for self-catering (some hostels have cooking facilities) are **wet markets** – so called because the floors are perpetually wet or at least damp, thanks to being hosed down from time to time. Probably the most popular, well-stocked and atmospheric of the ones downtown is the **Tekka Market** at the start of Serangoon Road, a worthwhile stopover on any trip to Little India (see page 52). Singapore has plenty of **supermarkets**, of course, some of which are franchises of Western or Japanese chains; all stock imported beers and wines and have a deli counter. For more unusual imports, including organic produce, try Market Place (one convenient outlet is on level B1 at the Raffles City mall; daily 8am–11pm; City Hall MRT), which is popular with expats.

is correspondingly Modern British with a few Asian touches. Four-course set meals (not Sun) are priced according to your choice of main dish, which could be smoked haddock (from $65), with Eton mess for pudding, for example. Mains from $50; four-course Sunday lunches $90. Mon–Sat noon–2.30pm & 6pm–midnight, Sun noon–3pm & 6–9pm.

Flutes National Museum, 93 Stamford Rd ☎ 6338 8770, ⊛ flutes.com.sg; Bras Basah or Dhoby Ghaut; map p.36. An upmarket choice for modern European and fusion cuisine, with main courses starting at $45 – about the same as the weekday two-course executive lunch. There's a separate brunch menu at weekends, including an English Sunday roast. Mon–Fri 11.30am–2pm & 6.30–10pm, Sat 10.30am–2.30pm & 6.30–10.30pm, Sun 10.30am–4pm.

Privé Asian Civilisations Museum, Empress Place ☎ 6776 0777, ⊛ priveacm.com.sg; Raffles Place MRT; map p.36. Sleek, contemporary affair serving up somewhat generic food – pancakes or eggs Benedict for breakfast, then burgers, pasta and the odd noodle dish the rest of the day. It's popular with museum visitors, though as much for the riverside location, generally much quieter than

Boat Quay opposite, as for the food. Mains from $20. Mon–Thurs 8.30am–10.30pm, Fri & Sat 8.30am–midnight, Sun 9am–10.30pm.

Sushi Tei #03-13 Raffles City ☎ 6334 7887, ⊛ sushitei. com; p.36. A stalwart of Singapore's Japanese dining scene, this chain features the obligatory conveyor belt and reasonably sized portions of eel, beef teriyaki, clams in broth and other dishes. Around $35 per person, with cheaper bento options available. Daily 11.30am–10pm.

TOP 5 CAFÉS AND DESSERT PLACES

Singapore has any number of Western-style cafés for sandwiches, pastries and cakes, plus places serving either gloopy local desserts or specialist ice cream.
Ah Chew Desserts see below
Baker & Cook see below
Chye Seng Huat Hardware see page 133
Cedele see page 130
The Daily Scoop see below

11

BRAS BASAH ROAD TO ROCHOR ROAD

The area sandwiched between the Colonial District and Little India includes plenty of well-established restaurants, including a good cluster close to *Raffles Hotel*.

★ **Ah Chew Desserts** #01-11, 1 Liang Seah St ☎ 6339 8198, ⊛ ahchewdesserts.com; Esplanade or City Hall MRT; map p.50. *Ah Chew* confronts you with nothing but unusual local sweets containing beans or other unexpected ingredients. The cashew-nut paste is not bad if a gloop made of nut butter appeals; also available are the likes of *pulot hitam*, made with black sticky rice and better warm than with the optional ice cream. Most items cost $4 or so. Mon–Thurs 12.30–midnight, Fri 12.30am–1am, Sat 1.30pm–1am, Sun 1.30–midnight.

Alley On 25 Andaz Singapore, 5 Fraser St ☎ 6408 1288; Bugis MRT; map p.50. If your hotel doesn't offer you a big breakfast spread as standard, consider treating yourself to the lazy breakfast – really a brunch buffet – at this hotel, with panoramic views. At weekends, three of the four restaurants on level 25 unite to offer eggs cooked to order, sausages, a huge range of salads, fruit and breads, plus noodles and rice, and you get to order one main dish from a list of six, ranging from burgers to steak and eggs. It's great value at $42, or you can pay double to indulge in unlimited Prosecco, wine and beer as well. Lazy breakfast Sat & Sun 11.30am–2.30pm.

★ **Artichoke** 161 Middle Rd ☎ 6336 6949, ⊛ bjornshen.com/artichoke; Bencoolen or Bugis MRT; map p.50. No restaurant in Singapore packs as much attitude – in the hippest possible way – as *Artichoke*. Housed in an airy bungalow, it serves fabulous Middle Eastern-tinged fusion food as conceived by the idiosyncratic

Bjorn Shen (woe betide you if you want minor tweaks to the dishes, ketchup with your fries or would like to split the bill using more than two cards – all three are likely to be verboten). For weekend brunch, there are mains such as the superbly rich lamb shakshouka or lamb shoulder alongside spicy baked eggs; in the evenings, choose from quirky meze such as burnt miso hummus or more predictable mains like lamb kebab. Mains from around $35. Tues–Fri 6–9.45pm, Sat & Sun 11.30am–2.45pm & 6–9.45pm.

Baker & Cook InterContinental Hotel, North Bridge Rd ☎ 6825 1502, ⊛ bakerandcook.biz; Bugis MRT; map p.50. Burgeoning artisanal café chain run by a Kiwi and featuring New Zealand coffee, great croissants, brownies, plus quiches, open sandwiches and salads. Daily 8am–7.30pm.

Chin Chin 19 Purvis St ☎ 6337 4640; Esplanade or Bugis MRT; map p.50. This likeably old-fangled Chinese shophouse diner with a cheap and cheerful menu of Hainanese standards like breaded pork chops and more generic faves, including chicken sautéed with cashew nuts and spicy mapo tofu. Around $20 per head, minus drinks. Daily 7am–9pm.

The Daily Scoop School of the Arts, opposite the start of Bras Basah Rd ☎ 6509 4875, ⊛ thedailyscoop.com. sg; Dhoby Ghaut or Bras Basah MRT; map p.50. One of a number of quality ice-cream makers boasting some distinctly Asian flavours (such as *chendol*, the coconut milk dessert, or *maoshanwang* – a variety of durian) alongside creations such as lychee Martini. Just $3.50 will get you a fancy takeaway cone; if you eat in, you can pair your scoop

HAWKER AND KOPITIAM FOOD

For taste and value, the inexpensive cooking served up by stalls in **hawker centres** and at the roadside diners called **kopitiams** simply can't be beaten. While not the healthiest food you could eat – much of it is fried, and cooks use salt and sugar liberally – it is likely to form an abiding and highly favourable impression of Singapore cuisine.

The most basic meal is **mixed rice** (also advertised as "economy mixed rice" to stress that it's good value, or "mixed vegetable rice" even though it's far from vegetarian), basically rice with toppings. Widely served up by Chinese, Malay and some Indian stalls, it's instantly recognizable by the trays of stir-fries and stews behind the glass. Order simply by pointing at what you fancy, and expect plenty of entertaining culinary cross-fertilization – the Chinese stalls all serve curry, the Indian stalls have tofu, and so on. It's best at mealtimes when the dishes will be freshly prepared, though food never really goes cold in Singapore's climate, so will be palatable at any time of day.

Otherwise, stalls offer literally dozens of classic one-plate rice and noodle dishes, plus other, more elaborate dishes. Our menu reader (see page 144) lists some of the most popular ones.

11

with waffles, brownies and the like. Sun–Thurs 11am–10pm, Fri & Sat 11am–10.30pm.

Fatty's Wing Seong #01-31 Burlington Square, 175 Bencoolen St (entrance on Albert St) ☎ 6338 1087; Rochor or Bugis MRT; map p.50. Famously run by an avuncular chubby cook in bygone decades, *Fatty's* was an institution on the now-vanished foodie paradise that was Albert St. Today this touristy restaurant maintains the original's no-frills *zichar* approach, and also does standards such as chicken rice. Around $20 a head. Daily noon–2.30pm & 5.15–10.15pm.

Herbivore #01-13 Fortune Centre, 190 Middle Rd ☎ 6333 1612, ⓦ herbivore.sg; Bencoolen or Bras Basah MRT; map p.50. There's a cluster of vegetarian restaurants near Waterloo St's Kwan Im Temple, particularly at the Fortune Centre building, where the star is this excellent place serving well-presented tempura, "chicken" teriyaki and so forth. Good-value sets (from $25) with noodles or rice plus accompaniments like soya sashimi, pickle and salad, plus dessert. Mon–Fri 11.30am–3pm & 5–9.30pm, Sat & Sun 11.30am–9.30pm.

Rochor Original Beancurd 2 Short St; Rochor or Bencoolen MRT; map p.50. This bare-bones shophouse joint is great for late-night attacks of the munchies, although you'll need to be attuned to Chinese snacks such as silken beancurd in syrup and *yew char kuay* (savoury doughnuts, like big, elongated versions of Spanish *churro*); if you're not, stick to their Portuguese-style custard tarts. Mon–Thurs 11am–1am, Fri 11am–3am, Sat noon–3am, Sun noon–1am.

The Tiffin Room Raffles Hotel, 1 Beach Road ☎ 6412 1816; Esplanade or City Hall MRT; map p.50. A fixture at *Raffles Hotel* since the 1890s, *Tiffin Room* has had its wood panelling and floors restored to evoke its early appearance, and continues to serve up skilfully spiced North Indian cuisine. Note, however, that the much-loved high teas it used to host will in future move to the lobby; contact the hotel for details.

★ **Xiang Cao Yunnan Original Ecology Hotpot** 26 Liang Seah St ☎ 6635 8243; map p.50. Hotpot can be amazing comfort food on a coolish, cloudy day, and Liang Seah St is lined with restaurants that serve nothing else. The principle is simple: help yourself from a buffet spread of meat and vegetables (around $25 per person here, plus a few dollars extra for soup stock refills), and then cook everything in the bubbling pot at your table, with chilli, garlic and tahini dips for added zest. Both veggie and non-veggie stock are available, and you can order small plates of raw seafood too, at no extra cost. The atmosphere in the evening is terrific, when cars are barred and tables set up outside, but book ahead or avoid the 6.30–8pm peak, when people can wait half an hour for a table. Daily at least noon to midnight.

Yhingthai Palace #01-04, 36 Purvis St ☎ 6337 1161, ⓦ yhingthai.com.sg; Esplanade or Bugis MRT; map p.50. A smartly turned-out Chinese-influenced Thai restaurant, where you can't go wrong with the deep-fried pomfret with mango sauce, herby fishcakes or deboned chicken wings stuffed with asparagus and mushroom. Around $45 per head, excluding drinks. Daily 11.30am–2pm & 6–10pm.

LITTLE INDIA TO LAVENDER STREET

Little India is paradise if you're after maximum flavour for minimum outlay; the first part of Serangoon Rd and its side streets, as well as Race Course Rd, are packed with inexpensive, excellent curry houses specializing in South Indian food, often dished out onto banana leaves and with plenty of vegetarian options; some places offer South Indian renditions of North Indian and Nepali dishes too. For other cuisines, you generally need to venture outwards to Lavender Street and Jalan Besar.

★ **Banana Leaf Apolo** 54 Race Course Rd ☎ 6293 8682; Little India MRT; map p.50. Pioneering banana-leaf-type restaurant with a wide selection of Indian dishes, including fish-head curry (from $25 depending on size) plus chicken, mutton and prawn curries ($15). The "South Indian vegetarian meal", a huge thali of rice, poppadums, two main curries and several side ones, plus a dessert, is a weekday lunchtime steal at just $10. There's also a branch inside the Little India Arcade (☎6297 1595). Daily 10am–10pm.

★ **Chye Seng Huat Hardware (CSHH)** 150 Tyrwhitt Rd ☎6396 0609, ⓦcshhcoffee.com; Boon Keng MRT; map p.50. Part of the slow gentrification that's converting the area's hardware shops into restaurants and hostels, *CSHH* is a hip café-bar with all-day breakfasts and varied mains that include crab linguine (from $20). Coffee is blended and ground on the premises. In the evening the focus shifts to their craft-beer stall in the courtyard. Tues–Thurs & Sun 9am–10pm, Fri & Sat 9am–midnight.

Gokul 19 Upper Dickson Rd ☎6396 7769; Rochor or Jalan Besar MRT; map p.50. Although they do serve standard Indian vegetarian dishes, *Gokul* buys into the Chinese vegetarian concept of mock meats in a big way, using them in emulations of street food classics such as *mee rebus*, the Malay noodle dish with a spicy/tangy sauce. The results are decent– if the place's popularity with non-carnivorous visitors from the Subcontinent is any yardstick. Around $15 per person. Daily 10.30am–9.45pm.

Hillman 135 Kitchener Rd ☎6221 5073, ⓦhillman restaurant.com; Farrer Park MRT; map p.50. A tiny, old-fangled restaurant that's unaccountably popular with rowdy Japanese businessmen, though don't let that put you off. They come, as you should, for the tiptop *zichar*

food. The claypot dishes are a particular speciality, ranging from noodles to, for the adventurous, sea cucumber – not a vegetable but a marine creature related to starfish and sea urchins. Reckon on $35 per head excluding drinks. Daily 11.30am–2.30pm & 5.30–10.30pm.

Komala Villas 76–78 Serangoon Rd ☎6293 6980; Rochor or Little India MRT; map p.50. A veteran, rather cramped vegetarian establishment with more than a dozen variations of *dosai* at just a few dollars each, plus fresh coconut water to wash it down. They also do more substantial rice-based meals from 11am to 4pm. There's also a branch nearby at 12–14 Buffalo Rd (☎6293 3664; open from 8am). Daily 7am–10.30pm.

MTR 438 Serangoon Rd ☎6296 5800, ⓦmavalli tiffinrooms.com/singapore; Farrer Park MRT; map p.50. It's small and charmlessly modern, but still has people lining up at peak times for its South Indian vegetarian snack meals: spicy one-bowl rice, lentil and nut combos, plus daily specials and lunchtime thalis. Most items cost between $4 and $8. Tues–Sun 8.30am–3pm & 5.30–9.30pm.

Saravanaa Bhavan 84 Syed Alwi Rd ☎6297 0770, ⓦsaravanabhavan.com.sg; Farrer Park MRT; map p.50. This South Indian vegetarian franchise, gone global out of Chennai, has a modern Singapore venue that offers all the staples, from *vada* (dhal-flour doughnuts) to *dosai*, plus their popular Indian take on Chinese food, typified by Gobi Manchurian (oddly not on the menu but usually available): stir-fried battered cauliflower with a spicy, tangy sauce. Also good for non-Tamil cuisine, such as *bisibelabeth*, a gooey

11

INDIAN FOOD

As befits a country whose Indian community is largely Tamil, **Indian food** in Singapore tends to be synonymous with South Indian cooking, which is generally spicy, makes heavy use of coconut and tamarind and emphasizes starchy and vegetarian food. The classic southern Indian dish is the **dosai** or *thosai*, a thin rice-flour pancake. It's usually served accompanied by *sambar*, a watery vegetable and dhal (lentil) curry; *rasam*, a spicy clear soup flavoured with tamarind; and perhaps a few small helpings of vegetable or dhal curries, plus coconut or mint chutney. Also very common are **rotis** – griddle breads – plus the more substantial *murtabak*, thicker than a roti and stuffed with egg, onion and minced meat. The latter is a particular speciality of Indian Muslim *kopitiams* and stalls, which form a sideshoot of the South Indian eating scene and tend to place much more emphasis on meat.

One endearing aspect of South Indian restaurants is that they often serve food on a **banana-leaf** "platter", the waiters dishing out replenishable heaps of various curries along with mounds of rice. In some restaurants you'll find more substantial dishes such as the popular fish-head curry (don't be put off by the idea – the "cheeks" between the mouth and gills are packed with tasty flesh).

South Indian restaurants tend to be very reasonably priced. North Indian food is usually more expensive (though some cheap South Indian places will offer attempts at northern cooking) and tends to be richer, less fiery and more reliant on mutton and chicken. In Singapore, tandoori dishes – the *tandoor* being the clay oven in which the food is cooked – are the most common North Indian offerings, particularly tandoori chicken marinated in yoghurt and spices and then baked. Breads such as nan also tend to feature rather than rice, though just about every restaurant has a version of biryani (usually spelt *briyani* here).

11

MALAY AND INDONESIAN FOOD

Though Malays form the largest minority in Singapore, the **Malay eating scene** is a bit one-dimensional, mainly because the Malays themselves don't have a tradition of elaborate eating out. Every hawker centre has several Malay stalls, but these tend to serve fairly basic rice and noodle dishes. It's a shame, because Malay cuisine is a spicy and sophisticated affair with interesting connections to China in the use of noodles and soy sauce, but also to Thailand, with which it shares an affinity for such ingredients as lemon grass, the ginger-like galangal and fermented fish sauce (the Malay version, *budu*, is made from anchovies). Malay cooking also draws on Indian and Middle East cooking in the use of spices, and in dishes such as biryani rice. The resulting cuisine is characterized by being both spicy and a little sweet. *Santan* (coconut milk) lends a sweet, creamy undertone to many stews and curries, while *belacan*, a pungent fermented prawn paste (something of an acquired taste), is found in chilli condiments and sauces. Unusual herbs, including curry and kaffir-lime leaves, also play a prominent role.

The most famous Malay dish is arguably satay; another classic, and this time ubiquitous, is *nasi lemak* (see page 144), standard breakfast fare. Also quintessentially Malay is *rendang*, a dryish curry made by slow-cooking meat (usually beef) in coconut milk flavoured with galingale and a variety of herbs and spices.

For many visitors, one of the most striking things about Malay food is the bewildering array of *kuih-muih* (or just *kuih*), or sweetmeats, on display at markets at street stalls. Often featuring coconut and sometimes *gula melaka* (palm-sugar molasses), *kuih* come in all shapes and sizes, and in as many colours (often artificial nowadays) as you find in a paints catalogue – rainbow layer cakes of rice flour are about the most extreme example.

INDONESIAN FOOD

Worth mentioning in the same breath as Malay food is **Indonesian cuisine** – the two can have much in common, given that native Malay speakers live in many parts of what is now Indonesia. One style of Indonesian cuisine is widespread in Singapore – *nasi padang*, associated with the city of Padang in Sumatra. Like mixed rice (see page 132), it's largely served up as trays of curries and stir-fries used as toppings for steamed rice.

rice, lentil and vegetable concoction from Karnataka. Daily 9am–11.30pm.

★ **Swee Choon** 183–191 Jalan Besar ☎6225 7788, ⓦsweechoon.com; Jalan Besar or Farrer Park MRT; map p.50. In business for more than half a century, *Swee Choon* is a busy, no-frills dim sum joint that now occupies several consecutive shophouses and stays open all night. Order by ticking boxes on a form, guided by the picture menu. Standards like *loh mai kai* (steamed chicken with glutinous rice) and *chee cheong fun* (rice noodle rolls with a soy sauce dressing) come off pretty well. Lunch costs as little as $15 per head, without drinks; evening prices are higher. Mon & Wed–Sat 11am–2.30pm & 6pm–6am, Sun 10am–3pm & 6pm–6am.

★ **Tekka Food Centre** Start of Serangoon Rd; Little India MRT; map p.50. Alongside Tekka market is one of the best old-school hawkers' centres on the island, generally steamy hot and busy. The Indian and Malay stalls are especially worthwhile; look out for exceptional Indian *rojak* – assorted fritters with sweet dips. Daily 7am till late.

Tiramisu Hero 121 Tyrwhitt Rd ☎6292 5271; map p.50. Popular indie café with black-and-white cartoon artwork and three sizes of tiramisu in a multitude of flavours (like matcha green tea, Baileys and durian). Also loads of waffles, breakfasts and unusual mains such as Thai seafood pizza (from $15). Daily 11am–10pm.

ARAB STREET AND AROUND

It seems logical that Arab St should boast a profusion of Middle Eastern and North African restaurants, but these places are all recent interlopers; the mainstay of the area's dining has long been Malay and Indonesian food.

Blu Jaz Café 11 Bali Lane ☎8126 2936, ⓦblujazcafe. net; Bugis MRT; map p.50. Easily spotted thanks to its gaudy decor, this was the venue that led the gentrification of Kampong Glam, and it now runs two other similarly colourful venues close by. The menu combines Turkish, East Asian and European food at affordable prices – a beef kebab will set you back $18, seafood noodles $12. Mon–Thurs noon–1am, Fri noon–2am, Sat 4pm–2am.

★ **Bumbu** 44 Kandahar St ☎6392 8628, ⓦbumbu. com.sg; Bugis MRT: map p.50. The entire shophouse is festooned with antique Peranakan tiles and carved wooden screens; the cuisine is a terrific mix of Thai and Indonesian, all fragrantly spiced. Standouts include the inky stir-fried squid, chilli basil chicken, beef *rendang* and bean sprouts with salted egg yolk, plus traditional desserts such as sago with palm molasses. Eminently affordable at around $30 per person, without drinks. Tues–Sun 11am–3pm & 6–10pm.

Hajjah Maimunah 11 & 15 Jalan Pisang ☎ 6297 4294, ⊛ hjmaimunah.com; Bugis MRT; map p.50. A cosy diner that's great for inexpensive Malay food, including good desserts and snacks. Mon–Sat 7am–8pm (may close during Ramadan).

Islamic Restaurant 745 North Bridge Rd ☎ 6298 7563; Bugis MRT; map p.50. The bland, modernized premises of today don't hint at this restaurant's impeccable pedigree, for which check out their photos of functions they catered for in the 1920s. Biryanis are the trademark offering ($8) though they also do a huge range of North Indian chicken, mutton, prawn, squid and veg curries, with good-value set meals at around $10. Daily 10am–10pm; closed Fri 1–2pm.

★ **Kampong Glam Café** 17 Bussorah St; Bugis MRT; map p.50. Fantastic roadside *kopitiam* serving inexpensive rice and noodle dishes, cooked to order, plus curries. Come not just for the food but for a good chinwag with friends over *teh tarik* late into the evening. Daily 8am–3am, but closed every other Mon.

★ **Rumah Makan Minang** 18A Kandahar St ☎ 9384 4484, ⊛ minang.sg; Bugis MRT; map p.50. A tiny street-corner place serving superb *nasi Minang* – the cuisine of the Minangkabau people of Sumatra, similar to *nasi padang* – including the mildly spiced chicken *balado* and more unusual curries made with offal. Just $10 per head for a good feed. Mon–Fri 8.30am–8pm, Sat & Sun 8.30am–5pm.

Windowsill Pies 17 Haji Lane ☎ 9772 5629, ⊛ windowsillpies.sg; Bugis MRT; map p.50. With just a handful of tables downstairs and a dozen seats upstairs, this little boutique shop only serves scrumptious dessert pies and tarts in varieties such as pumpkin and pecan, and grasshopper (actually mint and dark chocolate), plus coffee and tea. Pie slices from $8. Mon–Thurs & Sun 11am–8pm, Fri & Sat 11am–10pm.

Zam Zam 697/699 North Bridge Rd ☎ 6298 7011; Bugis MRT; map p.50. Staff at this venerable Indian Muslim *kopitiam* have the annoying habit of touting for custom even though the place draws crowds, especially on Fridays, with its decent enough *murtabak* and biryani offerings (there's even a venison version of the latter). Avoid the sickly speciality drink, *air katira* – it's like one of Singapore's syrupy ice desserts, only melted. Daily 8.30am–10pm.

CHINATOWN

Singapore's Chinatown is no Chinese ghetto, of course, and the range of food on offer here is pretty diverse, although the central Sago, Smith, Terengganu and Pagoda streets tend to be dominated by touristy Chinese restaurants – seldom the best in their class.

Amoy Street Food Centre Block 531A, southern end of Telok Ayer St; Tanjong Pagar MRT; map p.64. One of Chinatown's most popular hawker places, on two floors and serving standards as well as fresh creations. Highly rated stalls include *A Noodle Story*, with Cantonese *wonton* (dumpling) *mee* unusually topped with a soft-boiled egg (they can sell out by 1.30pm); *Lagoon in a Bowl*, which does a highly non-traditional salmon on blue rice; and *J2 Curry Puff*, whose crisp half-moon pastries are deep-fried and come with a range of moist, spicy fillings. The weekday lunchtime office crowd can be phenomenal, whereas the place may be half-dead at weekends. Daily 7.30am–late.

Annalakshmi #01-04 Central Square, 20 Havelock Rd ☎ 6339 9993, ⊛ annalakshmi.com.sg; Clarke Quay MRT; map p.64. Come here for excellent Indian vegetarian buffets served up by volunteers, with no prices specified; you pay what you feel the meal was worth. Profits go to Kala Mandhir, an association promoting South Indian culture. Note that they take a dim view of customers helping themselves to more than they can finish. There's also a branch at 104 Amoy St (☎ 6223 0809; Telok Ayer MRT; Mon–Sat 11am–3pm). Mon 11am–3pm, Tues–Sun 11am–3pm & 6.15–9.30pm.

Bacchanalia 39 Hongkong St ☎ 6909 6360, ⊛ bacchanalia.asia; Clarke Quay MRT; map p.64. The fanciest of French food, assembled out of cosmopolitan ingredients such as Shanghai hairy crab. Dinner is a multi-course degustation menu at $350, while a two-course lunch will set you back $115. Reserve two weeks in advance. Tues–Sat noon–2.30pm & 6.30–10.30pm.

Breakthru Café #01-02C People's Park Centre (at the back of the building), 101A Upper Cross St ☎ 6533 5977; Chinatown MRT; map p.64. A church-run cafeteria might seem an odd idea, but this one gives employment to former drug users and people convicted of drug possession. It's a great place to refuel cheaply on rice and noodle meals and dim sum selections (mostly under $10), and to do a bit of people-watching: judges from the courts opposite have lunch here and interact quite amicably with staff they may have previously sentenced. Mon–Thurs 7am–6pm, Fri 7am–5pm, Sat 7am–3pm.

Chao Shan Cuisine #01-01 Grand Building, 17 Phillip St, opposite the Yueh Hai Ching temple ☎ 6336 2990; Raffles Place or Telok Ayer MRT; map p.64. Once an informal suburban joint, this Teochew restaurant has certainly come up in the world. They do marvellous standards such as braised goose on a bed of beancurd, oyster omelette (in two styles, crispy or regular), fish maw soup (rather gelatinous) and cold crab. Around $40 a head, minus drinks. Daily 11.30am–2.30pm & 6–10.30pm.

11

11

CHINESE FOOD

The range of **Chinese cooking** available in Singapore represents a mouthwatering sweep through China's southeastern seaboard, reflecting the historical pattern of emigration from Fujian, Guangzhou and Hainan Island provinces. There aren't always clear-cut differences between each province's style; it's more that each has its signature dishes (including some that were actually created by hawkers in Singapore and have subsequently become local standards). You'll also come across food from further afield in China, notably northern Beijing (or Peking) and western Sichuan cuisines.

Some popular Chinese *kopitiams* and restaurants are what's termed **zichar** places – which basically means that their food has a home-cooked slant, with less attention to the classic repertoire or fancy presentation. They're always worth trying because they have more scope to be creative using ingredients to hand, and can tailor dishes to your cravings.

CANTONESE

Cantonese food dominates in formal restaurants, reflecting that cuisine's pre-eminence in Chinese cooking. It's noted for its subtleties of flavour and memorable sauces, most famously sweet-and-sour. Fish and seafood weigh in heavily, either fried or steamed, and other specialities include pigeon, roast meats and frogs' legs. Dim sum is also a classic Cantonese meal: literally translated as "to touch the heart", it's a blanket term for an array of dumplings, cakes and tidbits steamed in bamboo baskets. Though you do occasionally see it on lunch menus, traditionally dim sum is eaten for breakfast, with one basket (of three or four morsels) costing as little as $3.

HAINANESE

Hainanese cuisine in Singapore is synonymous with chicken rice, a simple but tasty platter featuring, predictably enough, slices of chicken laid on rice that has been cooked in chicken stock, with a chilli and ginger dip. Historically, though, the Hainanese were chefs to the British and kept their colonial employers happy with a range of fusion dishes such as breaded pork chops, still found on menus.

HOKKIEN

The Hokkien chef relies heavily upon sauces and broths to cook meat and (primarily) seafood. Without doubt, the cuisine's most popular dish in Singapore is Hokkien *mee*, though confusingly it comes in two styles. The classic hawker version consists of not just *mee* – yellow noodles – but also white vermicelli, the combination fried with prawns and pork for flavour. In restaurants, however, Hokkien noodles tend to be braised in a savoury brownish sauce.

TEOCHEW

Chaozhou (or Teochew) is a city in Canton province where steaming is the most commonly used form of cooking, producing light flavourful dishes such as fish steamed with sour plums. Other Teochew classics are braised goose, steamed crayfish and, at hawker stalls, *mee pok* – a spicy dish of flat noodles with round fishball dumplings.

BEIJING

The sumptuous presentation of Beijing cuisine reflects that city's opulent past as the seat of emperors. Meat dominates, typically flavoured with garlic and spring onions, though the dish for which Beijing is most famous is roast duck, eaten in a pancake filled with spring onion, and smeared with plum sauce.

SICHUAN

Sichuan (or Szechuan) food is famously spicy and greasy, with chilli, pepper, garlic and ginger conspiring to piquant effect in classic dishes such as camphor-and-tea-smoked duck and chicken with dried chilli. One of the most common offerings in this vein in Singapore is the hotpot, akin to a fondue; you order raw ingredients, such as slices of meat and fish, and cook them at your table in a pot of boiling stock.

Chinatown Complex Behind the Buddha Tooth Relic Temple; Maxwell or Chinatown MRT; map p.64. The hawkers upstairs are much preferable to anything on the ersatz "food street" of Smith St, and one of their number, *Liao Fan Hong Kong Soya Sauce Chicken Rice & Noodle* (at #02-126; irregular hours but at least late morning until 3pm), has shot to fame as one of the island's two Michelin-starred stalls. If you don't fancy waiting for up to half an hour to pay $2 for a plate, then eat at their pricier, fast-food-style outlet at 78 Smith St (Thurs–Tues until 9pm). Daily 7am–late.

Chongwen Ge Café 168 Telok Ayer St ☎9129 1625; Telok Ayer MRT; map p.64. Next to Thian Hock Keng, this little place has a short, satisfying menu of spicy Peranakan classics like *mee siam* (vermicelli in a tamarind/coconut milk sauce) and *otah* (fish dumplings). You can eat indoors or outside at the base of the pagoda. Nothing costs more than $12. Daily 11am–5.30pm.

Hong Lim Food Centre Block 531A, Upper Hokkien St; Clarke Quay or Chinatown MRT; map p.64. Another unsung municipal estate collection of hawker stalls that are much-prized by those in the know. Cherished outlets include *Outram Park Fried Kway Teow Mee*, for dark, sweetish flat rice noodles; *Tai Wah Pork Noodle*, for *bak chor mee* (its impossibly busy sister operation near Lavender MRT is Michelin-starred); and *Hokkien St Famous Hokkien Prawn Mee*, once a pushcart operation famed for yummy prawn noodles in broth. Daily 7.30am till late.

★ **Kok Sen** 30 & 32 Keong Saik Rd ☎6223 2005; Outram Park MRT; map p.64. Open to the street at the front and back, with the odd pigeon loitering between basic tables, this *zichar* place serves food as exemplary as the decor is plain: try their *har cheong kai* (fried chicken seasoned in fermented prawn paste), black bean beef *hor fun* noodles, and perhaps the claypot fish head or even the very spicy *kung pao* frog. Note that the English name on their sign is hard to spot. Daily noon–2.30pm & 5–11.30pm.

Lime House 2 Jiak Chuan Rd ☎6222 3130, ⊛lime house.asia; Outram Park MRT; map p.64. An impressively renovated shophouse where the lack of a/c seems apt given the culinary focus on another balmy corner of the earth – the Caribbean. The menu includes jazzed up versions of standards like curry goat and rice and peas. Plenty of rum-based cocktails, too, with a bar section in the back garden. Mains (large enough to share) from $28. Tues–Sat 5pm–midnight.

Maxwell Food Centre Corner of South Bridge Rd & Maxwell Rd; Chinatown or Tanjong Pagar MRT; map p.64. One of Singapore's first hawker centres and home to a clutch of popular Chinese stalls, including Tian Tian for Hainanese chicken rice, plus others that are good for satay or *rojak*. Daily roughly 7am–midnight.

My Awesome Café 202 Telok Ayer St ☎6222 2007, ⊛www.myawesomecafe.com; map p.64. This verging-on-hipster café, in a former Chinese shophouse clinic, constantly draws a crowd with its jumbo salads, sandwiches and wraps (around $20); sharing platters and a few mains also available. Daily 9.30am–midnight.

★ **Park Bench Deli** 179 Telok Ayer St ☎6815 4600, ⊛parkbenchdeli.com; Telok Ayer or Tanjong Pagar MRT; map p.64. They do breakfasts, light bites and weekend brunches here, but there's one thing they're famed for:

TOP 5 BLOWOUT JOINTS

The best way to stuff yourself silly in Singapore is to take advantage of **buffet** spreads. Several restaurants offer these, often for Sunday brunch or for **high tea** – a colonial tradition now elastically recast to cover just about any cuisine that seems to work as part of a mid-afternoon banquet.

L'Espresso see page 140
Paulaner Bräuhaus see page 139
Spices Cafe see page 142
Straits Kitchen see page 142
Annalakshmi see page 135

---

jumbo gourmet sandwiches (from $14). Pick from various fillings, including pulled pork, cheese and mustard, and double fried egg with bacon and mashed potato. You may face a wait on weekdays as people buy lunchtime takeaways for their entire office. Mon–Fri 7.30am–9pm, Sat & Sun 9am–3pm.

Savanh Bistro & Lounge 47 Club St ☎6325 8529, ⊛indochine-group.com; Telok Ayer or Chinatown MRT; map p.64. Classy Vietnamese, Lao and Cambodian cuisine in chic surroundings sums up the Indochine chain, and their Club St venue is no exception. The Vietnamese *chao tôm* (minced prawn wrapped round sugar cane) and deep-fried Vietnamese spring rolls are mouthwatering starters, while the Lao *larb kai* (spicy chicken salad) is one of many excellent mains. Around $40 per person, minus drinks. Mon–Sat noon–midnight.

★ **Spring Court** 52–56 Upper Cross St ☎6449 5030, ⊛springcourt.com.sg; Chinatown MRT; map p.64. With a prewar pedigree, *Spring Court* is now a mammoth occupying multiple floors of adjacent shophouses. Its popularity hasn't blunted the quality of the cooking; must-tries include the excellent if expensive *popiah* (steamed spring rolls, hand-wrapped by staff at a counter outside; $9), steamed chicken with Chinese ham and greens, and the braised tofu stuffed with vegetables and crowned by a scallop. Plenty of seafood options, plus dim sum, too. At least $30 per person without drinks. Daily 11am–3pm & 6–10.30pm.

Teh Tarik Time 43 New Bridge Rd ☎6338 9547; Clarke Quay MRT; map p.64. Dirt cheap snack-and-chill joint for those local standards, frothy sweet tea and *roti prata* – griddle bread, which is available in three dozen wacky modern variants, such as with chocolate or cheese. Also basic rice and noodle meals, nothing costing more than a few dollars. Daily 24hr.

Urban Bites 161 Telok Ayer St ☎6327 9460, ⊛urban bites.com.sg; Telok Ayer MRT; map p.64. It's nothing much to look at, but this little restaurant serves an impressive range of Lebanese standards, including meze favourites such as *rakakat* (like spring rolls but stuffed with cheese) and

11

kibbeh (bulgar wheat and minced lamb). Mains range from home-cooking favourites like *mujadara* (rice with lentils, fried onions and – their own twist – quinoa) to, of course, wraps ($20) and kebabs ($30). Mon–Sat 11am–3pm, 5–9.30pm.

Ya Kun Family Café #01-31 The Central, 6 Eu Tong Sen St ☎ 6534 7332, ⓦ yakun.com; Clarke Quay MRT; map p.64. Now a ubiquitous chain, *Ya Kun* started out in the war years as a Chinatown stall offering classic *kopitiam* breakfast fare – *kaya* toast plus optional soft-boiled eggs eaten with white pepper and soy sauce. Of course there's strong local coffee too, normally drunk with condensed or evaporated milk. Daily 7am–10pm.

Yixin 43 Temple St; Chinatown MRT; map p.64. Workaday vegetarian *kopitiam* that turns out dishes such as mock Peking duck ($8), plus rice and noodle standards like *lor mee* (noodles in a yummy, tangy, gloopy sauce), with a few organic options, too. A picture menu makes ordering easy. Barely signed in English, but easy to spot across from the *Inn on Temple Street* hotel. Daily 8am–9pm.

Zhonghua Bao Ding 241 South Bridge Rd, opposite the Sri Mariamman Temple ☎ 6323 2696; Chinatown MRT; map p.64. Barely signed in English, the "Explosion Pot Barbecue" (as it styles itself) specializes, unusually for a Chinese restaurant, in grills. Most of the clientele are mainland Chinese, here for spicy mutton and beef kebabs, pork crackling, duck necks and other greasy but tasty delights. Around $20 per person, minus drinks. Daily noon–10pm.

BOAT QUAY AND RIVERSIDE POINT

The south bank of the Singapore River is packed with busy restaurants and bars, at their most touristy in the restored shophouses of boisterous Boat Quay, though even the modern complexes can be a more enticing prospect than overpriced Clarke Quay on the north bank.

★ **Café Iguana** #01-03 Riverside Point, 30 Merchant Rd ☎ 6236 1275, ⓦ cafeiguana.com; Clarke Quay or Fort Canning MRT; map p.64. This open-fronted restaurant features fajitas, tacos, burritos – basically, all the standards, with plenty for veggies; light mains start at $25. The avocado ice cream makes a tasty dessert. Popular as a drinking venue, too (see page 150). Mon–Thurs 4pm–midnight, Fri 4pm–3am, Sat noon–1am, Sun noon–midnight.

Hans Im Glück 71 Boat Quay ☎ 9738 5310, ⓦ hansim glueck-burgergrill.sg; Clarke Quay or Raffles Place MRT; map p.64. A German burger chain with copious veggie and vegan options sounds like an oxymoron, but this one truly has something for everyone – even a choice of sourdough or multigrain buns. The lunch deal (until 5pm) is exceptional: add $5 on to the cost of your burger and you also get a generous portion of salad or potato/sweet potato fries, plus a soft drink and coffee or tea. Standalone burgers from $18. Mon–Thurs & Sun 11am–midnight, Fri & Sat 11am–1am.

Rendezvous #02-72 The Central, 6 Eu Tong Sen St ☎ 6339 7508, ⓦ rendezvous-hlk.com.sg; Clarke Quay MRT; map p.64. For decades *Rendezvous* has been serving up revered *nasi padang*, first as the Rendezvous *kopitiam* at the start of Bras Basah Rd, then in the hotel of that name that replaced it. The current location in a mediocre mall doesn't suit at all, but the curries have stayed the course, in particular the superb chicken korma, here a stew of just the right degree of richness, derived from coconut milk rather than cream or yoghurt. A couple of curries with rice and side dishes are unlikely to cost more than $25 a head. Daily 11am–9pm.

TANJONG PAGAR AND THE FINANCIAL DISTRICT

You're unlikely to head to these areas bordering Chinatown for the food alone, but they do boast some excellent, if often pricey, independent restaurants.

Blue Ginger 97 Tanjong Pagar Rd ☎ 6222 3928, ⓦ theblueginger.com; Tanjong Pagar MRT; map p.64. In a smartly renovated shophouse, this trendy Nonya restaurant has become a firm favourite thanks to such dishes as *ikan masak asam gulai* (mackerel in a tamarind

---

STREET ICE CREAM

A couple of generations ago, **ice cream** in Singapore often meant stuff sold by hawkers from pushcarts, in exotic flavours like sweetcorn, red (*aduki*) bean and yam. This was so-called **potong** ("cut" in Malay) ice cream because it came in bricks, and the seller would use a meat cleaver to turn it into slabs, to be served either between wafers as the classic ice cream sandwich or, oddly, rolled up in a slice of white bread.

The general elimination of street stalls put paid to that trade in Singapore, but in recent years the ice-cream vendors have made a comeback. They're now to be seen at Cavenagh Bridge, on Orchard Road, outside Bugis MRT and at a few other downtown locations. You can also find mass-produced versions of same unusual flavours in the freezer cabinets of convenience stores (look for Potong, "cut", on the wrapper), but it's never as good as the real thing, for which you can expect to pay just $1.50 or so per serving. Incidentally, the bread option is a surprisingly good foil for the ice cream, serving as a sort of neutral sponge.

and lemon-grass gravy), and that benchmark of Nonya cuisine, *ayam buah keluak* – chicken braised in soy sauce together with savoury black nuts. At least $25 per head, minus drinks. Daily noon–2.30pm & 6.30–10pm.

Clifford Pier 80 Collyer Quay ☎ 6597 5266, ⓦ fullerton bayhotel.com/dining; Raffles Place MRT; map p.64. This upmarket restaurant majors on a refined take on pan-Asian classics and street food: *bak chor mee*, *sup kambing* (Malay mutton soup), plus Hokkien *kong bak bao* (soy sauce pork eaten with steamed buns). Noodle dishes start at around $28, about five times what you'd pay at a food court, but then food courts don't feature the lofty, arched ceiling of this former boat terminal, marble floors and live piano music. Set menus abound, including for afternoon tea (daily; $55 but more at weekends), a weekend dim sum brunch and a buffet dinner (weekends; $70). Daily noon–2.30pm, 3.30–5.30pm & 6.30pm–10pm.

★ **Lau Pa Sat** 18 Raffles Quay; Telok Ayer or Raffles Place MRT; map p.64. The food court at this historic market building offers a panoply of Singapore hawker food, but the best thing about it is Malay satay in the open air – at least a dozen vendors set up their barbecues on neighbouring Boon Tat St in the evenings. Open 24hr.

Lucha Loco 15 Duxton Hill ☎ 6226 3938, ⓦ luchaloco. com; Outram Park or Maxwell MRT; map p.64. Popular with young expats, this Mexican joint does tacos and burritos at lunchtime, with the burritos dropped in favour of quesadillas and sharing platters in the evenings. Portions are on the small side, but they make amends with a buzzing garden drinking area where you can down their vast range of margaritas. Mon–Thurs noon–4pm & 5pm–midnight, Fri noon–4pm & 5pm–1am, Sat 6pm–midnight.

★ **The Populus Café** 146 Neil Rd ☎ 6635 8420, ⓦ thepopuluscafe.com; Outram Park MRT; map p.64.

> ## TOP 5 FOR HAWKER FOOD
> **Lau Pa Sat** see below
> **Maxwell Food Centre** see page 137
> **Newton Food Centre** see page 142
> **Tekka Food Centre** see page 134
> **Tiong Bahru Market** see page 146

This slick, contemporary café is popular with young professional types for its gourmet coffee blends and fusion meals such as cod with soba noodles (from $25). Mon 9am–7pm, Tues 9am–4pm, Wed–Fri 9am–10.30pm, Sat 9.30am–10.30pm, Sun 9.30am–7pm.

Sabio 5 Duxton Hill ☎ 6690 7562, ⓦ dhm.com.sg/ sabio; Outram Park or Maxwell MRT; map p.64. This tiny but elegant restaurant serves delicious tapas, including excellent pan-fried calamari and aged ham from acorn-fed pigs, the last sold by weight (most tapas $10–20). Also weekday set lunches for $22. Wash your meal down with sangria or Estrella Galicia beer. Mon–Fri noon–11.30pm, Sat 5pm–midnight, Sun 11.30am–10.30pm.

Xiao Ya Tou 6 Duxton Hill ☎ 6226 1965, ⓦ xyt.sg; Outram Park or Maxwell MRT; map p.64. *Xiao Ya Tou* looks like some kind of oriental fairyland, decked out in coloured lights and what appears to be 1960s East Asian showbiz photos. The food, for the most part, is good old Hokkien standards, real comfort food for locals – except that everything has had an upgrade; thus Hokkien *mee* comes with jumbo prawns and even clams instead of a few weedy shrimp. Correspondingly pricey compared with hawker joints, but worth it; mains from $18. Mon–Thurs noon–11pm, Fri noon–midnight, Sat 10am–midnight, Sun 10am–5pm.

11

MARINA BAY

Lavo Marina Bay Sands SkyPark ☎ 6688 8591, ⓦ lavo singapore.com; map p.79. The cheapest way to bypass the steep admission fee to level 57 of *Marina Bay Sands* is to pop up to this basically Italian restaurant at lunchtime, when you can have a frittata brunch or pizza from around $30. Prices ratchet up noticeably in the evening. Smart-casual dress. Daily 5pm–2am.

Nostra Cucina #B1-42 Marina Bay Sands shopping mall, 1 Bayfront Ave ☎ 6688 8522; Bayfront MRT; map p.79. An excellent range of reasonably priced thin-crust pizzas starting at $30, with plenty of salads, pasta options and soups, plus good desserts. Daily noon–11pm.

Paulaner Bräuhaus #01-01 Millenia Walk, 9 Raffles Blvd ☎ 6883 2572, ⓦ paulaner.com.sg; Promenade MRT; map p.79. The cavernous ceiling with a maypole sticking up into it is impressive, as is the menu of Bavarian delights such as the bitty *spätzle* pasta, but the best reason to come is the terrific Sunday brunch spread, including superb pork knuckle,

sausages and salads, and desserts like strudel and cheesecake. It's good value at $68 with unlimited soft drinks, or $80 with unlimited beer from their microbrewery. Restaurant Mon–Fri 11am–2.30pm & 6–10.30pm, Sat 6.30–10.30pm, Sun 11.30am–2.30pm & 6–10.30pm; bar daily 11am–1am.

TWG Tea Garden #B2-65 The Shoppes at Marina Bay Sands, Bayfront Ave ☎ 6565 1837, ⓦ twgtea.com; Bayfront MRT; map p.79. Founded in Singapore in 2008 (and not 1837 as the logo would have you believe), TWG Tea is now an international luxury brand, with teashops as far afield as London's Harrods. This teahouse is the grander of their two outlets at *Marina Bay Sands*, with tables arced around a glossy semicircular counter, and actually does a full range of mains, most flavoured with tiny amounts of tea. Many people, though, come for a straight tea (there are at least two dozen Darjeelings, for instance) and sumptuous desserts, including the excellent chocolate truffle tart. Pots of tea and desserts each start at $15. Mon–Thurs & Sun 10am–11pm, Fri & Sat 10am–midnight.

11

COOKERY CLASSES

There are three places offering half-day courses in the rudiments of Southeast Asian and other cooking styles. **Food Playground** (24A Sago St, Chinatown; ☎9452 3669, ⦿foodplayground.com.sg) is an unusual set-up where senior citizens, among others, get a chance to interact with people and teach local recipes, including ones for many hawker favourites ($120). Out in the eastern suburbs, Ruqxana at **Cookery Magic** (☎9665 6831, ⦿cookerymagic.com) teaches all of Singapore's native cuisines at her own home (117 Fidelio St; bus #42 from Kembangan MRT; $110). For a broader culinary palette, try the courses at **Coriander Leaf** (see page 130), largely run by the restaurant's owner Samia Ahad; she covers Indian and Indochinese cuisine, among others ($160).

ORCHARD ROAD AND AROUND

Eating in the heart of Singapore's shopping nexus – Orchard Rd, Tanglin Rd and Scotts Rd – is almost completely about hotel and mall restaurants, although it's worth checking out the shophouse-based venues at Cuppage Terrace (next to the Centrepoint mall) and on Killiney Rd.

Bistro Du Vin #01-14 Shaw Centre, Claymore Hill ☎6733 7763, ⦿bistroduvin.com.sg; Orchard MRT; map p.84. Informal French restaurant that does an exceptional duck leg confit, plus standards such as escargots and coq au vin. The lunch deals are great value at $48 for three courses, less than certain mains. Daily noon–2.30pm & 6.30–10pm.

★ **Brunetti** #01-35 Tanglin Mall, 163 Tanglin Rd ☎6733 9088, ⦿brunetti.com.sg; Orchard Boulevard MRT (15min walk); map p.84. This incredible Australian café boasts cabinet after cabinet stuffed with exquisite macaroons, cakes, pastries and ice creams that together come in almost as many colours as you find in a paint catalogue. Not too pricey – cheesecake costs $8 – though the light meals and savoury snacks aren't such good value. Daily 9am–9pm.

★ **Crystal Jade La Mian Xiao Long Bao** #B2-36A Ngee Ann City ☎6733 3229, ⦿crystaljade.com; Orchard MRT; map p.84. *Crystal Jade* is an umbrella for several linked Chinese restaurant chains, each with a different emphasis. Their mid-priced *La Mian Xiao Long Bao* outlets focus on Shanghai and northern Chinese cuisine, as exemplified by *xiao long bao*, succulent Shanghai pork dumplings, and the northwestern *lamian*, literally "pulled noodles", the strands of dough stretched and worked by hand. Around $30 per person, without drinks. No reservations. Daily 11am–10pm.

★ **Dancing Fish** Level 4, Tangs Department Store, 310 Orchard Rd; Orchard MRT; ☎6339 1048, ⦿dancingfish.asia; map p.84. Kuala Lumpur eating houses seldom manage to take root south of the Causeway, but this impressive Indonesian restaurant looks to have a decent shot. The titular fish and house speciality is a deep-fried tilapia, served splayed out as if balletically posed ($42). Other must-tries include *gulai pucuk paku*, jungle ferns stewed in spiced coconut milk; and the Balinese crispy duck.

Reckon on $40 per person without drinks. Daily 11.30am–10.30pm.

Food Republic Level 5, 313@Somerset, 313 Orchard Rd; Somerset MRT; map p.84. One of the nicest examples of this all-conquering food court chain, spacious, good for conversation and with a wealth of decent stalls, including one that does reliable *nasi padang*. Daily 10am–10pm.

Kiseki #08-01 Orchard Central mall, 181 Orchard Rd ☎6736 1216, ⦿kisekirestaurant.com.sg; Somerset MRT; map p.84. If you come here often enough you might end up as rotund as the sumo wrestler statue at the entrance. The food at this "mega Japanese buffet" is merely adequate, but what it excels at is variety – everything from sushi to Japanese curry pizza, via tempura, yakitori and (at dinner) steak and chicken teriyaki. Prices range from $28 weekday lunchtimes to nearly double that Friday to Sunday evenings. Daily 11.30am–3pm & 6–10.30pm.

Korea House 87 Killiney Rd ☎6734 3010; Somerset MRT; map p.84. Cosy place with tasty one-plate lunch specials such as *bibimbap* (rice with vegetables, a meat or egg topping and spicy sauce) and saba fish (grilled mackerel) starting at $11. They also do a wide range of standards like beef *bulgogi* (from $18) and that latter-day classic, army stew, a postwar concoction of US military rations such as spam and tinned beans, spiced up with Korean seasonings ($40 for two). Daily 11.30am–10.30pm.

L'Espresso Goodwood Park Hotel, 22 Scotts Rd ☎6730 1743, ⦿goodwoodparkhotel.com/dining; Orchard MRT; map p.84. A legendary array of English cakes, scones and speciality coffees, not to mention chocolate fondue, for high tea – so successful have they've extended it to lunchtimes at weekends. $53 (Fri–Sun $57). Daily 10am–midnight; high tea Mon–Thurs 2–5.30pm, Fri–Sun noon–2.30pm & 3–5.30pm.

★ **Lingzhi** #05-01 Liat Towers, 541 Orchard Rd ☎6734 5788, ⦿lingzhivegetarian.com; map p.84. This long-established Chinese vegetarian restaurant can be a bit too nouvelle cuisine for its own good, but their lunch offer sweeps that aside. It's confusingly named an "à la carte buffet", basically a forty-item menu from which you can keep ordering until you burst (or, more likely, they shut).

SINGAPOREAN BLACK PEPPER CRAB DISH

PERANAKAN FOOD

Peranakan cuisine, also called Nonya/Nyonya food (see page 44), is the product of the melding of Chinese and Malay/Indonesian cuisines. It can seem more Malay than Chinese thanks to its use of spices – except that pork is widely used.

Nonya popiah (spring rolls) is a standard dish: rather than being fried, the rolls are assembled by coating a steamed wrap with a sweet sauce made of palm sugar, then stuffed mainly with stir-fried bangkwang, a crunchy turnip-like vegetable. Another classic is laksa, noodles in a spicy soup flavoured in part by daun kesom – a herb with a distinctive taste and fittingly referred to in English as the laksa leaf. Other well-known Nonya dishes include asam fish, a spicy, tangy fish stew featuring tamarind (the asam of the name); otak-otak, fish mashed with coconut milk and chilli paste, then put in a narrow banana-leaf envelope and steamed or barbecued; and ayam buah keluak, chicken cooked with "black nuts" which are actually the large, creamy seeds of a local plant.

11

Try the surprisingly meaty monkey head mushroom, cooked with whole chillies, and the delicate vegetarian satay. No alcohol. Lunch buffet $28 (slightly more Fri–Sun). Daily 11am–3pm, 6–10pm.

★ **Marché** Ground floor and basement, 313@ Somerset, 313 Orchard Rd ☎6834 4041, ⓦmarche-movenpick.sg; Somerset MRT; map p.84. Never mind that Mövenpick's Marché restaurants are formulaic: what a formula, when you can have rösti, sausages or crêpes cooked to order in front of you, or help yourself to the superb salad bar. Daily lunch specials offer a meal and drink for around $15, while the bakery counter does takeaway sandwiches (from $5), bread sticks and Berliners – doughnuts with a range of fillings. Mon–Thurs & Sun 11am–11pm, Fri & Sat 11am–midnight; bakery from 7.30am.

Newton Food Centre Clemenceau Ave North; Newton MRT; map p.84. Instantly recognizable in the hawker meal scene of Crazy Rich Asians, Newton Food Centre has been one of the island's most well-known eating spots since it was built in the 1970s. The food isn't necessarily better than elsewhere and prices are a bit elevated as the place is very much on the tourist trail, but it does offer a cross-section of local favourites like oyster omelette, biryanis and satay. Best of all, many of the tables are out under the stars, a rarity in Singapore. You can eat well here for $10, but expect to pay quite a bit more if you go for the seafood, for which Newton is noted. Daily from late afternoon till midnight or so.

★ **PS Café** Level 2, Palais Renaissance, 390 Orchard Rd ☎9834 8232, ⓦpscafe.com/pscafe-at-palais-renaissance; Orchard MRT; map p.84. Since opening up in a clothing store elsewhere on Orchard Rd, PS Café has blazed a spectacular trail with its constantly evolving menu of inventive fusion food and great desserts, and now has several branches downtown; this is one of the nicest, set in something resembling a glasshouse. Weekend brunches never fail to disappoint, featuring the likes of a superfood salad with quinoa and goji berries, a portobello mushroom and poached egg plate, and king prawn spaghetti. Mains

from $30. Mon–Fri 11.30am–11pm, Sat & Sun 9.30am–11pm.

★ **Spices Café** Concorde Hotel, 100 Orchard Rd ☎6739 8370; Somerset MRT; map p.84. Buffets galore: an evening seafood feast (Mon–Thurs $68, Fri–Sun $74), afternoon tea (Sat & Sun noon–4.30pm; $46), and outshining them both, the best-value lunch spread of Peranakan and other local cooking anywhere in town (Mon–Fri $46). Daily 6am–11pm.

★ **Straits Kitchen** Grand Hyatt, 10 Scotts Rd ☎6732 1234; Orchard MRT; map p.84. Straits Kitchen is a tour de force of Singapore food, covering hawker favourites like satay, murtabak, savoury carrot cake and prawn mee, all expertly prepared. A vast range of desserts too, including Nonya classics like the eggy kueh lapis layer cake. Note, though, that the restaurant is halal so dishes that would normally contain pork have been modified/left out. Buffets: lunch $66, dinner $78. Mon–Fri noon–2.30pm & 6.30–10.30pm, Sat & Sun noon–3pm & 6–10.30pm.

Swensen's #03-23 Plaza Singapura, 68 Orchard Rd ☎6837 0650, ⓦswensens.com.sg; Dhoby Ghaut MRT; map p.84. Wins no prizes for trendiness, but for what is essentially a chain of ice-cream parlours, the food menu is extensive – salads, pasta dishes, noodles and so on. Prices are reasonable, with soups and many of the huge range of ice-cream concoctions weighing in at around $10. Daily 10.30am–10.30pm.

Thai Express #03-24 Plaza Singapura, 68 Orchard Rd ☎6339 5442, ⓦthaiexpress.com.sg; Dhoby Ghaut MRT; map p.84. A modern chain with plenty of wood and chrome fittings and where everything is chop-chop. The menu is packed with Thai rice and noodle standards (from $12) plus lots of desserts. Daily 11am–10pm.

Warung M Nasir 69 Killiney Rd ☎6734 6228; Somerset MRT; map p.84. Tiny but venerable Indonesian nasi padang joint, with standards such as fried chicken balado, beef and chicken rendang and tofu or beans fried with sambal, plus one or two sticky dessert options. Daily 10am–10pm.

DEMPSEY HILL AND AROUND THE BOTANIC GARDENS

Dempsey Hill (⊛dempseyhill.com), also called Tanglin Village or just Dempsey, is close to the Botanic Gardens and a couple of kilometres west of Orchard Rd. A sprawling collection of lawns and fields dotted with bungalows, it was originally a British military camp; later it housed Singapore's Ministry of Defence, and nowadays it's home to a jumble of posh restaurants and bars, plus health spas, antique shops and so forth. It's not too far from the main road, and can be reached using buses #7, #77 and #174 from Orchard Blvd, or by heading west on foot from Napier MRT (15–20min).

Adam Road Hawker Centre Corner of Adam and Dunearn rds; Botanic Gardens MRT; map p.87. This small 1970s hawker centre is well worth a visit if you're at the northern end of the Botanic Gardens or at Bukit Brown. The Chinese food is indifferent, but the Malay and Indian stalls are great – look out for the *Selera Rasa Nasi Lemak* stall (closed Fri), which the sultan of Brunei apparently sends his chauffeur to buy takeaways from whenever he's in town. Daily 7am–late.

Candlenut Block 17A, Dempsey Rd ☎6304 2288, ⊛comodempsey.com; map p.87. It doesn't look especially upmarket, but this restaurant lofts Peranakan food towards haute cuisine, with dishes like barramundi *asam pedas* (with chilli and tamarind). Everything still tastes recognizably Peranakan, just with all the flavours cranked up to eleven. Prices are correspondingly on the high side, too, at around $40 per head, minus drinks. Mon–Thurs Sun noon–3pm & 6–10pm, Fri & Sat noon–3pm & 6–11pm.

Casa Verde Visitor Centre, Botanic Gardens ☎6467 7326, ⊛casaverde.com.sg; map p.87. Right in the midst of the gardens near Symphony Lake, this casual Italian restaurant serves the expected pizza and pasta variations (from $25), but often it's the non-Italian dishes that stand out. They do sizeable Western cooked breakfasts (until 11am, with one all-day option), and there are luxury versions of local favourites like *nasi lemak* and *laksa* throughout the day (from $15). Mon–Fri 7.30am–8pm, Sat & Sun 7.30–9pm.

Long Beach Seafood Block 25, Dempsey Rd ☎6323 2222, ⊛longbeachseafood.com.sg; map p.87. Once you had to trek to the coasts to find Singapore's finest Chinese-style seafood, but these days the old beachside eating houses have set up all over, including here. The best dishes really are magic, including treacly crisp baby squid, chunky Alaska crab in a white pepper sauce, steamed *soon hock* (goby) and, of course, chilli crab. Worthwhile but pricey – you can pay anything from a few tens of dollars per head to a hundred or more if you order nothing but seafood. Daily 11am–3pm & 5pm–1am.

Open Farm Community 130E Minden Rd ☎6471 0306, ⊛openfarmcommunity.com; map p.87. It's gimmicky to call yourself a farm when all you have are a few vegetable and herb plots to supply the kitchen, but the cooking here is no gimmick: mains such as the wagyu burger and the roast pork are seriously top-notch. The place itself is suitably styled like an ultra-smart country bungalow. Mains from $30. Daily at least noon–4pm & 6–11pm.

Samy's Block 25, Dempsey Rd ☎6472 2080; map p.87. Housed in a colonial-era hall with ceiling fans whirring overhead, *Samy's* is an institution that's been serving super banana-leaf meals for decades; choose from curries of jumbo prawn, fish-head, crab or mutton, and either plain rice or the delicate, fluffy biryani. The service isn't what it was, but you can still eat well for $20 a head, excluding drinks. Wed–Mon 11am–3pm & 6–10pm.

GEYLANG AND KATONG

328 Katong Laksa 51 East Coast Rd, at the corner of Ceylon Rd ☎9732 8163; Marine Parade MRT; map p.101. The brash, modern appearance conceals the pedigree of this brother-and-sister-run place, famed for its classic *laksa*. It features noodles cut into short strands so you can slurp them with a spoon, and adheres to the classic formula with just prawns and seafood (modern variants may include meat). Daily 10am–10pm.

Alwadi Ground floor, Tristar Complex, 970 Geylang Rd; Paya Lebar MRT; map p.101. This food court is great for Malay and Indian Muslim food, with a wide range of noodle offerings such as *mee siam*, plus *lontong* (sticky-rice cakes with curry), *murtabak* and assorted fritters. Look out also for the popular *putu piring* stall, where you can line up to pay $2 for five little spongy rice-flour puddings, flavoured with palm molasses and individually steamed in metal cups. Daily 24hr.

Glory 139 East Coast Rd ☎6344 1749; Marine Parade MRT; map p.101. Run by the firm that manufactures Peranakan goodies sold in supermarkets across Singapore, this cafeteria-style place has the standard Nonya dishes, as well as an amazing range of sweet treats. Meals seldom come to more than $15 per person. Tues–Sun 8.30am–8.30pm.

★ **Guan Hoe Soon** 38/40 Joo Chiat Place ☎6344 2761, ⊛guanhoesoon.com; map p.101. Open in one form or another for more than half a century, this restaurant turns out fine Nonya cuisine in home-cooked style, including *ngoh hiang*, a yummy sausage-like item in which minced prawn is rolled up in a wrapper made from beancurd, and *satay babi* – not as in Malay satay, but a sweetish, spicy pork stew. Around $25 per head, excluding drinks. Daily 11am–3pm & 6–9.30pm.

★ **Hajjah Maimunah** 20 Joo Chiat Rd ☎6348 5457, ⊛hjmaimunah.com; Paya Lebar MRT; map p.101. One of very few truly Malay diners in Singapore, this place tends to fly under the radar but is much loved by those in the know. It serves good breakfasts (*nasi lemak, lontong*) and a fine *nasi campur* spread, featuring the likes of *ayam bakar sunda* (Sundanese-style barbecued chicken). For something more adventurous, order the *siput lemak sedut* (snails with coconut milk), and remember to save space for the *kuih*, starchy sweetmeats. Expect some queues at weekends. Around $15 per head. Tues–Sun 8am–9pm (may open later in Ramadan, with buffets).

A MENU READER

NOODLES (MEE) AND NOODLE DISHES

Bee hoon/mee fun	Thin rice noodles, like vermicelli.
Bak chor mee	Yellow noodles with minced pork and a spicy vinegar sauce, or in broth.
Hokkien fried mee	Yellow and white noodles fried with pieces of pork, prawn and vegetables.
(Char) kuey teow	*Kuey teow* (*hor fun* in Cantonese) are flat rice noodles, like tagliatelle.
Char	indicates the noodles are stir-fried, usually with prawns, Chinese sausage, egg and greens.
Lamian	"Pulled noodles", made by spinning dough skipping-rope-style in the air.
Laksa	Noodles, beansprouts, fishcakes and prawns in a spicy coconut soup.
Mee	Yellow wheat noodles
Mee goreng	Spicy Indian/Malay fried noodles.
Mee rebus	Classic Malay dish of boiled *mee*, the Singaporean version being served in a sweet sauce based on yellow-bean paste, garnished with tofu, boiled egg and bean sprouts.
Sar hor fun	Flat rice noodles served in a chicken stock soup, to which prawns fried shallots and bean sprouts are added.
Wonton mee	Roast pork, noodles and vegetables in a light soup.

RICE (NASI) DISHES

Biryani	Saffron-flavoured rice served with curries or fried chicken.
Claypot rice	Rice topped with meat, cooked in an earthenware pot over a fire to create a smoky taste.
Hainanese *chicken rice*	Steamed or boiled chicken slices on rice cooked in chicken stock, served with chicken broth and chilli and ginger sauce.
Lontong	Rice cakes made by boiling rice wrapped tightly in leaves; served with curries.
Mixed rice	The simplest and most popular choice at food courts, this is a spread of meat, fish and vegetable dishes which you point at to order; a large portion of plain rice comes as standard.
Nasi goreng	Malay- or Indian-style fried rice with diced meat and vegetables.
Nasi lemak	A classic Malay breakfast: fried anchovies, cucumber, peanuts and fried or hard-boiled egg slices served on rice cooked in coconut milk.
Nasi padang	Mixed rice featuring dishes cooked in the style of Padang, the town in Sumatra, Indonesia.
Nasi puteh	Plain cooked rice.

OTHER SPECIALITIES

Ayam goreng	Malay-style fried chicken.
Bak kut teh	Literally "pork bone tea", a Chinese broth of pork ribs in soy sauce, herbs and spices.
Chye tow kueh	Also known as "carrot cake", this is a sort of scramble made with white radish, flour and egg; it's available plain ("white") or "dark", the latter cooked with sweet soy sauce.
Congee	Watery rice gruel, either unsalted and eaten with slices of egg and salt fish, or else boiled up with chicken, fish or pork.
Dosai/thosai	South Indian pancake, made from ground rice and sometimes other ingredients, and stuffed with dhal or other fillings.
Fishballs/fishcake	Fish-flavoured dumplings, round or in slivers (the "cake" version), used to add substance to noodle dishes and stews.
Fish-head curry	Another Singapore classic, the head of a red snapper (usually), cooked in a

11

Sandwich Saigon 93 East Coast Rd ☎6440 5440, ⓦsandwichsaigon.com; Marine Parade MRT; map p.101. Katong has played host to a number of Vietnamese restaurants in recent years. This one stands out for its yummy Vietnamese baguettes, using bread baked on the premises and with fillings such as garlic chicken or pork chop (around $10). Also well-executed spring rolls and noodle dishes ($12), plus drip coffee. Daily 11.30am–3pm & 5.30–10pm.

11

	spicy curry sauce with tomatoes and okra.
Gado gado	Malay/Indonesian salad of lightly cooked vegetables, boiled egg, sticky-rice cubes and a crunchy peanut sauce.
Ikan bilis	Anchovies, usually deep-fried.
Kai pow/bao	Similar to *char siew pow* (see below), but contains chicken and boiled egg.
Kaya	A coconut and egg curd "jam", great with toast.
Keropok	Originally a kind of fish or prawn dumpling, but used in Singapore to mean crackers made of the dumpling mixture, sliced thinly and fried.
Murtabak	A much more substantial take on *roti prata*, stuffed with onion, egg and chicken or mutton.
Otak-otak	Fish mashed with coconut milk and chilli paste and steamed in a banana leaf; a Nonya dish.
Popiah	Spring rolls, steamed rather than fried, and filled with egg, vegetables and a sweet sauce; sometimes known as *lumpia*.
Pow/bao	Cantonese steamed bun; the most popular variety is *char siew pow*, filled with sweet roast pork.
Rendang	Dry, slow-cooked curry of beef, chicken or mutton.
Rojak	A salad of greens, beansprouts, pineapple and cucumber in a peanut-and-prawn paste sauce, similar to *gado gado*. There's also a totally different Indian version, comprising a selection of fritters (as ever, order by pointing) served with sweet spicy dips.
Roti john	French bread spread with egg, chopped onion and spicy chilli sauce (sometimes meat too), then shallow-fried.
Roti prata	Indian griddle bread served with a thin meat or fish curry sauce or dhal – a standard breakfast or snack.
Satay	Marinated pieces of meat, skewered on small sticks and cooked over charcoal; served with peanut sauce.
Sop kambing	Spicy Malay/Indian mutton soup.
Steamboat	Chinese fondue: raw vegetables, meat or fish dunked into a steaming broth until cooked. The spicy Sichuan version is called hotpot.

DESSERTS

Bubor cha cha	Sweetened coconut milk with pieces of sweet potato, yam and tapioca balls.
Cheng tng	Surprisingly refreshing Chinese sweet stew of unusual dried fruits and fungi, served hot or iced.
C(h)endol	Coconut milk, palm sugar syrup and pea-flour noodles poured over shaved ice.
Ice kachang	Slushy ice with beans, cubes of jelly, sweet corn, rose syrup and evaporated milk.
Pisang goreng	Battered bananas, fried.

DRINKS

Bandung	Sickly pink drink made with rose-flavoured syrup and a little milk.
Chinchow	Looks like cola gone flat but is actually a sweet drink made from a kind of seaweed, with bits of agar jelly floating around inside.
Kopi	Coffee, normally served with sweetened condensed milk.
-o	Suffix meaning "black" – so say *kopi-o* for black coffee.
-c	Suffix referring to unsweetened evaporated milk.
-kosong	Meaning "zero"; can mean either without sugar or milk
Lassi	Sweet or sour Indian yoghurt drink.
Tarik	Meaning "pulled" (*tarik*), it refers to pouring tea or coffee between two cups to produce a frothy drink.
Teh	Tea, usually with condensed milk.

Sik Bao Sin Desmond's Creation 592 Geylang Rd ☎ 6744 3757; map p.101. Having helped run one of Geylang's best loved *zichar* establishments for many years, Desmond here now cooks just a dozen or so dishes at his very own restaurant. The ginger chicken, braised tofu with prawns and bittergourd with pork are all especially good, though expect to line up for a table at times. Around $30 per head, excluding drinks. Tues–Sun 11.45am–2.30pm & 5.45–9.30pm.

TIONG BAHRU

40 Hands #01-12 78 Yong Siak St ☎ 6225 8545, ⓦ 40handscoffee.com; Tiong Bahru MRT; map p.107. With colourful tiled walls, *40 Hands* was in the vanguard of Singapore's indie café scene and serves locally roasted coffee that nicely complements its popular all-day breakfasts and toasted sandwiches (both from $18). Also salads and mains such as Korean fried chicken burgers. Mon–Wed 7am–7pm, Thurs & Fri 7am–10pm, Sat & Sun 7.30am–7pm.

Bakalaki 3 Seng Poh Rd ☎ 6836 3688, ⓦ bakalaki.com; Havelock MRT or bus #123 from Orchard Rd; map p.107. There's little that's obviously Greek about this modern restaurant, but they do great versions of all the standard meze and *souvlaki* kebab wraps, and they have their own deli selling foods you might get in a neighbourhood grocer's in Athens. Meze from $12, mains from $20. Mon–Thurs 6–midnight, Fri–Sun noon to 2.30pm & 6pm–1am.

Loo's Hainanese Curry Rice 57 Eng Hoon St; Tiong Bahru MRT; map p.107. Launched at another location in 1946, this is now a Tiong Bahru institution, as the lines often seen outside the *kopitiam* the stall is part of attest. They basically do rice with just a handful of topping choices, including pork chops, chicken curry and the Nonya dish *chap chye* (a stew of mixed vegetables and fungi). Daily 8am until everything sells out (typically 2pm).

★ **Tiong Bahru Market** 30 Seng Poh Rd; Tiong Bahru MRT; map p.107. The market's upstairs deck holds dozens of mostly Chinese stalls, some of which have been in business for half a century. For snacks, try *Tiong Bahru Pow* (stall number #02-18) – their *pow* fillings range from chicken to sweet bean paste – or *Jian Bo Shui Kueh* (#02-05), beloved for their *chwee kueh*, steamed rice-flour mounds livened up with a topping of salted radish. For something more substantial you may not have tried elsewhere, bypass the fine oyster omelettes at stall #02-61 in favour of their sideline, *chee cheong fun*, pork-stuffed rice-dough coils doused in a sweet/savoury sauce; or head to 163 *Fish and Chicken Porridge* (#02-40), known for its smooth, chicken- or fish-flecked gruel. Daily 7am–late.

HOLLAND VILLAGE

Redevelopment has taken much of the shine off the former expat stronghold of Holland Village, but it is still worth a visit for its restaurants and bars, and the closure of the central Lorong Mambong to cars in the evenings helps retain some of the buzz. Get here on bus #7 from the Botanic Gardens, Orchard Boulevard and the Colonial District, or ride the Circle Line to Holland Village MRT, which is only a few stops from HarbourFront.

Cha Cha Cha 32 Lorong Mambong ☎ 6462 1650, ⓦ chachacha.com.sg; Holland Village MRT; map p.111. Classic Mexican dishes, including enchiladas and fajitas, at this vibrantly coloured restaurant. Book ahead for the few tables outside, ideal for posing with a Sol beer or margarita. Mains from $15. Mon–Thurs & Sun 11.30am–11pm, Fri & Sat 11.30am–midnight.

★ **Crystal Jade La Mian Xiao Long Bao** 241 Holland Ave ☎ 6463 0968, ⓦ crystaljade.com; Holland Village MRT; map p.111. This chain is best known for its Shanghai and northern Chinese dumplings and noodles, though in the evenings they also do a steamboat buffet, which involves diners cooking raw ingredients in boiling stock at the table (from $33 per head). Daily 11am–10pm.

Original Sin #01-62 Block 43, Jalan Merah Saga ☎ 6475 5605, ⓦ originalsin.com.sg; Holland Village MRT; map p.111. Singapore's only upmarket Western vegetarian restaurant focuses on Mediterranean cooking, though a little unadventurously – pizza and pasta dishes dominate, albeit ones making sophisticated use of prime ingredients. Often busy despite mains starting at $30. Daily 11.30–2.15pm & 6–10pm.

SENTOSA AND VIVOCITY

★ **Food Republic** Level 3 Vivocity, above HarbourFront MRT; map p.115. Perhaps the best example of this upmarket food court, the stalls styled to resemble something out of prewar Chinatown using chunks of an abandoned village in China. The cuisine, from hand-picked stallholders, is top-notch too. Try the *wu xiang* stall – it's a Chinese take on the morsels-plus-dips concept, with lots of sausages, dumplings and patties on display. Pick several you like the look of, and they will be speedily refried for you and served with sweet and/or spicy sauces. Note that the whole place can be rammed at peak times, though. Daily 10am–10pm.

Slappy Cakes Close to Universal Studios, Resorts World ☎ 6795 0779, ⓦ slappycakes.com; map p.115. This US pancake house is great for kids, as it makes you and the little 'uns make your own. Order a batter (chocolate or zucchini, say), plus something to liven up the mix (strawberries or ham, anyone?) and then cook it at your table's griddle. It's fun and if the results aren't up to scratch, well at least you won't have anyone to blame other than yourself (probably). One order (from $15) makes enough for two to snack on. Daily 8am–9.30pm.

★ **Soup** #02-141 Vivocity ☎6376 9969, ⓦ soup restaurant.com.sg; HarbourFront MRT; map p.115. So-called *samsui* women once sailed from China's Guangdong province in droves, incredibly, to work on Singapore building sites. This fine little restaurant celebrates the cuisine of these redoubtable women, most famously their ginger chicken – similar to the steamed chicken in chicken rice, with a gingery dip and iceberg-lettuce leaves to roll it up in. Reckon on $25 per head, excluding drinks. Daily 11.30am–10pm.

Trapizza Siloso Beach ☎6376 2662; map p.115. Of the eating places on Siloso Beach, *Trapizza* stands out for its excellent pizzas and pasta dishes, starting at $25. Daily 11am–10pm.

11

THE LONG BAR, RAFFLES HOTEL

Drinking and nightlife

Affluent, and with a large expat community, Singapore supports a huge range of drinking holes, ranging from elegant colonial chambers through indie cocktail bars to slightly tacky joints featuring karaoke or middling covers bands. There's a particular fondness for rooftop venues, for views as well as a sense of seclusion. There are also a few glitzy and vibrant clubs where people let their hair down to cutting-edge sounds minus – this being Singapore – any assistance from illicit substances. Some venues regularly manage to lure the world's leading DJs to play, too.

ESSENTIALS

Cover charges Most clubs have a cover charge, if not all week then at least on Friday and Saturday. The charge almost always includes your first drink or two, and varies between $15 and $30 (weekends are pricier, and men may pay slightly more than women). Some clubs advertise weekly "ladies' nights" (often Wed) when women can get in free or enjoy discounted drinks.

Dress code "Smart casual" is the watchword at swankier bars and clubs, which generally means no vests, shorts or sandals in the evening.

Drink costs Some surveys deem Singapore to be one of the world's most expensive cities for drinking, but the reality is more subtle. It's true that a 640ml bottle (1.1 imperial or 1.4 US pints) of Tiger beer at a bar or club typically costs around $14, but hawker centres (and supermarkets) charge around half that, and a handful of bars thrive on selling keenly priced drinks. During happy hour, which can last the whole first half the evening, you'll either get a considerable discount off drinks or a "one-for-one" deal (two drinks for the price of one), and some bars also have a "house pour", a discounted beer, wine or cocktail on offer all night. Standard cocktails generally start at $18.

Legal restrictions Laws introduced following the surprise Little India riot of 2013, which the government saw as aggravated by alcohol, make it illegal to drink in public – meaning anywhere on the street beyond the premises of restaurants, hawker centres, bars and clubs, plus beaches and parks – nightly from 10.30pm to 7am. Within Little India and Geylang, an additional ban applies throughout the weekend and until 7am on Mondays. Supermarkets and convenience shops like 7-11 are also unable to sell alcohol when the ban is in force.

Opening hours Bars tend to open in the late afternoon, or from lunchtime if they major on food, and close around midnight (certainly an hour or two later on Friday, Saturday and the day before a national holiday). A few don't open on Sunday, especially ones in commercial districts that are quiet at weekends. Nightclub hours are more predictable – many throw their doors open no earlier than 9pm and stay open until 2am or so.

Reservations It's worth calling ahead to reserve a table for Friday or Saturday evening as many bars will be packed, particularly select ones hidden away in shophouses or with elevated views.

12

BARS AND PUBS

Bars are spread throughout downtown but tend to cluster where expats like to hang out: in and around the financial district, including Chinatown and Boat Quay; on Orchard Road; and at Holland Village.

THE COLONIAL DISTRICT

★ **Aura Sky Lounge** Level 6, National Gallery, Coleman St ☎6866 1977, ⓦaura.sg; City Hall MRT; map p.36. Come here for one of the panorama out over the Padang taking in *Marina Bay Sands*, Esplanade, the Singapore Flyer, South Beach and the Financial District; after dark is best. Happy hour Mon–Thurs & Sun 5–8pm. Daily 11.30am–1am.

Wine Connection Cheese Bar #01-05 Robertson Walk, 11 Unity St ☎6238 1279; Fort Canning MRT; map p.36. *Wine Connection* is a good-value wine retailer that doesn't rest on its laurels; it also runs a few wine bars – two at Robertson Walk, one of which is this fine establishment stocking a range of delectable cheeses to go with your tipple. Treat yourself to their signature raclette ($42 per head for at least two people). Daily from 11.30am: Mon–Thurs until 2am, Fri & Sat until 3am, Sun until 11pm.

BRAS BASAH TO ROCHOR ROAD

The Alchemist #B1-16 South Beach, 26 Beach Rd ☎6386 4635, ⓦtab.com.sg; Esplanade or City Hall MRT; map p.50. This isn't the only Singapore bar to serve beer flavoured with infusions, but here it's their USP – hence the name, a reference to their "lab" out at

Changi where they steep fruit and herbs in towers of beer. They apply the same idea to some "draught cocktails" too, including an agreeable "piñata colada" [not piña colada] that's basically Malibu, mint and lemon juice on tap, with some pineapple soaking in it. Happy hour Mon–Thurs until 9pm, Fri & Sat until 7pm. Mon–Thurs 4pm–1am, Fri & Sat 4pm–2am.

★ **Loof** Top of the Odeon Towers Extension, 391 North Bridge Rd #03-07 ☎9773 9304, ⓦloof.com.sg; Esplanade or City Hall MRT; map p.50. This rooftop garden bar is an elegant place to chill out, with views of the back of the *Raffles* hotel opposite. There's a strong local flavour too, in the form of cocktails and bar food that use lots of Southeast Asian ingredients (with input from that enfant terrible of Singapore cuisine, Bjorn Shen at *Artichoke* – see page 131). Happy hour weekdays until 8pm. Mon–Thurs & Sun 5pm–1am, Fri & Sat 5pm–3am.

LITTLE INDIA, ARAB STREET & LAVENDER STREET

★ **Atlas** Ground floor, Parkview Square, 600 North Bridge Rd ☎6396 4466, ⓦatlasbar.sg; map p.50. Aptly located at the Gotham-esque Parkview Square, *Atlas* is a palatial evocation of Jazz Age glamour, all gilt Art Deco-style fittings. Cabinets stretching to the lofty ceiling hold a veritable library of wines and spirits, including some fiendishly expensive vintages. If you don't feel like indulging, just come for a daytime coffee and a long gawp. Staff are generally laidback and will seldom hassle you to order another drink, even in the evening. Smart-casual dress after 5pm. Mon–Thurs 10am–1am, Fri 10am–2am, Sat 3pm–2am.

Bar Stories Level 2, 55/57A Haji Lane ☏ 6298 0838; Bugis MRT; map p.50. This tiny venue, secreted away on the top floor of a couple of shophouses, majors on custom-made cocktails created to suit your tastebuds by a young and enthusiastic team of mixologists. It's somewhat pricey – concoctions cost around $25 – and yet quite domestic, with home-style low couches and armchairs to relax in. Mon–Thurs 5pm–1am, Fri & Sat 5pm–2am.

★ **Camp Kilo Charcoal Club** 66 Kampong Bugis ☏ 9830 6052, ⊛ kilokitchen.com; Lavender MRT, then use footbridge across the Rochor River from Crawford St; map p.50. Despite the address, this has nothing to do with Bugis St, nor is it a club. Kampong Bugis is presently a meadow, the fallow site of a former gasworks, awaiting major redevelopment, and the *Charcoal Club* is a sort of DIY open-air bar-restaurant at ground level in a partly disused building. They're big on Sapporo beers and ciders, while foodwise the star is the whole roast pig (Fri & Sat, from 6pm until polished off). It's all totally relaxed, family-friendly and faintly anarchic – there's hardly anything like it elsewhere in town. Fri 5.30–11pm, Sat & Sun 11am–late.

The Long Bar Raffles Hotel, 1 Beach Rd ☏ 6412 1816; Esplanade or City Hall MRT; map p.50. Don't be surprised to find your feet shuffling through peanut shells here – punters chucking the shells on the floor, in contravention of just about everything modern Singapore stands for, is just one of the traditions maintained at this institution. More famous, of course, is that of the Singapore Sling, invented here in 1915: very pink, a bit cloying and priced at an eye-popping $38. The green metal contraption with hand cranks at the bar, incidentally, mixes several Slings at one go. No happy hour. Daily 11am–11pm.

Mr Stork Level 39, Andaz Hotel, 5 Fraser St ☏ 6408 1255; Bugis MRT; map p.50. It concedes 23 storeys in height to *1-Altitude* (see page 151), but the deal is the same: glorious 360-degree views from the very top of a tower. They offer their own Andaz pale ale on draught, created in collaboration with the *Red Dot Brewhouse* (see page 151). Arrive early if you want to park yourself in one of their ten tepees. No happy hour. Mon–Thurs 5pm–midnight, Fri 5pm–1am, Sat 3pm–2am, Sun 3pm–midnight.

CHINATOWN

Bitters & Love 118 Telok Ayer St ☏ 6438 1836, ⊛ bittersandlove.com; Telok Ayer MRT; map p.64. By day a cramped café called *Free The Robot* (hence the wall drawings), the place transforms by night into one of Singapore's most informal, relaxed cocktail bars. There's the usual menu of standard cocktails, with cutesy names such as Nonya Confessions, and staff can mix up pretty

much anything you want. Mon–Thurs 6pm–midnight, Fri 6pm–2am, Sat 7pm–2am.

Rooftop at Screening Room 12 Ann Siang Hill ☏ 6221 1694; Maxwell or Telok Ayer MRT; map p.64. It's less glitzy than most of its nearby rivals, but this unpretentious rooftop bar has long been a convivial spot for an evening drink, with the bonus of views of Chinatown's shophouses and towers, plus plenty of snacks, kebabs and burgers. Signature drinks include rum slushies and cocktails with an Asian twist, incorporating banana or green tea, for instance. Happy hour Mon & Tues all eve, Wed–Sat until 8pm. Mon–Thurs 5.30pm–2am, Fri 5pm–3am, Sat 5pm–4am.

Spiffy Dapper Upstairs at 73 Amoy St ☏ 8742 8908, ⊛ spiffydapper.com; Telok Ayer MRT; map p.64. This tiny indie cocktail bar must be the darkest venue in town, its thick drapes keeping out any extraneous lighting. There are at least fifteen standard cocktails on offer (from $25), and the mixologists can talk through these and other options based on your tastes. Mon–Fri 5pm–late, Sat & Sun 6pm–late.

Stickies 11 Keng Cheow St ☏ 6221 1694, ⊛ stickiesbar. com; Clarke Quay MRT; map p.64. No fancy decor or fittings here, but the place is often packed with a young, mainly local, crowd thanks to its many discount deals. The most striking offer is hourly pricing on its daily house pour (including beer): they charge $2 at 2pm, $3 at 3pm and so on (plus taxes), the idea being to get people to ease off late at night. Daily noon–midnight.

BOAT QUAY TO RIVERSIDE POINT

BQ Bar 39 Boat Quay ☏ 6536 1571, ⊛ bqbar.com; Raffles Place MRT; map p.64. One of Boat Quay's cooler venues, thanks to the friendly staff, memorable views of the river from upstairs and diverse sounds, anything from dance to rock. Kebabs available too from a nearby outlet run by the same management. Happy hour until 8pm. Mon–Thurs 11am–midnight, Fri 11am–3am, Sat 5pm–3am.

Brewerkz #01-05/06 Riverside Point, 30 Merchant Rd ☏ 6438 7438, ⊛ brewerkz.com; Fort Canning or Clarke Quay MRT; map p.64. Offers a range of highly rated beers from its own microbrewery, plus dozens of speciality imports, accompanied by a generically American food menu – burgers, pizza, ribs and the like. No happy hour as such, but drink prices dip before 7pm and after 10pm. Mon–Thurs & Sun noon–midnight, Fri & Sat noon–1am.

★ **Café Iguana** #01-03 Riverside Point, 30 Merchant Rd ☏ 6236 1275, ⊛ cafeiguana.com; Fort Canning or Clarke Quay MRT; map p.64. A great selection of tequilas and margaritas, plus beers from the microbrewery of sister venue *Brewerkz* two doors away; happy hour until 7pm. Mon–Thurs 4pm–midnight, Fri 4pm–1am, Sat noon–1am, Sun noon–midnight.

12

Harry's 28 Boat Quay ☎ 6538 3029, ⊕ harrys.com. sg; Raffles Place MRT; map p.64. Singapore's most ubiquitous chain of bars started out here and now has some twenty branches islandwide. Popular with locals as well as foreigners, it does half a dozen draught beers and ciders, plus light meals and snacks; happy hour is until 8pm. Mon–Thurs & Sun 11.30am–1am; Fri & Sat 11.30am–2am.

The Penny Black 26 & 27 Boat Quay ☎ 6538 2300, ⊕ pennyblack.com.sg; Raffles Place MRT; map p.64. Not a convincing evocation of a "Victorian London pub" as their sign states, but pleasant enough, with one table built around a red pillar box to evoke the UK. There's Strongbow cider and Old Speckled Hen on draught, plenty of pub grub – fish and chips, cottage pie, even chicken tikka masala (mains from $18) – and live British football on TV. Happy hour until 8pm. Mon–Thurs & Sun 11.30am–midnight, Fri & Sat 11.30am–2am.

Red Dot Brewhouse 33 & 34 Boat Quay ☎ 6535 4500, ⊕ reddotbrewhouse.com.sg; Raffles Place MRT; map p.64. Many of Singapore's slicker bars are expat-run, but not the *Red Dot Brewhouse*, the brainchild of one local who got bitten by the homebrew bug many years ago. Among their range of beers and ales, the most radical is the Monster Green Lager, rich in blue-green algae regarded by some as a superfood. Mon–Thurs noon–midnight, Fri noon–2am, Sat 3pm–1am.

TANJONG PAGAR AND THE FINANCIAL DISTRICT

★ **1-Altitude** Levels 61-63, One Raffles Place ☎ 6438 0410, ⊕ 1-altitude.com; Raffles Place MRT; map p.64. Even if this isn't "the world's highest alfresco bar", as it proclaims, but merely one of the loftiest, the views of the Colonial District, Marina Bay and Chinatown from the roof of the One Raffles Place tower are simply stunning. Perhaps best to drop by towards the end of your stay, when you can make sense of the cityscape and ponder the myriad changes that half a century of rapid growth has wrought. Cover charge $35 ($45 after 9pm) including two drinks. Daily from 6pm: Sun–Tues until 2am, Wed & Thurs until 3am, Fri & Sat until 4am.

Forest Darts Café 2 #01-05 Shenton House, 3 Shenton Way ☎ 6224 5631; Downtown MRT; map p.64. Amid the banker-dominated bars of the Financial District is this down-to-earth darts bar with electronic boards that save you doing lots of arithmetic. Mon–Fri 4pm–1am, Fri & Sat 4pm–2am.

MARINA BAY

Cé La Vi North tower, SkyPark at Marina Bay Sands, 1 Bayfront Ave ☎ 6508 2188, ⊕ sg.celavi.com; Bayfront MRT; map p.79. The bar at the SkyPark's fanciest venue is one of the best ways to get round the 57th-floor admission fee and enjoy fabulous views over downtown Singapore.

Stella and Hoegaarden on draught; curiously, happy hour is Tues only (6–9pm). Daily noon–late.

Orgo Roof terrace, Esplanade – Theatres On The Bay ☎ 6336 9366, ⊕ orgo.sg; Esplanade or City Hall MRT; map p.79. They make a big thing of their huge range of cocktails, which emphasize fresh fruit and herbs, but the views of the spires of the Financial District sell themselves. Happy hour until 8pm. Mon–Wed & Sun 6pm–1am, Thurs–Sat 6pm–2am.

Tap Craft Beer Bar #01-02 One Raffles Link, Raffles Link ☎ 6219 0676, ⊕ tapthat.com.sg; Esplanade MRT; map p.79. This generically modern bar gets attention for its truly eclectic range of imported beers and ciders, with draught beer at $12 a pint all day. Bar bites include teriyaki meatballs and their famed spam fries. Daily 11.30am–11.30pm.

ORCHARD ROAD

Alley Bar Peranakan Place, corner of Orchard Rd and Emerald Hill Rd ☎ 6732 6966, ⊕ alleybar.sg; Somerset MRT; map p.84. The most interesting of the three bars at the start of Emerald Hill Rd, *Alley Bar* slots into a narrow, high-ceilinged space and does a good range of cocktails and spirits, plus draught Erdinger and Kilkenny. The food menu is extensive, too, ranging from fried spicy squid to satay. Happy hour until 9pm. Mon–Thurs & Sun 5pm–2am, Fri & Sat 5pm–3am.

Ice Cold Beer 9 Emerald Hill Rd ☎ 6735 9929, ⊕ ice-cold-beer.com; Somerset MRT; map p.84. Noisy, happening place where the beers are kept in ice tanks under the glass-topped bar. Shares kitchen and menu with *No. 5 Emerald Hill*. Leffe Blond and Fuller's London Pride on tap, among others. Happy hour until 9pm and again after 1am. Mon–Thurs 5pm–2am, Fri & Sat 2pm–3am.

Manhattan Regent Hotel, 1 Cuscaden Rd ☎ 6725 3377; Orchard Boulevard MRT; map p.84. It's hard to see why *Manhattan* has been winning international awards in recent years: it's no better stocked than other posh cocktail bars in town, and its vaguely Jazz Age styling is a poor second to what you get at *Atlas* (see page 149). That said, the cocktail list is extensive and the sensibly pitched music level and comfy sofas are conducive to conversation. Mon–Thurs & Sun 5pm–1am, Fri & Sat 5pm–2am.

Martini Bar Grand Hyatt Hotel, 10 Scotts Rd ☎ 6732 1234; Orchard MRT; map p.84. Choose from several dozen martini variations at this plush bar, ranging from their trademark lychee martini to some that include local ingredients such as sugar cane. Happy hour 5–9pm. Mon–Thurs 5pm–midnight, Fri & Sat 5pm–1am, Sun 3pm–midnight.

★ **No. 5 Emerald Hill** 5 Emerald Hill Rd ☎ 6732 0818, ⊕ emerald-hill.com; Somerset MRT; map p.84. Set in one of Emerald Hill Rd's restored houses, *No. 5* is not only a feast for the eyes but also offers speciality cocktails plus

12

great chicken wings and thin-crust pizzas. Asahi Black and Kronenbourg on tap, among others. Happy hour until 9pm, with especially low prices before 5.15pm. Mon–Thurs noon–2am, Fri & Sat noon–3am, Sun 2pm–2am.

DEMPSEY HILL

The Rabbit Hole 39C Harding Rd ☎ 6473 9965, ⓦ thewhiterabbit.com.sg; map p.87. From house of God to gin palace: that's the tale of the *Rabbit Hole*, the marvellous open-air garden bar at the back of the restored church which now holds its upmarket sibling, the *White Rabbit* restaurant. There are two dozen gin and a dozen gin-based cocktails to navigate your way around. Mon–Thurs & Sun 6–11.30pm, Fri & Sat 6pm–12.30am.

KATONG

The Cider Pit 328 Joo Chiat Rd ☎ 6344 5759; map p.101. Down-to-earth neighbourhood watering hole with a good range of apple and pear ciders, plus British-style pub grub. Mon–Fri 3pm–1am, Sat & Sun 1pm–1am.

HOLLAND VILLAGE

Wala Wala Café Bar 31 Lorong Mambong, Holland Village ☎ 6462 4288, ⓦ walawala.sg; Holland Village MRT; map p.111. In business for a quarter-century, this rocking joint has a host of draught beers, including San Miguel and Stella, to wash down snacks like spicy chicken wings. The a/c section upstairs hosts acoustic and electric covers bands. Happy hour until 9pm. Mon–Thurs 4pm–1am, Fri 4pm–2am, Sat 3pm–2am, Sun 3pm–1am.

SENTOSA

Ola Beach Club 46 Siloso Beach Walk ☎ 6250 6978, ⓦ olabeachclub.com; map p.115. Sentosa's beach bars are generally rather tame and feel like a missed opportunity. *Ola Beach Club* is fractionally better than the rest on Siloso Beach, with its own small pool, high-tech water sports programme and a Hawaiian-themed menu that's big on pork, seafood and *poke* (raw fish salad). Daily 10am–9pm, later at weekends.

DISCOS AND NIGHTCLUBS

Singapore's once-vibrant **clubbing** scene has come off the boil in recent years. A smattering of cutting-edge **Western-style clubs** remain, although allegiances are incredibly fickle, with venues prone to plummeting out of the limelight after just a few years. Some places feature **bands** playing covers of current hits and pop classics, as opposed to bands playing their own material or seriously into old-school genres like jazz (see page 156). There are also plenty of Chinese karaoke bars, usually signed in both English and Chinese; a few of these can have a slightly seedy side.

Camp Kilo Lounge 21 Tanjong Pagar Rd ☎ 9824 9747, ⓦ campkilo.com; Maxwell or Tanjong Pagar MRT; map p.64. An intimate venue with occasional big-name DJs or indie gigs, at which times a cover charge may apply. Happy hour until 8pm (not Sat); ladies' night is Thursday. Wed 5.30pm–midnight, Thurs & Fri 5.30pm–3am, Sat 9.30pm–4am.

Canvas #B1-06 The Riverwalk, 20 Upper Circular Rd ☎ 8125 0166, ⓦ canvasvenue.sg; Clarke Quay MRT; map p.64. On the south bank of the Singapore River, *Canvas* is a cosy space where you may get hip-hop, electronica, Latin or other sounds depending on the evening, but Tuesdays sees stand-up comedy rule the roost. Tues 8–11pm, Wed–Sat 8pm–late.

Cé La Vi North tower, SkyPark at Marina Bay Sands, 1 Bayfront Ave ☎ 6688 7688, ⓦ sg.celavi.com; Bayfront MRT; map p.79. One of Singapore's fanciest places to party, attracting noteworthy DJs from time to time. Cover charge Wed, Fri & Sat (ladies' night is Wed) from $33; on Sun you pay $20, redeemable against food and drink. Daily noon–late.

Tanjong Beach Club Tanjong Beach, Sentosa ☎ 6270 1355, ⓦ tanjongbeachclub.com; map p.115. If you needed a reason to trek to Tanjong Beach, this would be it. Styled like a luxury beach bungalow, it boasts a quirky ground-level infinity pool, a bar and pricey restaurant, monthly beach parties (usually Sun from 3pm) featuring guest DJs, and occasional film screenings, too. Mon–Fri 11am–10pm, Sat & Sun 9am–10pm.

Zouk The Cannery (aka Block C), Clarke Quay ☎ 6738 2988, ⓦ zoukclub.com; Clarke Quay MRT; map p.36. In business since 1991, *Zouk* is the one constant in Singapore's clubbing firmament, specialising in house and other dance sounds. Its sizeable Clarke Quay premises ooze post-industrial chic and hold four venues, including two bars and its little-sister club *Phuture*, where the emphasis is more on hip-hop and R&B. Photo ID required. Zouk Wed, Fri & Sat 10pm till late, Phuture Wed–Sat 10pm till late.

LGBTQ VENUES

Singapore's **LGBTQ scene**, though modest, is lively by Southeast Asian standards, and in recent years the country has seen the annual Pink Dot rally (a gay pride event by another name; June; ⓦ pinkdot.sg) grow into one of the most well-attended civil-society events on the island. That said, attitudes toward homosexuality remain mixed.

Colonial-era legislation banning sex between men remains on the statute book following a failed attempt in 2007 to get parliament to repeal it. The matter reared its head again in 2018, when India finally rescinded its version of the law and a noted Singapore diplomat suggested it was time the city state followed suit. Although the government has essentially said it regards the law as a dead letter, it appears to have little appetite to take on what it sees as more conservative/religious groups within Singapore society, nor to recognise any form of gay union or partnership, nor in allowing international trends to influence local opinion: it's noteworthy that the authorities have banned multinational firms from sponsoring Pink Dot and foreigners from attending. That said, the old "don't ask, don't tell" attitude is shifting, with the media less reluctant to cover LGBTQ issues such as the landmark 2018 Singapore court ruling allowing a local gay man to adopt a child he fathered with a surrogate mother in the US. Still, bars and clubs keep a low profile, scarcely using the word "gay" in their publicity, for example.

The scene centres on Chinatown and Tanjong Pagar, where there are a handful of bars and clubs; note that they only really get busy at weekends, and even then only after 10pm. In addition, mainstream clubs do host gay nights, for example, those organized by Hypertainment (ⓦ hyper.com. sg) at *1-Altitude* (see page 151). Ladies' nights promotions may see some lesbians attending; lesbians can also try ⓦ facebook.com/twoqueensasia for details of forthcoming events. Another source of information is a small gay library

project, the Pelangi Pride Centre (ⓦ pelangipridecentre. org).

Backstage Bar 80 Neil Rd ☎ 6423 9232, ⓦ homeof thebluespin.com; Maxwell or Outram Park MRT; map p.64. Like its sister bar, the slightly larger *Tantric* next door, *Backstage* is a chilled-out venue where you can hang out indoors or in the courtyard. Happy hour Mon–Thurs & Sun until 8pm. Daily 6pm–midnight.

Dorothy's 13A Trengganu St ☎ 6221 6806; Chinatown MRT; map p.64. Entered through a side door in Temple St (look for the rainbow flag above the street), this tiny upstairs bar displays the cutout figure of a certain *Wizard of Oz* character and offers a view over Temple St. Daily 6pm–late.

Tantric 78 Neil Rd ☎ 6423 9232, ⓦ homeofthebluespin. com; Outram Park MRT; map p.64. Likeable shophouse bar with a clientele that's slightly more reflective of Singapore's multi-ethnic make-up than the largely Chinese crowd you find elsewhere. There's outdoor seating on a slick terrace, and upstairs, a nominally separate bar that's a mini-shrine to the prewar American Chinese actress Anna May Wong. Mon–Fri & Sun 8pm–3am, Sat 8am–4am.

12

TRADITIONAL CHINESE OPERA

Entertainment and the arts

Even on a brief visit it's hard not to notice how much money has been invested in the arts: Singapore offers an excellent range of cultural events in all genres, drawing on both Asian and Western traditions. Prime downtown property has been turned over to arts organizations in areas like Waterloo Street and Little India, and prestige venues like Theatres on the Bay bring in world-class performers – at top-dollar prices. This isn't to say that all is hunky-dory: questions remain over whether creativity is truly valued when censorship lingers, if not as overtly as in the 1970s and 1980s, then in terms of there being well-established red lines concerning party politics, ethnicity and religion which no one dare cross. More cynically, some say that support for the arts is a way to keep Singapore attractive to expats and its own occasionally restive middle class.

STREET THEATRE

Walk around Singapore long enough and you're likely to stumble upon some sort of streetside cultural event, most usually a wayang – a Malay word used in Singapore to denote Chinese opera. Played out on outdoor stages next to temples and markets, or in open spaces in the new towns, wayangs are highly dramatic and stylized affairs, in which garishly made-up characters enact popular Chinese legends to the accompaniment of the crashes of cymbals and gongs. They're staged throughout the year, but the best time to catch one is during the Festival of the Hungry Ghosts, when they are held to entertain passing spooks. Another traditional performance, **lion-dancing**, takes to the streets during Chinese New Year, and **puppet theatres** may appear around then, too. Chinatown and the Bugis/Waterloo Street area are good places to stumble upon performances.

ESSENTIALS

Festivals There are two major international arts festivals annually: the Singapore International Festival of the Arts (calendar online; Ⓦ sifa.sg), running the gamut from theatre through dance and film to concerts; and the Singapore Fringe Festival (Jan or Feb; Ⓦ singaporefringe. com), which concentrates on theatre, dance and the visual arts. There's also the annual Singapore Writers' Festival (Ⓦ singaporewritersfestival.com), featuring international as well as local writers working in all four of the country's official languages.

Information Events are widely advertised in the press, ticketing websites and in listings magazines, the best of which by far is the weekly *SG* (free in print, and at Ⓦ sg. asia-city.com).

Tickets You can buy tickets directly from venues or the SISTIC agency, which has outlets in many downtown malls (Ⓣ 6348 5555, Ⓦ sistic.com.sg). Some events are advertised on Ⓦ peatix.com and Ⓦ eventbrite.sg, which are also good places to look out for free-to-attend book launches, activist talks and civil-society forums.

THEATRE AND COMEDY

Singapore's arts scene is probably at its best when it comes to **drama**: a number of independent theatre companies have sprung up over the years, performing works by local playwrights which dare to include a certain amount of social commentary; productions may be in Chinese or other languages, with English subtitles. Foreign theatre companies tour regularly too, some putting on lavish Western musicals. There's also a low-key **comedy** scene that manages to stutter along. One venue to check it out is the *Canvas* club (see page 152), where you might catch the best-known home-grown performer, the drag act Kuma. Gigs by foreign comedians are sometimes listed on Ⓦ comedyfest.asia, while Ⓦ thecomedyclub.asia runs open-mic nights.

THEATRE COMPANIES

The Necessary Stage Marine Parade Community Building, 278 Marine Parade Rd; Ⓣ 6440 8115,

Ⓦ necessary.org; Marine Parade MRT. Pioneering socially conscious theatre group. Their premises are out near Katong though some productions are staged downtown.

Singapore Repertory Theatre KC Arts Centre, 20 Merbau Rd; Ⓦ srt.com.sg; Fort Canning or Clarke Quay MRT. New work by Western playwrights plus the odd children's production.

Theatreworks 72-13 Mohamed Sultan Rd Ⓣ 6737 7213, Ⓦ theatreworks.org.sg; Fort Canning MRT. Another of the early pioneers of the Singapore stage.

Wild Rice Ⓦ wildrice.com.sg. Locally written plays tackling themes such as press censorship and sexuality; a lot of productions are staged during their own mini-theatre festival (July/Aug, but not yearly). At the time of writing they were raising funds for their own theatre space at the reconstituted Funan shopping mall set to open in late 2019 (see page 162).

CLASSICAL AND TRADITIONAL MUSIC AND DANCE

At the heart of Singapore's healthy Western classical music scene is the **Singapore Symphony Orchestra**, whose concerts often feature stellar guest soloists, conductors and choirs from around the world. Dance is an another thriving art, with several active local troupes and regular visits by international companies.

COMPANIES AND ORCHESTRAS

Chinese Opera Teahouse 5 Smith St Ⓣ 6323 4862,

Ⓦ ctopera.com; Chinatown MRT. For an interesting culinary and musical experience, come here for the *Sights and Sounds of Chinese Opera* (Fri & Sat 7pm), a set dinner followed by performances of excerpts from Chinese operas. The package costs $40, though you can watch the opera selections alone for $25 (includes tea and snacks; admission at 7.50pm).

City Chinese Orchestra Ⓦ cityco.com.sg. Chinese classical and folk music recitals, at various venues.

13

Singapore Chinese Orchestra ⓦsco.com.sg; Tanjong Pagar MRT. Performances of traditional Chinese music through the year, plus occasional free concerts. Assorted venues.

Singapore Dance Theatre ⓣ6338 0611, ⓦsingapore dancetheatre.com. Contemporary and classical works at a range of venues, including in the open air at Fort Canning Hill.

Singapore Lyric Opera ⓣ6336 1929, ⓦsingapore opera.com.sg. Western opera and operetta, with one big production a year.

Singapore Symphony Orchestra ⓦsso.org.sg. Performances at Esplanade – Theatres on the Bay and the Victoria Concert Hall. Occasional free concerts at the Botanic Gardens and hour-long daytime shows for children.

Siong Leng Musical Association ⓦsiongleng.com; Outram Park MRT. A unique body dedicated to preserving *nanyin* (literally "southern sound") – distinctive folk music and opera from southeast China, sung in dialect. They put on sporadic concerts, including three free shows a year against the temple backdrop of Thian Hock Keng.

Temple of Fine Arts ⓣ6535 0509, ⓦtfasg.org. This Indian cultural organization puts on occasional shows of classical music and dance.

FILM

Postwar Singapore was the nexus of the Malay-language movie industry, with some films in Chinese also shot here. That flowering lasted all of twenty years until, following independence, Malay film-making drifted off to Kuala Lumpur while in Singapore censorship grew more problematic as tastes were, in any case, gravitating away from locally made films towards slicker efforts from the West and Hong Kong. It wasn't until the 1990s that local film-making saw a renaissance, and today a thriving independent scene unleashes a handful of full-length features, shorts and documentaries each year.

The best time to appreciate locally made movies is at the **Singapore International Film Festival** (dates may vary year to year; ⓦsgiff.sg). If you intend to be in Singapore for a while, you might want to join the Singapore Film Society (ⓦsfs.org.sg), which puts on its own private monthly screenings and mounts occasional mini-festivals. Otherwise, Singapore's cinemas offer up all the latest blockbusters from Hollywood, Bollywood and Hong Kong, with English subtitles as appropriate. Turn up early or book in advance to secure tickets (starting at $10, but two or three times that for new releases at downtown cinemas). Take a sweater, as the air-conditioning is often on at full blast, and be prepared for some chatter during the film.

MULTIPLEX CHAINS

Cathay Cinemas include: Cathay Cineplex, 2 Handy Rd, Dhoby Ghaut MRT; Cineleisure Orchard, 8 Grange Rd, Somerset MRT; ⓦcathay.com.sg. The Art Deco Cathay Cineplex is a city landmark and includes a gallery of memorabilia from Cathay's own involvement in local film-making in the mid-twentieth century (see page 85).

Golden Village Cinemas include: Level 7, Plaza Singapura, 68 Orchard Rd, Dhoby Ghaut MRT; Levels 2 & 3, VivoCity, HarbourFront MRT; plus one due to open at the rebuilt Funan SG mall on North Bridge Rd, City Hall MRT; ⓦgv.com.sg.

Shaw Cinemas include: Lido Cineplex, Shaw House, 350 Orchard Rd, Orchard MRT (IMAX-equipped); ⓦshaw.sg.

INDEPENDENT CINEMAS

Alliance Française 1 Sarkies Rd ⓦalliancefrancaise .org.sg; Newton MRT (exit C). Weekly French-language films with English subtitles at their Ciné-Club; tickets online.

Filmgarde Cineplex Level 5, Bugis+, 201 Victoria St ⓦfgcineplex.com.sg; Bugis MRT. Relatively commercial for an indie, with both English- and Chinese-language flicks.

National Museum 93 Stamford Rd ⓦnationalmuseum. sg; Bras Basah or Dhoby Ghaut MRT. Occasional open-air screenings of global films. Tickets from the museum itself or SISTIC.

Omni-Theatre See page 112. One of Singapore's two IMAX cinemas.

★ **The Projector** Level 5, Golden Mile Tower, 6001 Beach Rd ⓣ6337 8181, ⓦtheprojector.sg; Nicoll Highway MRT. Lurking next to a concrete parking deck is the island's best cinema, an unmodernized 1970s affair lovingly revived with just some fresh coats of paint and cool murals. It screens cult films of the past and left-field new releases and hosts festivals dedicated to the movies of regions and individual nations, including the Singapore edition of Malaysia's Freedom Film Fest, focused on democratic, LGBTQ and other human rights issues in East Asia.

The Screening Room 12 Ann Siang Hill ⓣ6221 1694, ⓦscreeningroom.com.sg; Chinatown MRT. The restaurants and bars here seem to have eclipsed the cinema, but the place still shows a mainstream film favourite, often several years old, each night.

LIVE MUSIC

Singapore is an established part of the East Asian circuit for **Western stadium-rock outfits** as well as indie bands, though gigs can be marred by a slightly staid atmosphere as locals are still uncomfortable about letting their hair down. Home-grown bands singing in English do exist and some aren't at all bad, but the scene is small and suffers from a dwindling number of venues prepared to support original music. A terrific place to watch bands – indeed one of the best events to catch in Singapore – is the series of street parties called Urban Ventures (4 yearly; ⓦfacebook.com/urbanventuressg), which sees historic downtown streets converted into mini-festival sites. Meanwhile, gigs do take place monthly at the Projector cinema and also periodically under the Another Indie Gig banner (@facebook.com/radiusnoise). The two best music festivals were arguably the **Singapore Jazz Festival**, which spans soul and a bit of world music as well (@sing-jazz.com) and **Laneway** (@singapore.lanewayfestival.com), a satellite of the well-established Australian indie event; unfortunately the future of both was in doubt at the time of writing. Also worth investigating are two festivals focusing on local and East Asian indie, namely **Baybeats**, an Esplanade event spanning everything from punk to hip-hop; and **Sundown** featuring Asian hip-hop (@sundownfestival.sg). Electronic dance music fans should watch out for **Ultra** (@ultrasingapore.com). Rivalling Western music in local popularity are **Mando- and Canto-pop**, bland hybrids of Chinese lyrics and Western pop; superstars of both genres visit periodically, as do stars of **K(orean)-pop**, and the rapturous welcome they receive makes their shows quite an experience. In addition to the venues listed below, some restaurants and bars do host live music.

Crazy Elephant #01-03 Block E, Clarke Quay ☎6337 7859, @crazyelephant.sg; Clarke Quay or Fort Canning MRT; map p.36. Of the hotchpotch of brash venues at Clarke Quay, this bar has more street cred than most, with live music – old-school blues and rock – practically every night and an open-mike jam session on Sundays. Some tables are by the water's edge. Happy hour until 9pm. Mon 5pm–1am, Tues–Thurs & Sun 5pm–2am, Fri & Sat 5pm–3am.

Timbre Substation arts centre, 45 Armenian St ☎6338 8030, @timbregroup.asia; Bras Basah or City Hall MRT; map p.36. Open-air bar-restaurant by the car park at the back of *Substation*, with house bands and singer-songwriters serving up slightly derivative material nightly. Open-mic night Tues. Mon & Sun 6pm–midnight, Tues–Thurs 6pm–1am, Fri & Sat 6pm–2am.

Timbre The Arts House, 1 Old Parliament Lane ☎6336 3386, @timbregroup.asia; Raffles Place MRT; map p.36. Similar to its set-up at Substation, though with a slicker feel in view of the high-vis riverside location. Mon–Thurs 6pm–1am, Fri & Sat 6pm–2am.

ARTS CENTRES AND GENERAL-PURPOSE VENUES

In addition to the venues listed here, the two casino-resorts of *Marina Bay Sands* (see page 80) and *Resorts World* (see page 114) also play host to some concerts and musical extravaganzas.
The Arts House 1 Old Parliament Lane, near Empress Place ☎6332 6919, @theartshouse.com.sg; Raffles Place MRT. Plays, concerts, films and art exhibitions.
Drama Centre Level 3, National Library, 100 Victoria St @dramacentre.com; Bugis or Bras Basah MRT. Mainly plays by local companies.
Esplanade – Theatres on the Bay 1 Esplanade Drive ☎6828 8222, @esplanade.com.sg; Esplanade or City Hall MRT. Hosts many international stars and its own programme of free gigs, recitals, dance performances and so forth, well worth checking out.
NAFA Lee Foundation Theatre Campus 3, Nanyang Academy of Fine Arts, 151 Bencoolen St ☎6512 4000;

Rochor or Bencoolen MRT. Plays and other performances.
Sports Hub In the Kallang district, either side of Stadium MRT @sportshub.com.sg. The National Stadium and Indoor Stadium here host plenty of big-selling bands.
The Star Performing Arts Centre 1 Vista Exchange Green, @thestar.sg; Buona Vista MRT. Ultramodern, megachurch-owned venue that doubles as worship space and big-name concert venue, its biggest theatre seating 5000.
Substation 45 Armenian St ☎6337 7535, @substation. org; Bras Basah or City Hall MRT. Self-styled "home for the arts" with a theatre as well as a gallery hosting art, sculpture and photography exhibitions.
Victoria Concert Hall and Theatre 11 Empress Place ☎6908 8810, @vtvch.com; Raffles Place MRT. Colonial-era venue for concerts and plays (see page 37).

MEN IN TRADITIONAL CHINESE COSTUME

Festivals

With so many ethnic groups and religions present in Singapore, it would be unusual if your trip didn't coincide with some sort of traditional festival, ranging from exuberant, family-oriented pageants to blood-curdlingly gory displays of devotion. Below is a chronological round-up of Singapore's major festivals, with suggestions of where best to enjoy them; the list doesn't include commercial events themed around shopping, such as the Great Singapore Sale (see page 161), or arts and cultural festivals (see page 154). The dates of many of these change annually according to the lunar calendar; we've listed rough timings, but for specific dates it's a good idea to check with the Singapore Tourism Board (ⓦyoursingapore.com). Some festivals are also public holidays, when many shops and restaurants may close (see page 31).

JANUARY–MARCH

PONGGAL (OR PONGAL)
Mid-Jan A Tamil thanksgiving festival marking the end of the rainy season and the onset of spring. In Hindu homes, rice is cooked in a new pot and allowed to boil over, to symbolize prosperity. At the Sri Srinivasa Perumal Temple on Serangoon Rd, food is prepared against a cacophony of drums, bells, conch shells and chanting, offered up to the gods, and then eaten by devotees as a symbol of cleansing.

CHINESE NEW YEAR
Jan/Feb Singapore's Chinese community springs spectacularly to life to welcome in the new lunar year over fifteen days (the first two are public holidays). The festival's origins lie in a Chinese legend telling of a horned monster that was awoken by the onset of spring, terrorizing nearby villagers until they discovered it could be held at bay by noise, light and the colour red. Essentially, Chinese New Year is a family affair – old debts are settled, friends and relatives visited, mandarin oranges exchanged, red envelopes (*hong bao*) containing money given to children, and papers bearing the character for good fortune are attached to front doors. Although festivities are a muted affair compared to

elsewhere in Asia thanks to a ban on individuals setting off fireworks, Chinatown can be worth visiting for its lanterns and fairy lights. Two major celebrations take place at Marina Centre: the traditional Chingay procession, a carnival-like display with dragon and lion dancers that has now grown into a major ticketed event including international performers; and River Hongbao, with displays of lanterns and yet more performances of music and dance.

THAIPUSAM
Jan/Feb Not for the faint-hearted, this Hindu festival sees entranced penitents walking the 3km from Little India's Sri Srinivasa Perumal Temple to the Chettiar Temple on Tank Road, carrying *kavadis* – elaborate steel arches decorated with peacock feathers and attached to their skin by hooks and prongs – and with skewers spiked through their cheeks and tongues – to honour the Lord Murugan. Some join the procession to pray for assistance, others to give thanks for heavenly aid already granted. Coconuts are smashed at the feet of the penitents for good luck as they set off, and friends and relatives jig around them en route, singing and chanting to spur them on.

14

APRIL–AUGUST

QING MING (OR CHING MING)
April At the beginning of the third lunar month, the Chinese remember their ancestors by cleaning and restoring their graves and making offerings of joss sticks, incense papers and food.

VESAK DAY
May Saffron-robed monks chant sacred scriptures at packed Buddhist temples, and devotees release caged birds to commemorate the Buddha's birth (May), enlightenment and the attainment of Nirvana; in the evening, candlelit processions are held at temples.

RAMADAN
April/May/June Muslims spend the ninth month of the Islamic calendar fasting from dawn to dusk (during which time they also abstain from drinking anything, smoking and sex) in order to intensify awareness of the plight of the poor and to identify with the hungry. By late afternoon, stalls set up to sell Malay sweetmeats and snacks in preparation for the fast-breaking; one such group of stalls can be found around the Sultan Mosque. Muslims mark Hari Raya Puasa (Eid-al-Fitr), the end of Ramadan, by feasting, donning their best traditional clothes and visiting family and friends.

DUMPLING/DRAGON BOAT FESTIVAL
June Pyramid-shaped parcels of sticky-rice, wrapped up in leaves and steamed, are sold at stalls all over Singapore,

but are especially common in the run-up to the Dumpling Festival, celebrated on the fifth day of the fifth lunar month. The festival commemorates Qu Yuan, a Chinese scholar who drowned himself in protest against political corruption. Local people, it is said, tried to save him from sea creatures by beating drums, disturbing the waters with their oars, and throwing in rice dumplings to feed them, but to no avail. Qu Yuan is also commemorated with dragon boat races, the rowing boats bearing a dragon's head and tail; in Singapore crews race across Bedok Reservoir in the east of the island.

HARI RAYA HAJI (OR EID AL-ADHA)
July/Aug This Muslim festival marks the culmination of the annual Hajj pilgrimage to Mecca and Medina; in Singapore, unlike in the Arab world, it carries slightly less significance than the end of Ramadan. Goats are sacrificed and their meat is given to those in need.

NATIONAL DAY
Aug 9 Singapore's acquisition of statehood in its own right after splitting from Malaysia in 1965 is marked by a huge show at the Padang and Marina Bay, featuring military parades and fireworks.

FESTIVAL OF THE HUNGRY GHOSTS
Aug/Sept Sometimes called Yue Lan, this festival is meant to appease the souls of the dead released from Purgatory

during the thirty days of the seventh lunar month, and thereby forestall unlucky events. Chinese street operas and concerts are held for the entertainment of the "wandering spirits", and joss sticks – some the size of a man – red candles and paper money are burnt outside Chinese homes.

Paper effigies of worldly goods such as houses, cars and servants are sometimes burnt, too. Elsewhere, marquees are set up in the street to hold festive banquets, followed by auctions of pieces of charcoal, cake and flowers – all thought to be auspicious.

SEPTEMBER–DECEMBER

14

BIRTHDAY OF THE MONKEY GOD
Sept Processions and evening street opera shows may take place close to Tiong Bahru's Qi Tian Gong (see page 107) to mark the birthday of one of the most popular deities in the Chinese pantheon, the Monkey God.

MOON CAKE FESTIVAL
Sept Held on the fifteenth day of the eighth lunar month, and also known as the Mid-Autumn Festival, this basically marks the harvest moon. At this time the Chinese celebrate by eating (and gifting elaborately packaged) moon cakes – generally made from aduki-bean paste and sometimes stuffed with salted egg yolk for good measure, though in Singapore durian-flavoured and other weird tropical variants are available. One story is that the cakes commemorate the fall of the Mongol Empire, plotted, so legend has it, by means of messages secreted in cakes. Others say the cakes represent the full moon, said to be at its brightest at this time of year. Besides seeing the cakes on sale all over the island, by night you may come across children strolling around with multicoloured candlelit lanterns in the open areas around high-rise estates.

NAVARATHIRI
Sept/Oct Hindu temples such as the Chettiar Temple on Tank Road, and Chinatown's Sri Mariamman Temple, devote nine nights to classical dance and music in honour of Durga, Lakshmi and Saraswathi, the consorts of the Hindu gods Shiva, Vishnu and Brahma. On the tenth night, a silver horse is carried at the head of a procession that begins at the Tank Road temple.

FESTIVAL OF THE NINE EMPEROR GODS
Oct This festival has enjoyed a revival in Singapore of late and is marked at quite a few temples. It signifies the nine-day sojourn on earth of the Taoist Nine Emperor Gods, associated with the stars of the Big Dipper, who are thought to cure ailments and bring good health and longevity. The

best place to witness the rites is the 1921 Hougang Tou Mu temple (779A Upper Serangoon Rd; Kovan MRT then head back southwest on bus #101 or #107 for a couple of stops). There's a procession during which effigies of the nine gods are carried in sedan chairs, in some cases ending up at the seaside to send the gods back the way they are believed to have come. You may also see mediums in a trance state as they "channel" a deity, allowing them to see the future and to skewer their cheeks without apparently feeling pain. For more on the festival, see Ⓦ nineemperorgodsproject.com.

DEEPAVALI (DIWALI)
Oct/Nov Serangoon Road is festooned with colourful lights during this, the most auspicious of Hindu festivals, celebrating the victory of the Lord Krishna over Narakasura, and thus of light over dark. Oil lamps are lit outside homes to attract Lakshmi, the goddess of prosperity, and prayers are offered at all temples.

THIMITHI
Oct/Nov Another dramatic Hindu ceremony, this one sees devotees proving the strength of their faith by running across a four-metre-long pit of hot coals at the Sri Mariamman Temple in Chinatown. Outside the temple, devotees in their hundreds line up awaiting their turn, and building up their courage by dancing, shouting and singing.

PILGRIMAGE TO KUSU ISLAND
Oct/Nov Locals visit Kusu island in their thousands to pray for good luck and fertility at the island's temple and Muslim shrine. See page 119.

CHRISTMAS
Dec 25 December in Singapore is generally very wet, which is about as "wintry" as a tropical Christmas gets. It's a particularly colourful and atmospheric time for shopping though, with some enormous, fabulously decorated Christmas trees along Orchard Rd.

ARAB STREET

Shopping

Choice and convenience make the Singapore shopping experience a rewarding
one, but the island's affluence and generally strong currency mean most things
are priced at Western levels. The Great Singapore Sale (June & July) is still
promoted as the best time to bargain-hunt, but online shopping and sales linked
with major festivals have blunted its appeal. Unsurprisingly, Orchard Road boasts
the biggest cluster of malls, bulging with designer names, some with multiple
outlets. Malls elsewhere tend to be more informal; the most interesting ones
in Chinatown are like multistorey markets, home to a few traditional outlets
stocking Chinese foodstuffs, medicines, instruments and porcelain. Singapore's
remaining shophouses are worthy of attention too, as some are still home to
independent stores selling books, jewellery, souvenirs and so on.

15

ESSENTIALS

Bargaining Haggling is not as widespread as you might assume – it's expected in smaller family-owned or independent shops, but nowhere else.

Complaints In the unlikely event that you encounter a problem with a retailer that you cannot resolve mutually, you may be able to recover your money by initiating proceedings at Singapore's Small Claims Tribunal. It costs $10 to submit your case online; see the relevant section at ⓦ statecourts.gov.sg for more information.

Opening hours Department stores and other big retailers are typically open daily from 10am to 9pm (perhaps 10pm in the biggest malls), while hours vary for smaller shops. In the reviews that follow, times are not given for shopping malls as the buildings themselves are accessible from the early morning until late at night, but their tenants keep hours as they please.

Tax refunds On leaving the country by air, tourists can claim a refund of Singapore's goods and services tax (GST; 7 percent) on purchases over a certain amount (at least $100, though some retailers require a larger outlay), provided the shop in question is participating in the tax refund scheme. These days it's recommended to go the electronic route, meaning that you ask the shop to link your purchases to one of your debit or credit cards; the tax is refunded to that card when you head to a booth at the airport and swipe it (or scan the barcode on a ticket that the shop will have issued). For detailed information on the intricacies of this, have a look at the "Tourist Refund Scheme" section of ⓦ iras.gov.sg, or pick up the appropriate leaflet from a tourist office. An app, Tourego, now promises to streamline the whole process if you are buying from one of their member retailers.

SHOPPING MALLS AND DEPARTMENT STORES

ORCHARD ROAD AND AROUND

313@Somerset 313 Somerset Rd (above Somerset MRT) ⓦ 313somerset.com.sg; Somerset MRT; map p.84. Zara, Muji and Sony are the star names at this newish mall.

Forum the Shopping Mall 583 Orchard Rd ⓦ forum theshoppingmall.com.sg; Orchard MRT; map p.84. Plenty of items for pampered brats – upmarket kids' clothes, toys and so forth.

The Heeren 260 Orchard Rd; Somerset MRT; map p.84. There's really only one reason to come here – it's home to the flagship outlet of Robinsons, a department store chain dating back to the 1850s.

ION Orchard 2 Orchard Turn ⓦ ionorchard.com; Orchard MRT; map p.84. Despite the impressive hyper-modern facade and a sprinkling of designer brands, Prada included, by far the most popular section of this cavernous mall is the *Food Opera* food court on basement 4.

Ngee Ann City 391A Orchard Rd ⓦ ngeeanncity.com.sg; Orchard MRT; map p.84. A brooding twin-towered complex, home to the Japanese Takashimaya department store (some people simply call this mall Takashimaya) and the excellent Kinokuniya bookshop, plus several jewellers.

Paragon Opposite Ngee Ann City ⓦ paragon.com.sg; Orchard MRT; map p.84. Small but swanky, Paragon is holding its own despite upstart competition. Come here for Calvin Klein, Gucci, Versace and many more big names.

Plaza Singapura 68 Orchard Rd ⓦ plazasingapura.com.sg; Dhoby Ghaut MRT; map p.84. Veteran mid-priced mall with a bit of everything: the UK department store Marks & Spencer, affordable sportswear and sports equipment, musical instruments and general electrical equipment. Always busy.

Tanglin Shopping Centre 19 Tanglin Rd (next to the Orchard Rendezvous hotel) ⓦ tanglinsc.com; Orchard MRT; map p.84. Some 30-plus years old, this relatively small development is dominated by little shops selling art, antiques and curios.

Tangs Junction of Orchard and Scotts rds ⓦ tangs.com; Orchard MRT; map p.84. Tangs is a department store founded in the 1950s, and the only one to have its own building on Orchard Rd, topped by a pagoda-style construction occupied by the *Marriott* hotel. Its clothes range includes some pieces by Singapore-based designers.

THE COLONIAL DISTRICT

Funan SG 109 North Bridge Rd ⓦ funan.com.sg; City Hall MRT; map p.36. To open in late 2019 after being rebuilt from scratch, this mall is a much larger version of its former self, which was the best place in town for electronic gear, cameras and computer equipment. The former tenants have dispersed to nearby buildings or up Orchard Road, but it's expected that some will return to their revamped old home.

Raffles City 252 North Bridge Rd ⓦ rafflescity.com; City Hall MRT; map p.36. Home to a branch of Robinsons department store with a Marks & Spencer within it, plus numerous fashion chains.

BRAS BASAH ROAD TO ROCHOR ROAD

Bugis Junction Junction Victoria St and Rochor Rd ⓦ bugisjunction-mall.com.sg; Bugis MRT; map p.50. Mall encasing several streets of restored shophouses, and home to the Japanese/Chinese department store BHG plus local electronics retailer Challenger.

LITTLE INDIA

★ **Mustafa** Syed Alwi Rd ⓦmustafa.com.sg; Farrer Park; map p.50. From humble 1970s clothes shop to enormous department store, Mustafa is a phenomenon and nothing like the glitzy malls of Orchard Rd. It sells electronics, fresh food, luggage, you name it – and it never closes. Daily 24hr.

MARINA BAY

The Shoppes at Marina Bay Sands 10 Bayfront Ave; ⓦmarinabaysands.com; Bayfront MRT; map p.79. A mall so vast it will do wonders for your daily step count if you properly explore its sprawl of swish designer outlets.

CHINATOWN

★ **People's Park Complex** 1 Park Rd; ⓦpeoplespark complex.com; Chinatown MRT; map p.64. The most entertaining place to browse in Chinatown because it's so workaday, a 1970s concrete hunk of shops, offices and apartments. Stalls outside at ground level sell amazing snacks; inside there are shops offering reflexology or agents

doing cash transfers to China. Also here is the Overseas Emporium on level 4, selling Chinese calligraphy brushes, lacquerwork and some dowdy clothes that could have been fashionable in China twenty years ago.

Yue Hwa Chinese Products 70 Eu Tong Sen St ⓣ6538 4222, ⓦyuehwa.com.sg; Chinatown MRT; map p.64. This department store sells some surprisingly pricey clothing in both Western and Chinese stylings, the latter including tops with loop fasteners rather than buttons and buttonholes, starting at $60. Also on sale are the obligatory Chinese medicinal and health products, plus snacks and confectionery. Mon–Fri & Sun 11am–9pm, Sat 11am–10pm.

HARBOURFRONT

★ **VivoCity** 1 HarbourFront Walk ⓦvivocity.com.sg; HarbourFront MRT; map p.115. A humdinger of a mall, containing a branch of Tangs department store, a cinema, three food courts and the Japanese electronics retailer Best Denki.

15

ANTIQUES, CRAFTS, CURIOS AND SOUVENIRS

Singapore bulges with stores selling Asian antiques and crafts, ranging from Chinese snuff bottles to Malaysian pewter. If it's antiques you're specifically after, try trawling through Tanglin Shopping Centre (see opposite). For souvenirs, besides the places listed below, it's worth visiting the new **Design Orchard** (see map, page 84), a low-rise showcase for local designers at the junction of Orchard and Cairnhill roads (and near Somerset MRT). Managed by Naiise (see below), it will stock Singapore-themed souvenirs and crafts, plus clothes and homeware; contact any tourist office for more details.

Antiques of the Orient #02-40 Tanglin Shopping Centre ⓣ6734 9351, ⓦaoto.com.sg; Orchard MRT; map p.84. Antiquarian books and maps, engravings and old photos. Mon–Sat 10am–5.30pm, Sun 11am–3.30pm.

★ **Arch** #B1-13 Capitol Piazza, 13 Stamford Rd ⓣ6384 6608, ⓦarchsingapore.com.sg; City Hall MRT; map p.79. Their secretive production process works magic on thin slices of wood, transforming them into intricate pieces of 2D or 3D artwork or to be worn as jewellery. A small shophouse facade starts at around $25, while a 20cm-wide Marina Bay panorama can cost $250 or more. Daily 11am–9pm.

Asian Arts & Crafts 180 Serangoon Rd ⓣ6299 0500; Little India; map p.50. A cornucopia of religious statuary: most of the deities are Hindu, but there are a few Buddhist ones, the odd Virgin Mary and some Arabic calligraphic carvings of "Muhammad" and "Allah". Daily 10am–10pm.

Aster By Kyra 168 Telok Ayer St ⓣ6684 8600, ⓦasterbykyra.sg; Telok Ayer MRT; map p.64. Part of Chongwen Ge (see page 69), this little shop sells

Peranakan-style scarves and porcelain, but its mainstay is lovely tiles of the kind you see on shophouse walls and floors. Indonesian factory replicas start at $12, whereas prices for originals salvaged from old buildings hit three figures if in good condition. Daily noon–5pm.

Cat Socrates #02-25 Bras Basah Complex, Block 231, Bain St ⓣ6333 0870, ⓦcatsocrates.wixsite.com/catsocrates; City Hall or Bras Basah MRT; map p.50. Earrings, trinkets and knick-knacks, some with a Singapore angle, others with a feline flavour. You may or may not get to meet the cat shopkeeper, currently one Chestnut, who spends quite a lot time snoozing in his own booth. Mon–Sat noon–8pm, Sun 1–7pm.

Crystal Creations #01-02A Tanglin Place, 91 Tanglin Rd ⓣ9154 0798, ⓦcrystalcreations.co; Orchard Boulevard MRT; map p.84. This small gallery stocks some impressive and expensive jadeite carvings, but they major on the delightful Chinese art of *neihua* – literally "internal drawing". For just a few tens of dollars you can pick up snuff bottles and miniature glass teapots, colourfully hand-painted with floral and other motifs on the inside. Daily 1–9pm.

East Inspirations 33 Pagoda St ⓣ6224 2993, ⓦeast-inspirations.com; Chinatown MRT; map p.64. The classiest of several antique shops in the heart of Chinatown, offering Asian furniture, porcelain-based lamps, and vases. Daily 10.30am–6.30pm.

Eng Tiang Huat 10 Lorong 24A Geylang ⓣ6734 3738, ⓦdunhuangmusic.com; Aljunied MRT; map p.101. Oriental musical instruments, opera costumes and props. Mon–Sat 11am–6pm.

The Heritage Shop 93 Jalan Sultan; Nicoll Highway or Lavender MRT; map p.50. An incredible range of bric-a-brac, from antique radios to beautiful enamelware tiffin carriers – little pots for cooked food, stacked and held together within a metal frame. Daily 1.30–8pm.

Jamal Kazura Aromatics 21 Bussorah St ☎ 6293 3320; map p.50. Veteran maker and seller of alcohol-free perfume, using various essential oils – a small Arabian-style bottle of scent starts at around $12. Daily 9.30am–7pm (Fri closed 1–2pm).

Kwok Gallery #03-01 Far East Shopping Centre, 545 Orchard Rd ☎ 6235 2516; Orchard MRT; map p.84. A broad inventory of traditional Chinese pottery, jade and sculpture. Mon–Sat 11am–6pm.

Lim's Legacy #02-324 Marina Square ☎ 6837 0028; Esplanade or City Hall MRT; map p.79. Asian-themed homeware, including decorative cabinets, vases and statuettes. Daily 11am–9.30pm.

Little Shophouse 43 Bussorah St, near Sultan Mosque ☎ 6295 2328; Bugis MRT; map p.50. Well named, this tiny outlet boasts some beautiful examples of Peranakan beaded slippers (from $300), plus replica Peranakan crockery. Daily 10am–6pm.

Malay Art Gallery 31 Bussorah St ☎ 6294 8051; Bugis MRT; map p.50. Stocks *kerises* (traditional daggers) from Malaysia and Indonesia. Mon–Sat 8.30am–5.30pm, sometimes also Sun noon–6pm.

Museum Label National Museum, 93 Stamford Rd ⓦ nationalmuseum.sg; Bras Basah or Bencoolen MRT; map p.84. A range of Singapore-specific souvenirs. Daily 10am–6.30pm.

★ **Naiise** #B1-08 The Cathay, 2 Handy Rd ⓦ naiise. com; Dhoby Ghaut or Bencoolen MRT; map p.50. This homeware/stationery shop has a whole section devoted to witty Singapore-themed souvenirs: Singapore Sling-flavoured marmalade, cushions in the shape of local snacks, even shophouse-tile Rubik's cubes. Daily noon–10pm.

Orchid Chopsticks 25 Trengganu St ☎ 6227 0662; Chinatown MRT; map p.64. You'd never have thought chopsticks could be this interesting: here they come in just about every material and hue, some fairly plain, others lustrous and ornamented. Daily 10am–10pm.

Pylones #B1-03 Wheelock Place, 501 Orchard Rd ☎ 6735 2705; Orchard MRT; map p.84. Incredibly colourful home accessories and knick-knacks, playfully decorated by this French design collective to look like something out of a children's picture book. Daily 10.30am–9.30pm.

Ratianah 23 Bussorah St ☎ 6392 0323; Bugis MRT; map p.50. Friendly Malay shop, now occupying neighbouring shophouses too, that offers Nonya-style fabrics and blouses, plus bangles and brooches. Mon–Sat 12.30–9pm, Sun 1–5pm.

Red Dot Design Museum 11 Marina Boulevard ☎ 6514 0111, ⓦ museum.red-dot.sg/shop; Downtown, Bayfront or Marina Bay MRT; map p.64. A good place for quirky, ergonomically designed gifts, including oddly shaped umbrellas and kitchenware, plus distinctive jewellery and "maker" kits combining electronics and art. Mon–Thurs 10am–8pm, Fri–Sun 10am–11pm.

Rishi Handicrafts 5 Baghdad St ☎ 6298 2408; Bugis MRT; map p.50. Specializes in a range of basketry made from rattan, bamboo and other materials, with some knick-knacks, too. Mon–Sat 10am–5.30pm, Sun 11am–5.30pm.

Rumah Bebe 113 East Coast Rd ☎ 6247 8781, ⓦ rumahbebe.com; map p.101. Peranakan products, including beaded shoes and handbags, costume jewellery and the traditional *kebaya* garb of Nonyas. Also offers courses in beading and Nonya cookery. Tues–Sun 9.30am–6.30pm.

Teajoy #01-05 North Bridge Centre, 420 North Bridge Rd ☎ 6339 3739; Bugis MRT; map p.50. Close to the National Library, this shop specializes in lustrous Chinese Song dynasty-style teacups. Daily 1–8pm.

Tong Mern Sern 51 Craig Rd ☎ 6223 1037, ⓦ tmsantiques.com; Tanjong Pagar or Outram Park MRT; map p.64. "We buy junk and sell antiques", proclaims the banner outside this great little establishment. The owner is quite a character and will gladly tell you all about the crockery, old furniture and other bric-a-brac he has amassed. Mon–Sat 9am–6pm, Sun 1–6pm.

True Blue Shoppe 51 Armenian St ☎ 6337 7454; City Hall or Bras Basah MRT; map p.36. Peranakan porcelain plus Nonya jewellery and fabrics. Daily 10am–7pm.

Vista & Co #02-30 Holland Rd Shopping Centre ☎ 6466 6276; Holland Village MRT; map p.111. A little emporium of lamps, woodcarving and Perakanan-style pottery. Mon–Sat 10am–6pm, Sun 10am–5pm.

Zhen Lacquer Gallery 1 Trengganu St ☎ 6222 2718; Chinatown MRT; map p.64. Specializes in colourful lacquerware boxes and bowls, including ones made from coconut shells. Daily 10.30am–9pm.

BOOKS, CDS AND DVDS

Singapore's bookshops are as well stocked as many in the West; all the larger outlets carry a good selection of Western and local fiction, plus books on Southeast Asia and a range of magazines. Online booksellers include ⓦ localbooks. sg and, for specialist or academic books on Singapore and elsewhere in the region, Select Books (ⓦ selectbooks. com.sg). CDs and DVDs are going the way of the dodo in Singapore even as vinyl enjoys a mini-resurgence – despite

15

the tropical weather being lethal to records, which readily go furry with mould. For Indian and Malay music and film, head to Little India and the Joo Chiat Complex in Geylang (see page 99), respectively.

Books Actually 9 Yong Siak St ☎ 6222 9195, �🌐 booksactuallyshop.com; Tiong Bahru MRT; map p.107. Singapore's leading indie bookshop, with its own imprint, Math Paper Press. Stocks some local indie albums, too. Tues–Sat 10am–8pm, Mon & Sun 10am–6pm.

Curated Records #01-53, 55 Tiong Bahru Rd ☎ 6438 3644; Tiong Bahru MRT; map p.107. A cramped, boxy outlet that manages to pack in a decent range of rock and indie CD and vinyl releases, including up-to-the-minute imports. Tues–Sun 1–8pm.

Grassroots Book Room 25 Bukit Pasoh Rd ☎ 6337 9208; Tanjong Pagar or Chinatown MRT; map p.64. Plush, mainly Chinese-language bookstore with a well-chosen set of English-language books of local interest. Mon, Wed & Thurs 11am–8pm, Fri & Sat 11am–9pm, Sun 11am–6pm.

★ **Kinokuniya** Level 4, Ngee Ann City ☎ 6737 5021, �🌐 kinokuniya.com.sg; Orchard MRT; map p.84. Singapore's largest and best bookshop, with titles on every conceivable subject and some foreign-language literature too. Daily 10.30am–9.30pm.

Littered With Books 20 Duxton Rd ☎ 6220 6824; Tanjong Pagar or Chinatown MRT; map p.64. Despite its name, this indie outlet has a neatly laid out, though somewhat random, selection of literary fiction, thrillers and travel writing. Daily at least noon–8pm, slightly longer hours Fri–Sun.

Roxy Records #02-15 Excelsior Shopping Centre (at the Hill St end of the Peninsula Excelsior hotel) ☎ 6337 7783; City Hall MRT; map p.36. A range of imported indie and other hard-to-find releases, plus secondhand vinyl – even covering Chinese opera. Mon–Sat noon–9pm.

That CD Shop #B2-48 The Shoppes at Marina Bay Sands ☎ 6688 7511; Bayfront MRT; map p.79. The only mainstream CD/DVD shop left in town. Daily 11am–10pm.

JEWELLERY

Singapore isn't a bad place to buy jewellery, particularly if you share the Chinese affinity for jade or the Asian fondness for high-purity gold (22 or 24 carat).

CT Hoo #01-22 Tanglin Shopping Centre ☎ 6737 5447; Orchard MRT; map p.84. Specializes in pearls. Mon–Sat 9.30am–6.30pm.

Flower Diamond #03-02 Ngee Ann City ☎ 6734 1221, �🌐 flowerdiamond.com; Orchard MRT; map p.84. Contemporary as well as more traditionally styled designer bling, at sensible prices. Daily 10am–9pm.

Poh Heng #01-17 People's Park Complex ☎ 6535 0960, �🌐 pohheng.com.sg; Chinatown MRT; map p.64. Old-fangled Chinese jewellers dating back to 1948, though now housed in modern premises. Daily 11am–9pm.

Risis National Orchid Garden, Botanic Gardens ☎ 6475 5104, �🌐 risis.com; Napier MRT; map p.87. Singaporeans tend to regard gold-plated orchids – available as brooches, pendants, earrings, even on tie clips – as clichéd, but tourists snap them up here as well as at a few malls and at Changi Airport. Daily 8.45am–6.30pm.

The Silver Triangle 16 Haji Lane ☎ 8440 9331; Bugis MRT; map p.50. This Singapore isn't the obvious place to shop for trinkets and jewellery made by hill tribes in Laos, but the proceeds from this cosy gallery, run by a garrulous Frenchman, play a big role in keeping crafts projects going. Tues 11am–7pm.

Wong's Jewellery 62 Temple St ☎ 6323 0236, ⚐ wongsjewellery.com; Chinatown MRT; map p.64. Chinese-style outlet, good for jade, gold and pearls. Daily 10am–7.30pm.

FABRICS AND FASHION

Arab Street and Jalan Serai are among the main areas for old-fashioned fabric stores packed with bolts of cloth. Some of these stock Malaysian and Indonesian **batik**, produced by applying hot wax to a piece of cloth with either a pen or metal stamp; patterns appear when dye is applied as it cannot penetrate the waxed areas. Also available is the exquisite style of brocade known as **songket**, made by handweaving gold and silver thread into plain cloth. Not cheap, it's traditionally worn as a *sampin*, a sarong-like garment. Chinese, Japanese and Thai silks are all available, too, and there are multi-hued silk **saris** on sale in Little India. Long gone are the days when Singapore rivalled Bangkok as a place to get made-to-measure clothes inexpensively, but there are still plenty of **tailors** downtown hoping to pick up tourist custom, for example on or off South Bridge Road in Chinatown and in the shopping centre below the *Peninsula Excelsior Hotel*. The standard of workmanship varies, so ask to see specimens before committing yourself. A pair of no-frills men's trousers costs $50–60.

Basharahil Brothers 101 Arab St ☎ 6293 6569; Bugis MRT; map p.50. A large range of off-the-peg batik tops, skirts and shirts. Mon–Sat 10am–6pm, Sun 11am–5pm.

Charles & Keith #B3-58 ION Orchard ☎ 6238 1840, ⚐ charleskeith.com; Orchard MRT; map p.84. Singapore's answer to Malaysia's Jimmy Choo, the brothers Charles and Keith Wong design stylish, affordable women's shoes and handbags. Daily 10am–10pm.

Dakshaini Silks 13 Upper Dickson Rd ☎ 6291 9969; Rochor MRT; map p.50. Indian embroidered silk textiles and garments. Mon–Sat 10am–9pm, Sun 10am–8pm.

★ **Dover Street Market** Block 18 Dempsey Rd, Dempsey Hill ☎ 6304 1388, ⓦ singapore.doverstreet market.com; Napier MRT, then a 1km walk west; map p.87. The latest outpost, after New York and Tokyo, of this high-end fashion retail concept, showcasing multiple labels in a series of artfully designed spaces. Daily 11am–8pm.

Malay Art Gallery 31 Bussorah St ☎ 6294 8051; Bugis MRT; map p.50. *Songket* cloth, suitable for wearing or framing. Mon–Sat 8.30am–5.30pm, some Sun noon–6pm.

Ong Shunmugam #01-76 Block 43 Jalan Merah Saga ☎ 6252 2612, ⓦ ongshunmugam.com; Holland Village MRT; map p.111. Ong Shunmugam is part of the new generation of home-grown (in this case by adoption – she hails from Malaysia) high-fashion designers, known for her innovative take on the cheongsam and East Asian motifs generally. Tues–Sat 11am–7pm; appointments required.

Toko Aljunied 91 Arab St ☎ 6294 6897; Bugis MRT; map p.50. Batik cloth and *kebaya* – the blouse/sarong combinations traditionally worn by Nonyas. Men's shirts start at $50, and there are some women's shawls starting at close to $200. Custom-made clothes too, by appointment. Mon–Sat 10.30am–7pm, Sun 11.30am–6pm.

OUTDOOR AND SPORTING GOODS

If you are using Singapore as a springboard for an expedition elsewhere in Southeast Asia, you may want to save money and pick up any gear you need in another country, though Singapore has the advantage of choice and more reliable quality.

Campers' Corner 51 Waterloo St ☎ 6337 4743, ⓦ campers corner.com.sg; Bras Basah or Bencoolen MRT; map p.50. A wide range of premium brands at lofty prices. Daily noon–8pm.

Decathlon #02-03 City Square Mall, 180 Kitchener Road ☎ 6225 4773, ⓦ decathlon.sg; Farrer Park MRT; map p.50. Reasonably priced sporting gear, rucksacks, waterproofs and camping equipment. Daily 10am–10pm.

15

STATUES AT HAW PAR VILLA

Kids' Singapore

Slick yet suitably exotic, Singapore can feel like a gigantic theme park to children, and just wandering Little India or even Orchard Road should unearth plenty to interest them. Reactions to the Hindu and Buddhist temples covered throughout this book will vary: some children are fascinated by them, while for others the colourful statuary and rites just sail over their heads. Traditional festivals are generally entertaining too, but Thaipusam (see page 159) is one event that might freak some kids out. Otherwise, the most obvious thing to do with kids is to head to Sentosa, essentially one giant theme park (see page 114). Upmarket shops geared to kids cluster within the Forum mall on Orchard Road (see page 84). For childcare products, try Mothercare, with various outlets in the city centre (ⓦmothercare.com.sg).

ATTRACTIONS FOR KIDS

Prices for children's tickets, where available, are given throughout this book after the adult prices, and generally weigh in at a third less.

Bukit Timah Nature Reserve See page 90. Come for the rainforest trails and macaques. The trails are probably a bit too strenuous for under-6s.

Cable cars to Sentosa See page 119. Not only is this the way to arrive in style at Sentosa, but the vertiginous views always go down well.

DuckTours and river cruises See page 27. Children love the amphibious DuckTour; the Singapore River cruise is fun but unlikely to make quite such an impression.

Far East Organization Children's Garden Gardens By The Bay; see page 81. One of the best dedicated children's play areas in Singapore, with separate sections for under-6s and under-13s; both have water features whose jets sense movement nearby (bring swimwear), while the under-13s also have two treehouses to clamber up to. Free. Tues–Fri 10am–7pm, Sat & Sun 9am–9pm.

Forest Adventure Bedok Reservoir Rd ☎8100 7420, ⊛forestadventure.com.sg; Bedok Reservoir MRT. There's a treetop obstacle course at Sentosa, but this one out in the eastern suburbs just might appeal if you are tackling, say, Changi on the same day. The park includes a children's course (ages 5–9; $36 plus $25 per accompanying adult) featuring the usual assortment of elevated bridges and two zip lines. Tues–Sun 9.30am–6.30pm.

Go-Go Bambini Block 8, Dempsey Rd ☎6474 4176, ⊛gogobambini.com. Near the Botanic Garden, this indoor playground features lots of bouncy playpens, climbing walls etc. Best reached by taxi. It costs $28 for each child (Mon–Thurs unlimited play, Fri–Sun 2hr) while accompanying adults get in free. Daily 9am–7pm.

Haw Par Villa See page 108. No rides at this Buddhist theme park, where lurid statues, murals and dioramas dramatize Chinese myths. The occasional shock-horror touch tends to amuse rather than scare.

Jacob Ballas Garden Off Evans Rd, near the northern end of the Botanic Gardens ⊛sbg.org.sg; Botanic Gardens MRT. Designed for those aged 14 and under, with a water-play area, a treehouse and a mini-farm and maze to explore. Free. Tues–Sun 8am–7pm.

Jurong Bird Park See page 111. Penguins and flamingos are among the obvious highlights, and do catch at least one bird show – the ones featuring birds of prey are especially good.

Kayaking See page 104. Kids over 7 may enjoy a few hours of kayaking out at Ubin Island.

Lost #03-01 Peace Centre, corner of Selegie Rd and Sophia Rd ☎6717 1668, ⊛lost.sg; Bencoolen or Dhoby Ghaut MRT. Best suited to teenagers rather than young children, this escape room with five scenarios of varying difficulty is a potential rainy-day distraction. Groups with fewer than seven members may need to pay for seven to play as a team, or else some people may be assigned to other groups. They don't take foreign cards, so try to reserve a slot on the phone rather than online. Mon–Fri $22 per person during the day, $28 eves and all weekend. Mon–Thurs & Sun 11am–10.45pm, Fri & Sat 11am–12.45am.

Marina Bay Sands Sampan Rides Level B2, The Shoppes at Marina Bay Sands; Bayfront MRT. The idea of navigating the shopping mall's "canal" system in little wooden boats sounds preposterous, but it actually goes down really well with children. $10, regardless of age. Daily 11.30am–8pm.

Singapore Flyer See page 78. This can be a space-age experience for kids, even though they're merely being raised aloft in a glass-and-metal cage. The views are incidental.

Singapore Science Centre See page 112. Uncover your children's latent scientific bent by setting them loose amid zillions of interactive displays.

Singapore Zoo, Night Safari and River Safari See page 96. Animal exhibits aside, the zoo also has a Rainforest Kidzworld section featuring pony rides and a water-play area, but it's the night safari that some young 'uns find magical.

Snow City 21 Jurong Town Hall Rd, close to the Omni-Theatre and Science Centre (see page 112) ☎6560 2306, ⊛snowcity.com.sg. Hi-tech machines let it snow year-round in this corner of equatorial Singapore, though the slope at this indoor centre is just 60m long and less than three storeys high, leaving scope only for tobogganing on rubber rings. $18/hr including use of their jackets and boots; glove rental costs extra. Daily 10am–6pm.

Super Park #02-477 Suntec City Tower 1, 3 Temasek Boulevard ☎6560 2306, ⊛superparkcom.sg; Promenade MRT. This Finnish activity space format allows adults and kids to play side by side as much as possible. Activities include pedal-car racing, trampolining and taking soccer penalties against a "robo-keeper", claimed to be nearly infallible. Half-day tickets from $22 (for an evening session); day tickets from $35 (weekdays). All prices rise at weekends. Mon–Fri 10am–9pm, Sat & Sun 9am–9pm.

Zero Latency VR #03-346 Suntec City (in between towers 2 & 3), 3 Temasek Boulevard ☎8862 8393, ⊛zerolatencyvr.com.sg; Promenade MRT. Australian virtual-reality gaming outfit with a choice of 30min shoot-em-ups; players navigate an open space, VR goggles donned and "weapons" at the ready, to bump off zombies or other nasties. Participants must be aged at least 13; glasses cannot be worn. $59. Daily at least 11am–10pm.

16

RAFFLES STATUE BY THE SINGAPORE RIVER

Contexts

History

Not much is known of Singapore's pre-colonial history. Third-century Chinese sailors could have been referring to Singapore in their account of a place called Pu-Luo-Chung, a corruption of the Malay for "island at the end of a peninsula". In the late thirteenth century, Marco Polo reported seeing a place called Chiamassie, which could also have been Singapore. By then the island was known locally as Temasek and was a minor trading outpost of the Sumatran Srivijaya Empire. According to the Sejarah Melayu (or Malay Annals, a historical document commissioned by the Malay sultans in the seventeenth century), by the late fourteenth century the island was called Singapura, meaning "Lion City" in Sanskrit, though the origins of the name are mysterious. The annals mention a Sumatran noble who saw what he took to be a lion while sheltering on the island from a storm, but this must be regarded as legend.

Around 1390, a Sumatran prince called **Paramesvara** broke with the Majapahit Empire of Java and escaped to what is now Singapore. There he ruled until a Javanese offensive forced him to flee up the Malay Peninsula, where he and his son, **Iskandar Shah**, founded the **Malacca sultanate**. With the rise of Malacca, Singapore declined into a low-key fishing settlement and remained so after the Portuguese and then the Dutch took Malacca in 1511 and 1641 respectively.

The founding of Singapore

In the late eighteenth century the **British East India Company** embarked on a drive to establish ports along the strategic Straits of Malacca. Penang was secured in 1786 and Malacca taken in 1795 at the request of the Dutch Republic (whose government was in exile in London after being brought down by French-backed revolutionaries), but a port was needed further south to counter the Dutch presence in what is now Indonesia. Enter the visionary **Thomas Stamford Raffles** (see page 40), the British lieutenant-governor of Bencoolen in Sumatra. In 1818 he was tasked with setting up a colony at the southern tip of the Malay Peninsula, and in January the following year he stepped ashore on the northern bank of the Singapore River, accompanied by Colonel William Farquhar, a former senior British official in Malacca who was fluent in Malay.

Swampland and tiger-infested jungle covered Singapore, and its population was probably no more than a thousand, but Raffles recognized that the area at the southern tip of the island could make a superb deep-water harbour. With a view to setting up a trading station, he quickly struck a treaty with Abdul Rahman, *temenggong* (chieftain) of Singapore and a subordinate of the sultan of Johor, the region occupying the southern part of the Malay Peninsula. Raffles also exploited a

7th century	14th century	c.1390
The Sumatran Srivijayan Empire, encompassing the Malay Peninsula, rises to prominence	Srivijaya is challenged by the Majapahit Empire of Java and declines	Prince Paramesvara, fleeing Majapahit, takes control of Singapore – then Temasek – which prospers for a few years

succession dispute in the ruling house of Johor, bypassing the man who had until then been ruling as sultan, and who was sympathetic to the Dutch. Instead Raffles recognized his half-brother as sultan and signed a second treaty with both him and the *temenggong*. This riled the Dutch, for whom Singapore was part of their domain, but Farquhar managed to divert a contingent of British troops to Singapore and an immediate confrontation was averted. The matter was settled by the **Anglo-Dutch treaty** of 1824, a classic colonial carve-up in which the Dutch let the British keep Malacca and Singapore in exchange for Bencoolen and British recognition of the Riau Archipelago, the islands just south of Singapore, as being part of the Dutch sphere of influence.

The early boom years

With its duty-free stance and ideal position at the gateway to the South China Sea, Singapore experienced a meteoric expansion. The population had reached ten thousand by the time of the first census in 1824, with Malays, Chinese, Indians and Europeans arriving in search of work and commercial opportunities.

Two years earlier, Raffles had begun dividing up what is now downtown Singapore, earmarking the area south of the Singapore River for the Chinese, while Muslims were settled around the sultan's palace near today's Arab Street. Sultan Hussein and the *temenggong* were bought out in 1824, and Singapore ceded outright to the British. Three years later, the fledgling colony united with Penang and Malacca to form the **Straits Settlements**, which became a British crown colony in 1867. Singapore's laissez-faire economy boomed throughout this time, though life was chaotic and disease was rife. By 1860 the population had reached eighty thousand; Arabs, Indians, Javanese and Bugis (from Sulawesi) all came, but most populous of all were the Chinese from the southeastern provinces of China.

The advent of steamships and the Suez Canal made Singapore a major staging post on the Europe–East Asia route at the close of the nineteenth century.

Singapore had also become a world centre for rubber exports thanks to **Henry Ridley**, who led a one-man crusade to introduce the rubber plant to Southeast Asia. As all of the Malay Peninsula gradually fell into British clutches, the island benefited further from its hinterland's tin- and rubber-based economy.

The Japanese occupation

Singapore's Asian communities began to find their political voice in the 1920s, but pro-independence activity had not gone far when the spectre of war reared its head. Within the space of a few hours in December 1941, the Japanese had bombed Pearl Harbor and landed on the Malay Peninsula, whose commodities were vital for their war effort. By the end of January 1942 they were at Johor Bahru, facing Singapore across the Straits of Johor. After bombing Singapore for a week, on February 7 the Japanese General Tomoyuki Yamashita launched an attack on Pulau Ubin. More landings from the north followed, and between February 11 and 14 the Japanese won decisive victories at Bukit Timah and Pasir Panjang, the site of today's museums at the old Ford car factory (see page 92), and Bukit Chandu (see page 108). On February

1511	1641	1795
The Portuguese capture Malacca, creating the first European outpost in the Malay Peninsula	The Dutch East India Company seizes Malacca	The British East India Company captures Dutch possessions in Southeast Asia, including Malacca

15, the Allied commander Lieutenant-General Arthur Percival went to Yamashita's new base at the Ford factory and surrendered.

Winston Churchill described it as "the largest capitulation in British history". Its causes have been endlessly argued over by historians, but at the risk of generalizing, it seems fair to say that the British proved surprisingly disorganized and underprepared when it mattered. They also underestimated their enemy – regarding the Japanese as "small and short-sighted and thus totally unsuited physically to tropical warfare", as one intelligence officer put it – and were caught off guard by the speed of their advance. Ironically, it later emerged that the Japanese forces had been outnumbered and their supply lines perilously stretched prior to their success.

Three and a half years of brutal Japanese rule ensued, during which Singapore was renamed Syonan, or "Light of the South", and Europeans were either herded into Changi Prison or sent to work on Thailand's infamous "Death Railway". Less well known is the vicious **Operation Sook Ching**, mounted by the military police force, or **Kempeitai**, during which upwards of 25,000 ethnic Chinese men were executed at Singapore's beaches as enemies of the Japanese.

Postwar transformation

Even though the island was back in British hands following the end of World War II in 1945, the aura of colonial supremacy had gone and Singaporeans were demanding a say in the island's administration. The subsequent quarter-century would be a time of enormous political upheaval in Singapore, whose resolution laid the foundations for the regimented and wealthy city-state of today.

Though Britain was beginning to divest itself of its colonial possessions, it was unsure what to do with Singapore. One "obvious" option, for Singapore and the Malay Peninsula to become a new state together, was fraught with difficulty: Singapore had so many Chinese that its inclusion would have led to the politically awkward result of Malays being in a minority in the new state. So it was that when the Straits Settlements were dissolved in 1946, Malacca and Penang joined the newly formed **Malayan Union** together with the rest of the Peninsula, while Singapore became a crown colony in its own right. However, even the Singapore-less union was opposed by Malay nationalists, who did not want the Chinese and Indian communities to be afforded citizenship under the terms of the union, arguing that the Malays should retain special privileges. The British caved in and reinvented the union in 1948 as the **Federation of Malaya**, with rights for the Chinese and Indians to be decided later. Now it was leftists that were disgruntled, and that same year a communist insurgency was launched in Malaya by largely Chinese guerrillas, who had gained experience of jungle warfare in resisting the Japanese. This created another area of potential friction between the two territories: Malayan Chinese politicians tended to be conservative and looked askance at Singapore, where many Chinese were developing leftist sympathies.

In April 1955, Singapore held elections for the newly created legislative assembly, 25 of whose 32 members were directly elected. The **Labour Front** emerged as the biggest party and its leader, **David Marshall**, an idealistic, British-trained lawyer of Iraqi Jewish stock, became the island's first chief minister. The elections were also notable for the emergence of the brand-new **People's Action Party (PAP)**, which came third. Led by

28 January 1819	**1824**	**1845**
Stamford Raffles sets foot on Singapore for the first time	The Anglo-Dutch treaty is signed, under which the British dominate the Malay Peninsula; the same year, the Malay rulers cede Singapore to the East India Company	*The Straits Times,* Singapore's oldest surviving newspaper, begins publication

another British-qualified lawyer, the shrewd, calculating **Lee Kuan Yew**, a Peranakan, the party had at its core several more graduates of British universities who were generally of the centre left. Lee's key insight was that to take power, the party had to reach out beyond the English-speaking elite. He steered the PAP into absorbing new members further to the left, chiefly trade unionists as well as Chinese activists who were unhappy over the lack of support for Chinese-language education.

Just before the elections, the PAP's left wing had been involved in mass action by ten thousand Chinese high-school students demanding recognition for their union. The following month the bus workers' union, led by two PAP activists, was embroiled in a strike that descended into violence, with a number of deaths. Marshall made concessions to restore order while attacking the PAP for fomenting disorder, but just a year later, he resigned over differences on defence after talks with the British on further constitutional reform. He was replaced by his deputy, **Lim Yew Hock**, who confronted the unions and the students and, in 1957, arrested several PAP left-wingers. Ironically, this aided his political rivals by strengthening the hand of the moderates in the PAP.

Marriage with Malaysia, and divorce

Malaya achieved independence in 1957, and two years later Singapore achieved full self-government, with the PAP winning 43 of the 51 seats in the newly enlarged, totally elected legislative assembly. Lee became Singapore's first prime minister and quickly looked for a merger with Malaya, with a high degree of autonomy for the island. The talk was of Singapore playing New York to Kuala Lumpur's Washington DC, and it made sense: Singapore was Malaya's financial hub and main port, as well as a centre for publishing and the arts. For its part, Malaya, still recovering from the communist insurgency, feared that PAP leftists could yet turn Singapore into an extremist hotbed and so wanted the island under its wing, though with its Chinese element diluted by having Sarawak and British North Borneo (now Sabah) join as well. That was duly achieved in September 1963 with the proclamation of a new country, the **Federation of Malaysia**. Soon afterwards Singapore went to the polls, with the PAP again winning despite a major challenge from ex-PAP left-wingers.

Singapore's presence within Malaysia, was, however, an uneasy one, with the PAP challenging the mainstream Malaysian parties over their ethnically based politics. Racial incidents in Singapore developed into full-scale riots, with several deaths. Within two years Singapore was given its marching orders from the Federation, in the face of outrage in Kuala Lumpur at the PAP's attempts to break into Peninsular politics in 1964.

The new nation takes shape

On August 9, 1965, hours after announcing that Singapore would be going it alone as an **independent state**, a tearful Lee Kuan Yew appeared on local TV and called the event "a moment of anguish". With no natural resources, the tiny island seemed destined to fade into obscurity. Against all the odds, the PAP's vision transformed Singapore into an Asian economic heavyweight, but this also meant the government orchestrating seemingly every aspect of life on the island as it saw fit, brooking little opposition.

1858	February 1915	15 February 1942
The British East India Company closes, its possessions transferred to direct British government control	Indian troops stationed in Singapore mutiny for more than a week, killing tens of British soldiers and civilians	The British surrender to the Japanese at the Ford factory near Bukit Timah

While the port and shipyards were thriving, the first task was for Singapore to diversify economically and lessen its dependence on Malaysia. For all its leftist credentials, the PAP went all-out to seek **foreign investment**, and new industries sprang up in Jurong and other areas. The government also clamped down on union militancy, a process that had begun in 1961 when it formed the National Trades Union Congress to replace a leftist union grouping; now the unions were told to swallow a **no-strike philosophy** in return for government intervention in resolving industrial disputes fairly.

Soon after the split with Malaysia, Singapore set up military **conscription**, modelled in part on the Israeli system (and, indeed, with Israeli help), but the stakes were raised after the surprise announcement, in 1968, that the British were to close all their military bases east of Suez. Singapore was still a major British outpost, an arrangement that boosted both the island's security and the local economy. While the vacuum left by the British was cushioned by new industries and American investment, conscription has remained a fundamental element of Singapore life ever since, with a sizeable chunk of the budget spent on defence.

There was also the pressing matter of the country's high birth rate and lack of decent housing. In 1966 the Land Acquisition Act was passed, enabling the government to buy land compulsorily for minimal compensation. This allowed the building of **new towns** all over the island, where people from kampongs (villages) or the slums of Chinatown could be resettled in affordable apartments within uniform concrete towers. However, ethnic quotas in each town, meant to prevent ghettoes forming, had the effect of breaking communities apart and of making one area much like another demographically – with electoral implications.

The 1970s and 1980s

Over the next two decades, the PAP consolidated its grip on Singapore as its project for the nation continued to roll. The economy largely enjoyed healthy growth, and by 1980 Singapore was practically an industrialized country. The opposition was moribund: between 1968 and 1980, the PAP held every seat in parliamentary elections, and when the opposition Workers' Party unexpectedly won a by-election in 1981, the new MP, **J.B. Jeyaretnam**, found himself charged with several offences and chased through the Singaporean courts for the next decade. The government was also not averse to using the colonial-era **Internal Security Act**, which allows detention without trial, and used it to keep the leftist Chia Thye Poh either in jail or under some form of detention for more than two decades for allegedly advocating violence.

Having transformed the trade unions, the government now turned its attention to the **press**, which they felt should articulate the policies of the party that the electorate had voted for rather than offering an independent perspective. Press reform culminated in the early 1980s with a wholesale restructuring of the industry: two established Chinese newspapers were closed and two new ones created out of their ashes, while papers in all languages were brought under the umbrella of a new company whose chairman, **S.R. Nathan**, was once a civil servant involved in security and intelligence matters.

Another significant development of the time was in **education**. Back in the 1950s, the PAP had appeased Chinese-speaking voters by permitting the launch of a Chinese-language university, Nantah, but thirty years on the public had largely decided that

September 1945	August 1957	1959
The Japanese occupation ends with the surrender at City Hall by the Padang	The Federation of Malaya – the Malay Peninsula, minus Singapore – gains independence from the British	Singapore attains full self-government under Lee Kuan Yew while remaining a British colony

English offered better prospects, and Chinese-language institutions were in decline. In 1980 the government absorbed Nantah into the new National University of Singapore, which used English, and a few years later the remaining state schools that taught mainly in Chinese were switched to English. Though most Singapore students still learn Chinese, Malay or Tamil as a subsidiary language, it is English that now reigns supreme – with all the potential implications that has for the island's identity, cultures and values.

The PAP's grip on power was cemented with a major change to the British-style electoral system with the introduction in the late 1980s of "group representation constituencies" or **GRCs**. These were essentially winner-takes-all super-constituencies where only one party wins all the seats in an area by gaining the largest share of the total vote. The system was brought in apparently to make parliament more diverse (candidates for a GRC must form an ethnically balanced slate), though considering how hard it was for the opposition to win any single seats, let alone a cluster, the change had the effect of raising the barrier faced by anyone wishing to challenge the PAP.

New leaders

As the 1990s began, Singapore was an obvious economic miracle, yet it was also bland and rigid, a consumerist showcase where the historic Chinatown had been partly demolished and the remnants sanitized, and where patronizing state campaigns exhorted citizens to, among other things, be nice to each other and not spit in the street. So when Lee Kuan Yew stepped down in 1990 in favour of his deputy, **Goh Chok Tong**, Singaporeans hoped for a degree of loosening up. Goh promised to lead in a more consultative way, and there were some liberalizing changes: films began to be rated so that they could be viewed intact instead of being cut to shreds in order to be family-friendly, and the arts scene began to take off. That said, there were still written and unwritten rules curbing freedom of expression, and the government has kept a lid on the press. Since 2004, when Lee's eldest son, **Lee Hsien Loong**, took over as prime minister, not much has fundamentally changed, although he comes across as much more managerial than his often ruthless father.

The banking crisis and its aftermath

The wisdom of the island's reliance on **financial services** was questioned when Singapore suffered a sharp recession in the wake of the banking crisis of 2008. Then **Temasek Holdings**, the state-owned company that helps to manage Singapore's huge foreign reserves, grabbed stakes in two foreign banks, but suffered huge losses. Amid a public outcry it was announced in 2009 that the company's head, Ho Ching – who also happens to be the prime minister's wife – was to step down, though in the event she clung on to her job.

But two years later, when the island went to the polls, the opposition managed to win six out of the 87 parliamentary seats, including its first ever GRC, with the foreign minister among government casualties. This was a minor political earthquake, and Lee Kuan Yew subsequently gave up his "minister mentor" post – a role created to give him continuing influence.

Sept 1963	9 August 1965	May/June 1987
Singapore plus Sarawak and Sabah in Borneo join Malaya to form a new federation, Malaysia	After protracted bickering with Malaysian political parties over economic and social policies, Singapore is forced to leave the Federation and goes it alone as an independent country	The government cracks down on an alleged Marxist conspiracy, imprisoning lawyers and Catholic activists

To the present

The 2011 election result was the surest sign yet of persistent internal disquiet, a sense that Singaporeans are sometimes far less sanguine about their prospects and the system that envelops their lives than is obvious from the state-run media. One overt sign of this is the howls of dismay whenever there is a breakdown on the **MRT** system, which had run flawlessly until recent years.

The most notable area of discontent concerns **immigration**, with people seeing the government's openness to new migrants as taking jobs from them at all levels. If only the island had a **minimum wage** policy, some argue, Singaporeans would be tempted to do more basic jobs and fewer migrants would be needed – not realizing that the cheap food and transport they take for granted are partly the result of migrant labour.

As it happens, immigrants were at the centre of one of the most startling events of recent years when, in December 2013, **Little India** witnessed Singapore's first major public unrest in at least thirty years after a migrant worker died in a road accident. Thankfully, the ensuing **riot** was soon brought under control and was not exploited to stoke the immigration debate further.

Singapore's fiftieth anniversary and beyond

In March 2015, **Lee Kuan Yew died**. Inevitably, there was a massive outpouring of grief, but the event had wider implications. Together with the republic's golden jubilee that August, his death effectively turned **September's elections** into a referendum on the PAP's track record since independence. The outcome confounded observers just as the 2011 result had: despite the opposition appearing better organized than ever, the PAP increased its share of the popular vote. The historic context to the polls aside, this was partly because the government had finally taken popular resentment on board; in particular, it was seen to be tightening immigration rules at last. Prior to the polls, it had also plied voters with unprecedented sweeteners, including healthcare and transport subsidies for the over-65s. Viewed in that light, the opposition did reasonably well not to lose any parliamentary seats compared with its 2011 showing.

Since then it has been largely business/politics as usual, but not without a few revealing twists. Relatively unsurprising was that several opposition MPs and councillors found themselves on trial in 2018 over alleged irregularities in the financial management of the island's sole opposition-run town council; a verdict is due in 2019. While the affair may have had echoes of past events for some observers, another was without precedent: the 2017 **social media spat** between the prime minister and his own siblings over the fate of Lee Kuan Yew's old home at **38 Oxley Road**, just five minutes' walk from Orchard Road. Lee Hsien Loong's siblings maintained that their father's will required that the house, its guard posts now vacant, to be knocked down to prevent it becoming a sort of shrine, and they accused the prime minister of being unwilling to countenance the demolition. They even went so far as to declare that they felt "big brother omnipresent" in Singapore and that "the system has few checks and balances to prevent the abuse of government". The row has since died down, but without any publicly announced settlement. A few months later, the prime minister's own nephew allegedly fell foul of the country's laws on criticizing Singapore's courts when he wrote in a friends-only Facebook post that the government was "litigious" and the courts "pliant". The case had yet to come to trial at the time of writing.

May 1989	May 2011	December 2013
After 23 years of imprisonment without trial, former left-wing opposition MP Chia Thye Poh is released to a kind of internal exile on Sentosa	Singapore's opposition enjoys its best electoral showing since independence	Rioting breaks out in Little India after a migrant worker dies in a road accident

With Singapore now in its sixth decade of independence, a mass of contradictions clearly remains. Ministers rule paternalistically, paying themselves handsomely for their supposed expertise, yet maintain they don't have all the answers and that citizens must show more initiative; capitalism appears to have trumped the welfare state, yet the state owns eighty percent of the land, and institutions that it dominates play a crucial role in shipping, property, banking and other key sectors of the economy. The nation is more at ease with itself and more culturally liberated than a generation ago – yet its **civil liberties** record still deserves scrutiny, something it is rarely subjected to as Western countries prefer to see Singapore as a wealthy trading partner and useful little ally in the so-called war on terror.

The country's success is not unqualified: Singapore too often feels not so much governed as "managed", with little of the messiness that full accountability often entails. Its wealth inequality is on a par with that of the US and worse than in, say, Australia and the UK, neither of which is a beacon in this regard. Commentators have wondered whether Singapore might follow in the reformist footsteps of neighbouring Malaysia, where the ruling coalition that had governed since independence was thrown out in 2017's polls, but that seems unlikely until the city-state's voters are presented with a better opposition or a worse government to choose between – probably both.

March 2015	**August 2015**	**September 2017**
Lee Kuan Yew dies, aged 91	Singapore celebrates its 50th anniversary of full independence	Singapore's ceremonial president is elected unopposed after a change in rules left a government MP as the sole eligible candidate

Religion

Singaporeans enjoy freedom of worship, and the island's multicultural nature is reflected in its wide range of creeds. More than half of the population are adherents of Buddhism, with elements of Taoism and Confucianism. Malays, who make up around fifteen percent of the population, are predominantly Muslim, while the nation's Indians are either Hindu, Muslim or Sikh. In addition, one in ten Singaporeans is Christian – belonging to traditional denominations as well as US-style evangelical megachurches – and there is a tiny Jewish community worshipping at two synagogues. This section gives an outline of traditional Chinese beliefs plus Islam and Hinduism, and their places of worship.

Chinese beliefs

The majority of Singaporean Chinese describe themselves as **Buddhist**, **Taoist** or **Confucianist**; in practice, they are often a mixture of all three. These different strands of Chinese religion ostensibly lean in different directions, but the combination amounts to a system of belief that is first and foremost pragmatic. The Chinese use religion to ease their passage through life, whether in the spheres of work or family, while temples double as social centres, where people meet and exchange views.

Buddhism

Buddhism states that the suffering of the world can only be relieved by attaining a state of personal enlightenment, or Nirvana, through meditation. The founder of Buddhism, **Siddhartha Gautama**, was born a prince in Lumbini in present-day Nepal, around 500 BC. Shielded from knowledge of suffering and death for the first decades of his life, he later renounced his pampered existence and spent years meditating before finding enlightenment under a bodhi tree. At this point he became the Buddha or "Awakened One". In Singapore and elsewhere in Southeast Asia he is sometimes called Sakyamuni, or "Holy Man of the Sakya tribe".

In his first sermon, Buddha taught the four noble truths: that suffering exists; that its source should be recognized; that one should strive for a cessation of suffering; and that this can be achieved by following the **Eightfold Path** – practising right views, intentions, speech, action, livelihood, effort, mindfulness and concentration. The religion is split into two schools: **Hinayana** (or Theravada) Buddhism, which focuses on people attaining enlightenment for themselves, and **Mahayana** Buddhism – more common in Singapore – which teaches that one who has become a Bodhisattva, that is, attained enlightenment, should then help others do the same.

Taoism

Unity with nature is the chief tenet of Taoism (also spelt Daoism), a philosophical movement dating from the sixth century BC, and propounded by the Chinese scholar **Lao Tze** or Laozi. Taoism advocates that people follow a central *Tao* or "way", and cultivate an understanding of the nature of things. This search for truth has often expressed itself in Taoism by way of superstition on the part of its devotees, who engage in fortune-telling and the like. The Taoist gods are mainly legendary figures – warriors, statesmen, scholars – with specific powers that can generally be determined by their form; others represent incarnations of the forces of nature.

Confucianism

Confucianism began as a philosophy based on piety, loyalty, humanitarianism and familial devotion. In the 2500 years since **Kongzi** or **Confucius**, its founder, died, it has transmuted into a set of principles that permeate every aspect of Chinese life. A blueprint for social and moral harmony, the Confucian ideology stresses one's obligation to family, community and the state, hinging on the individual's need to recognize his or her position in the social hierarchy and act accordingly – son must obey father, student must obey teacher, subject must obey ruler.

Chinese temples

The rules of **geomancy**, or **feng shui** (wind and water), are rigorously applied to the construction of **Chinese temples** to ensure they are free from malign influences. Visitors wishing to cross the threshold of a temple have to step over a low barrier intended to trip up evil spirits, and walk through doors painted with fearsome door gods; fronting the doors are two stone lions, providing yet another defence. Larger temples typically consist of a front entrance hall opening on to a walled-in courtyard, beyond which is the hall of worship, where joss sticks are burned below images of the deities.

Temples are usually constructed around a framework of huge, lacquered timber beams, adorned with intricately carved warriors, animals and flowers. More figures are moulded onto outer walls, which are dotted with octagonal, hexagonal or round windows. Elsewhere in the grounds, you'll see sizeable ovens stuffed constantly with slowly burning fake money, prayer books and other offerings. Pagodas – tall, thin towers thought to keep out evil spirits – are common too.

The most important and striking element of a Chinese temple is its roof. They are grand, multi-tiered affairs, with low, overhanging eaves, the ridges alive with auspicious creatures such as dragons and phoenixes and, less often, with miniature scenes from traditional Chinese life and legend. One particular feature of Singapore temple roofs is the use of **jiannian**, a southern Chinese art form in which pottery fragments in multicoloured pastel hues are used to create ornamentations such as finials.

Temples are open from early morning to early evening and devotees go in when they like, to make offerings or to pray; there are no set prayer times. They also play an important part in Chinese community life, and some hold occasional musical and theatrical performances.

Islam

Islam ("submission to God") was founded in Mecca in what is now Saudi Arabia by Muhammad (570–632 AD), the last in a long line of prophets that included Abraham, Moses and Jesus. Muhammad transmitted Allah's final and perfected revelation to mankind through the writings of the divinely revealed "recitation", the **Koran**. The official beginning of Islam is dated as 622 AD, when Muhammad and his followers, exiled from Mecca, made the **hijra**, or migration, north to Yathrib, later known as Medina. The *hijra* marks the start of the Islamic calendar.

All the central tenets of Islam are embodied in the Koran, with the most important known as the **Five Pillars of Islam**. The first pillar is *shahada* – the confession of faith, "There is no god but God, and Muhammad is his messenger." The *shahada* is recited at the *salat*, the second pillar, which enjoins the faithful to make five daily prayers facing in the direction of Mecca. The other three tenets are: giving alms (*zakat*); fasting during the ninth month of the Muslim lunar calendar, **Ramadan**; and making the great annual pilgrimage (**hajj**) to Mecca at least once in a devotee's lifetime.

The first firm foothold made by Islam in Southeast Asia was the conversion of the court of Melaka, in modern-day Malaysia, in the early fifteenth century. One after another, the powerful Malay court rulers of the region took to Islam, adopting the title sultan. Today, almost all of Singapore's Malays are Muslims, as well as a proportion of its Indian population. Islam as practised here may be devout but is not overt, largely because of the secularizing influence of the state, which has banned headscarves from government-run schools.

Mosques

While only a small proportion attends the mosque every day, all Muslims converge on their nearest **mosque** on Friday for the weekly congregational prayer at midday. Once there, the men wash their hands, feet and faces three times in the outer chambers, before entering the prayer hall to recite sections of the Koran. Standard fixtures in the prayer hall are the *minbar* (pulpit), from where the imam preaches, and women cannot enter the main prayer hall during prayers and must congregate in a chamber to the side of the hall. Visitors are welcome outside the set prayer times, provided that their shoulders and legs are covered.

Hinduism

Hinduism reached the Malay Peninsula and Singapore long before Islam, brought by Indian traders more than a thousand years ago. Its base of support grew in the nineteenth century, when large numbers of indentured workers and convicts arrived from the subcontinent to labour on rubber estates and in construction.

Hinduism had no founder, but grew slowly over thousands of years. Its central tenet is the belief that life is a series of rebirths and reincarnations (*samsara*) that eventually leads to spiritual release (*moksha*). An individual's progress is determined by his or her *karma*, very much a law of cause and effect, in which negative decisions and actions slow up the process of upward reincarnation and positive ones accelerate it.

A whole variety of deities are worshipped, which on the surface makes Hinduism appear complex, but even with a loose understanding of the **Vedas**, the religion's holy books, the characters and roles of the main gods quickly become apparent. The deities you'll come across most often are the three manifestations of the faith's Supreme Divine Being: **Brahma the Creator**, **Vishnu the Preserver** and **Shiva the Destroyer**. Other enduring favourites among Hindus include: elephant-headed Ganesh, the son of Shiva, who is evoked before every undertaking except funerals; Vishnu's consort, the comely Lakshmi, worshipped as goddess of prosperity and wealth; and Saraswati, wife to Brahma, and seen as a goddess of purification, fertility and learning.

Hindu temples

Step over the threshold of a Hindu temple and you enter a veritable Disneyland of colourful gods and fanciful creatures. In Singapore, the style is typically **Dravidian** (South Indian), as befits the largely Tamil population, with a soaring *gopuram*, or entrance tower, teeming with sculptures, and a central courtyard leading to an inner sanctum (off-limits to tourists) dedicated to the presiding deity.

Books

Singapore has a thriving English-language publishing industry, with indie imprints like Epigram and Ethos Books doing a fine job of publishing both fiction and books on social and cultural issues. Titles marked ★ are particularly recommended while o/p signifies out of print. Note that authors with Chinese names usually have their surname appearing first, as is the Chinese custom; Malay and Indian authors are alphabetized according to the given name, which appears first, the second name being the father's name.

TRAVEL WRITING AND MEMOIR

Charles Allen *Tales from the South China Seas*. Recollections of the last generation of British colonists in which predictable Raj attitudes prevail, though some of the drama of everyday lives, often in inhospitable conditions, is evinced with considerable pathos.

Isabella Bird *The Golden Chersonese*. The intrepid author's adventures in the Malay states in the 1870s ranged from strolls through Singapore's streets to elephant-back rides and encounters with alligators. Periodically reissued, it's also available from various websites as a free download.

Russell Braddon *The Naked Island*. Braddon's disturbing and moving first-hand account of the POW camps of Malaya, Singapore and Thailand displays courage in the face of appalling conditions and treatment.

Hidayah Amin *Gedung Kuning: Memories of a Malay Childhood;* **Hidayah Amin and Yahaya Sanusi** *Kampung Tempe. Gedung Kuning* is a simple, heartfelt account of life in the little yellow mansion on Kandahar Street, taking in Muslim festivals, family weddings, neighbourhood characters and intergenerational stories, abruptly ended by the author's family being turfed out in 1999 when the state acquired the property. *Kampung Tempe*, on the other hand, is quite literally a book of village history, achieving the rare feat of chronicling an unsung Malay hamlet that has been subsumed out of existence by a middle-class suburb.

Eric Lomax *The Railway Man*. An artless, redemptive and moving story of capture during the fall of Singapore, torture by the Japanese and reconciliation with the author's tormentor after fifty years.

★ **Lucy Lum** *The Thorn of Lion City*. You might think a memoir of a wartime childhood in Singapore would be dominated by the savagery of the Japanese, but for the author that was nothing compared to the torment inflicted on her at the hands of her manipulative and violent mother and grandmother. It's told with zero artifice, which only makes it more compelling.

HISTORY, SOCIETY AND POLITICS

Munshi Abdullah (aka Abdullah bin Kadir) *The Hikayat Abdullah* (o/p). Raffles' one-time clerk, Abdullah, kept a diary of some of the most formative years of Southeast Asian history, and his first-hand account is crammed with illuminating vignettes and character portraits.

Noel Barber *Sinister Twilight*. Documents the fall of Singapore to the Japanese by reimagining the crucial events of the period.

Graham Berry *From Kilts to Sarongs*. It wasn't just George Drumgoole Coleman and the architectural firm of Swan & MacLaren – this book relates how Scots played a major role in building some of Singapore's best-known enterprises.

Patrick Keith *Ousted*. Singapore's unhappy stint as part of Malaysia might seem something from the distant past, but the events of the mid-1960s, recounted in this excellent blow-by-blow account by a former advisor to the Malaysian government, still shape both countries and their relations today.

Colin Smith *Singapore Burning: Heroism and Surrender in World War II*. Highly detailed, definitive account of the fall of Singapore, written with a journalist's instinct for excitement.

★ **C.M. Turnbull** *A History of Modern Singapore 1819–2005*. Mary Turnbull had barely completed a major update of this standard work when she died in 2008, and what a fine legacy her swansong is: lucid, thorough, nearly always spot-on in its analysis and, as always, utterly readable.

Simon Vincent *The Naysayer's Book Club*. A collection of extended interviews with Singaporean activists, academics and writers who like to think outside the box. There's little in their views that comes across as genuinely radical but, if nothing else, the book proves just how easy it is to transgress that Singapore box.

★ **Nicholas Walton** *Singapore, Singapura: From Miracle to Complacency*. This dissection of Singapore's success story unfolds in episodes surrounding the author's incredible 52km day-walk from the Second Link with Malaysia to Tanah Merah Ferry Terminal at the other end of the island. Walton offers no new insights, nor does he predict when things might turn sour, if ever, but for comprehensiveness it's hard to fault this distillation of the numerous issues thrown up by the Singapore miracle and the unique way it was brought about.

★ **Teo You Yenn** *This is What Inequality Looks Like*. Who would have thought anthropology could have such mass appeal? Teo You Yenn's first-person account of three years of fieldwork among people at the bottom of the Singapore ladder finally gives them a voice and is told with such reforming zeal that crowds of young people, in particular, turned out when she gave public talks about her work.

ARCHITECTURE
★ **Julian Davison and Luca Invernizzi Tettoni** *Black & White: The Singapore House* and *The Singapore Shophouse*. *Black & White* celebrates the island's surviving colonial "Anglo-Malay" residences – such as at the Botanic Gardens – which marry mock Tudor and Southeast Asian elements. Even better is *The Singapore Shophouse*, dissecting its subject through the lens of stylistic era, district and so forth, with a cornucopia of dazzling photos of interiors as well as exteriors.

★ **Kang Ger Wen** *Decoration and Symbolism in Chinese Architecture: Understanding Singapore's Historic Chinese Buildings*. Picks apart the folkloric or religious significance of every motif you're likely to see at temples like Thian Hock Keng and Yueh Hai Ching, supported by exemplary photos.

Peter Lee and Jennifer Chen *The Straits Chinese House*. Packed with vintage images, this book on Peranakan homes, domestic artefacts and vanishing traditions makes an excellent memento after you've visited the Baba House or the Peranakan Museum.

Wan Meng Hao and Jacqueline Lau *Heritage Places of Singapore*. A compact, full-colour catalogue of the hugely diverse pre-independence architecture of Singapore, from Palladian colonial buildings to overlooked Art Deco edifices as well as traditional temples and shrines.

BIOGRAPHY
Victoria Glendinning *Raffles and the Golden Opportunity*. The first serious biography of Singapore's founder in decades does occasionally get bogged down in a surfeit of detail on Raffles' extended family, but offers plenty of enjoyable insights into the headstrong drive of a generally neglected figure of British colonialism.

James Harding and Ahmad Sarji *P. Ramlee: The Bright Star*. An uncritical but enjoyable biography of the singer, actor and director sometimes described as the Malay world's Harry Belafonte. More importantly, it's a window on to what seems like a different era, only half a century ago, when Singapore was the centre of the Malay entertainment universe.

Ilsa Sharp *Path of the Righteous Crane*. Eu Tong Sen, after whom one of Chinatown's main thoroughfares is named, was the founder of the Eu Yan Sang emporia of Chinese herbal medicines. This biography not only recounts the many successes of this prewar tycoon in Singapore and Malaysia but also unwraps migrant Chinese society of the time.

FOOD
Aziza Ali *Aziza's Creative Malay Cuisine; Sambal Days, Kampong Cuisine*. Singapore once had a celebrated posh Malay restaurant, run by Aziza Ali, and her *Creative Malay Cuisine* cookbook is crammed with impressive recipes. *Sambal Days, Kampong Cuisine* is a memoir of a middle-class Malay childhood that is also a reverie packed with special foods for just about every occasion.

★ **Sylvia Tan** *Singapore Heritage Food*. This book begins a little unpromisingly with passé colonial-era dishes – prawn cocktails and the like – but then comes a romp through all manner of classic Singapore restaurant and hawker food, from Hainanese chicken rice and chilli crab to less familiar standards that visitors seldom notice, such as *oh luak* (scrambled egg with oysters) and *chap chye* (Peranakan mixed veg and fungi braised in soy sauce). Plenty of vintage photos of now-vanished pushcart food stalls, too.

NATURE
Nick Baker and Kelvin Lim *Wild Animals of Singapore*. An illustrated pocket guide to just about any creature seen in Singapore in recent times, though crucial details of which are easy to spot and which virtually extinct are relegated to appendices.

A. Jeyarajasingam *A Field Guide to the Birds of Peninsular Malaysia and Singapore*. User-friendly and with oodles of glossy plates, this should help even the bird-blind sort out a black-naped oriole from a white-rumped shama.

FICTION
Alfian Sa'at *Malay Sketches*. Not so much short stories as vignettes, Sa'at's miniature tales – collected here under a title that deliberately echoes that of a classic work by a nineteenth-century British colonial official – attempt to capture the bittersweet experience of Singapore's Malay community. The stories aren't always brilliantly executed, but when they work they do pack a punch, exposing home truths concerning religion, ethnic stereotypes and competition with the Chinese.

★ **Anthony Burgess** *The Malayan Trilogy*. Published in one volume, *Time for a Tiger*, *The Enemy in the Blanket* and *Beds in the East* provide a witty and acutely observed vision of 1950s Malaya and Singapore, underscoring the racial prejudices of the period.

★ **James Clavell** *King Rat*. Clavell spins a gripping tale of survival in the notorious Changi Prison during the Japanese occupation.

Joseph Conrad *Lord Jim*. Southeast Asia provides the backdrop to the story of Jim's desertion of an apparently sinking ship and subsequent efforts to redeem himself; the main protagonist was modelled on the sailor A.P. Williams, who lived and died in Singapore.

★ **J.G. Farrell** *The Singapore Grip*. Lengthy wartime novel, the last of Farrell's empire trilogy, in which real and fictitious characters flit from tennis to dinner party as the countdown to the Japanese occupation begins.

Shamini Flint *Inspector Singh Investigates: The Singapore School of Villainy*; **William L. Gibson** *Singapore Black*. Two whodunnits: Flint's is about a rotund Sikh police detective probing a murder at the Singapore offices of an international law firm, albeit with all the depth of characterization of *Murder She Wrote*. Far better is *Singapore Black*, a meticulously researched trilogy opener set in the 1890s, with Detective Inspector Hawksworth investigating a murder that encompasses Chinese gangs and Indian Tantric ritual.

Liana Gurung, Chloe Tong and Ann Gee Neo *The Phantom of Oxley Castle*. This children's picture book, about two princes and a princess who live in a tropical castle along with their finicky butler, would appear to be a barely disguised satire on the public row over Lee Kuan Yew's old house (see page 174). Young readers won't mind that the book ends in anticlimax, with the castle denizens destined to "live happily ever after… for now".

Han Suyin *And The Rain My Drink*. Han is mainly remembered for her autobiographical novel which inspired the 1950s Hollywood hit *Love is a Many-Splendored Thing*, but *And The Rain My Drink* is an underrated gem; there is no better novel of 1950s Malaya and Singapore, with the Communist Insurgency its overarching theme.

★ **Sonny Liew** *The Art of Charlie Chan Hock Chye*. The winner of three Eisner awards, which are to comics what the Oscars are to film, this graphic novel appears to commemorate an overlooked genius of Singapore comic art. In reality, Liew's "retrospective" on the fictional Mr Chan's satirical work and struggle for recognition is an indictment of the autocratic trajectory of postwar Singapore politics – a useful antidote to establishment accounts.

Paul Theroux *Saint Jack*. The compulsively bawdy tale of Jack Flowers, an ageing American who supplements his earnings at a Singapore ship's chandlers by pimping for Westerners. The 1979 movie adaptation, filmed on the island through subterfuge – the crew knew the plot's sleaziness would never pass muster with the authorities – was only unbanned in Singapore in 2006.

Glossary

Ancestral tablet Small upright object representing a departed forebear in Chinese ancestor worship.

Baba Peranakan male, usually someone of mainly Chinese heritage.

Bumboat Small cargo boat.

Cheongsam Tight-fitting Chinese dress with a slit up the side.

Five-foot way Recessed ground-level walkway, substituting for a pavement; a standard feature of shophouses.

Godown Riverside warehouse.

Gopuram Pyramid of sculpted deities over the entrance to a Hindu temple.

Hajj Major annual Muslim pilgrimage to Mecca.

Halal Something permissible in Islam.

Hawker centre A cooked-food market containing a cluster of stalls under one roof and sharing common tables.

Istana A Malay palace.

Jalan Road or street.

Jiannian Use of multicoloured pottery shards to build up decorative tableaux, for example on Chinese temple rooftops.

Kampong/kampung Village.

Kavadi Steel frames hung from the bodies of Hindu devotees during Thaipusam.

Kempeitai The military police during the Japanese occupation.

Keramat Auspicious Malay site or shrine.

Kongsi Chinese clan association.

Kopitiam Inexpensive street-level diner, now increasingly rare.

Kris Wavy-bladed Malay dagger.

Lorong Lane.

Mahjong A Chinese game played with little brick-shaped "tiles".

Masjid Mosque.

Nonya Peranakan female (from the Malay nyonya).

Padang Field; used also for grassy town squares.

Pasir Sand, often used in names of areas with beaches.

Peranakan Person of mixed culture and/or race, born in the territories around the Straits of Malacca.

Pulau Island.

Ramadan Muslim fasting month.

Sari Traditional Indian woman's garment, worn in conjunction with a choli (short-sleeved blouse).

Shophouse Townhouse-like building, the oldest examples of which had living quarters upstairs and a shop space at ground level.

Songkok Stiff drum-like cap worn by Malay men.

Sook Ching The military operation under which the occupying Japanese rounded up and killed thousands of Singapore Chinese.

Sultan Ruler.

Tanjong/tanjung Promontory.

Telok/teluk Bay.

Temenggong Chieftain.

Tongkang Chinese sailing boat.

Trishaw Three-wheeled cycle-rickshaw.

Wayang Theatrical show; in the Singapore context, Chinese opera.

Small print and index

A ROUGH GUIDE TO ROUGH GUIDES

Published in 1982, the first Rough Guide – to Greece – was a student scheme that became a publishing phenomenon. Mark Ellingham, a recent graduate in English from Bristol University, had been travelling in Greece the previous summer and couldn't find the right guidebook. With a small group of friends he wrote his own guide, combining a contemporary, journalistic style with a thoroughly practical approach to travellers' needs.

The immediate success of the book spawned a series that rapidly covered dozens of destinations. And, in addition to impecunious backpackers, Rough Guides soon acquired a much broader readership that relished the guides' wit and inquisitiveness as much as their enthusiastic, critical approach and value-for-money ethos. These days, Rough Guides include recommendations from budget to luxury and cover more than 120 destinations around the globe, from Amsterdam to Zanzibar, all regularly updated by our team of roaming writers.

Browse all our latest guides, read inspirational features and book your trip at **roughguides.com**.

Rough Guide credits

Editors: Joanna Reeves, Siobhan Warwicker
Cartography: Ed Wright
Managing editor: Rachel Lawrence
Picture editor: Aude Vauconsant

Cover photo research: Aude Vauconsant
Senior DTP coordinator: Dan May
Head of DTP and Pre-Press: Rebeka Davies

Publishing information

Ninth Edition 2019

Distribution

UK, Ireland and Europe
Apa Publications (UK) Ltd; sales@roughguides.com
United States and Canada
Ingram Publisher Services; ips@ingramcontent.com
Australia and New Zealand
Woodslane; info@woodslane.com.au
Southeast Asia
Apa Publications (SN) Pte; sales@roughguides.com
Worldwide
Apa Publications (UK) Ltd; sales@roughguides.com
Special Sales, Content Licensing and CoPublishing
Rough Guides can be purchased in bulk quantities
at discounted prices. We can create special editions,
personalised jackets and corporate imprints tailored to
your needs. sales@roughguides.com.
roughguides.com

Help us update

We've gone to a lot of effort to ensure that this edition of
The Rough Guide to Singapore is accurate and up-to-
date. However, things change – places get "discovered",
opening hours are notoriously fickle, restaurants and
rooms raise prices or lower standards. If you feel we've got
it wrong or left something out, we'd like to know, and if
you can remember the address, the price, the hours, the
phone number, so much the better.

Please send your comments with the subject
line "**Rough Guide Singapore Update**" to mail@
uk.roughguides.com. We'll credit all contributions and
send a copy of the next edition (or any other Rough Guide
if you prefer) for the very best emails.

Reader's updates

Thanks to all the readers who have taken the time to write in with comments and suggestions (and apologies if we've
inadvertently omitted or misspelt anyone's name):

Grateful thanks to readers Larry Kaplan, Veerle Van de Catsye and Damien White, who all took the time to offer feedback
on the last edition.

Acknowledgements

The author would like to thank Susanah, Thaleia and Shermaine; Elizabeth T and colleagues; Gretchen and Shaiful; Natt
Haniff; Eric and Chloe; Jerome and Sharon; Jeannine; Alvin; Rex; Valencia; Brian; Deborah and Elaine; Jessica; George;
Shushanta; Nur Fathin; Suning; Beida; Fabrice; Leenu; Joyce; Grace; and Jerald. Special thanks to Ooi Kee Beng; John;
Fabian, Catherine and Yik Han; and David Leffman for their friendship and advice over the years. At Rough Guides, thanks
to Joanna Reeves, Aude Vauconsant and Ed Wright for their hard work.

ABOUT THE AUTHOR

Not to be confused with his namesake, the journalist at *Singapore's Straits Times*, **Richard
Lim** (@rltl17) is a London-based freelance editor and writer. He enjoys travelling around the
Middle East and Southeast Asia in particular, and is also keen on science, technology and
photography.

Photo credits
(Key: T-top; C-centre; B-bottom; L-left; R-right)

Index

Map symbols

The symbols below are used on maps throughout the book

✈	International airport	◆	Place of interest	🐘	Zoo	▨	Building
✈	Local airport	◆	Nature park	▲	Hill	⊣	Church
⊝	MRT station	✡	Synagogue	🗼	Lighthouse	▭	Market
★	Transport stop	☪	Mosque	▩	Expressway	◯	Stadium
⛴	Ferry terminal	♨	Hindu/Sikh temple	═══	Road	▦	Park
✉	Post office	♨	Chinese/Thai temple	▨	Pedestrianized road	▨	Beach
ⓘ	Tourist office	⛵	Swimming pool	▥	Steps	▨	Swamp
⊞	Hospital/clinic	⚲	Fountain	- - - -	Footpath	✝	Christian cemetery
⊙	Statue	⛳	Golf course	——	Ferry	▣	Chinese cemetery
P	Parking	⊠	Gate	▬▬▬	Railway	Y	Muslim cemetery
♟	Museum	♦	Checkpoint	- ▪ - ▪	Cable car		

Listings key

- ■ Accommodation
- ● Eating
- ■ Drinking and nightlife
- ● Shopping

City plan

The **city plan** on the pages that follow is divided as shown:

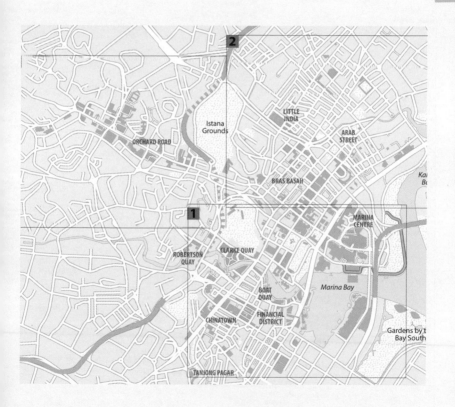

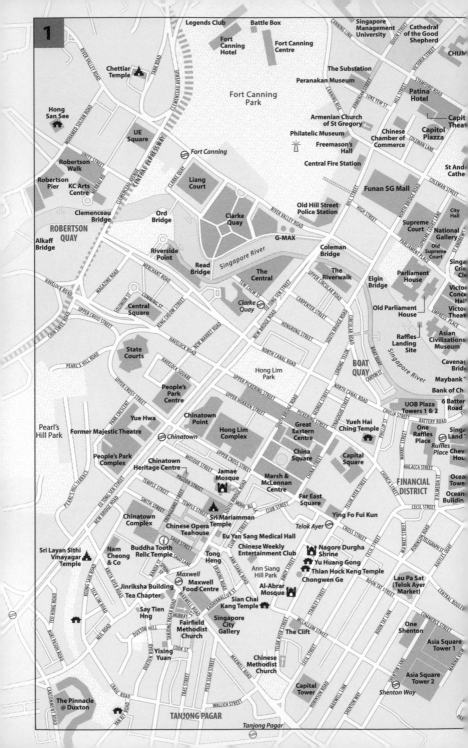

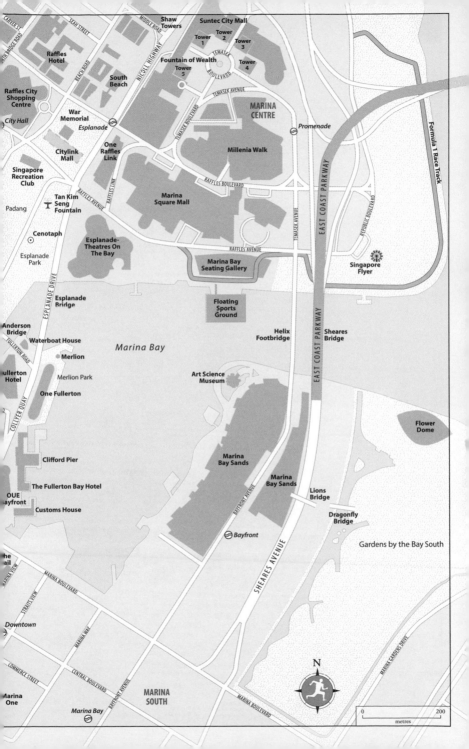

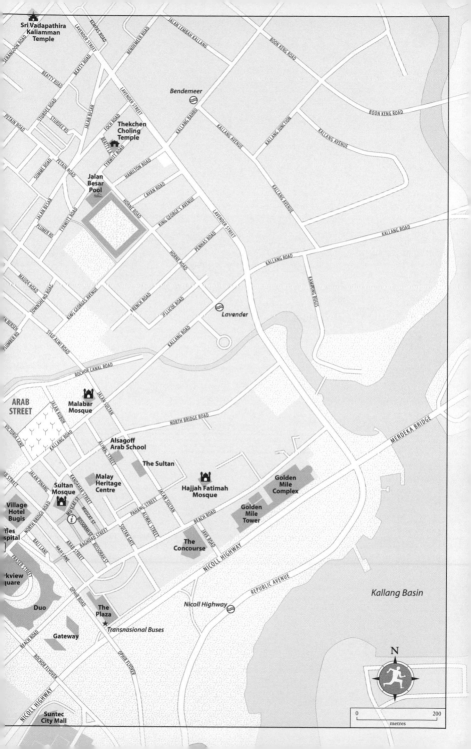

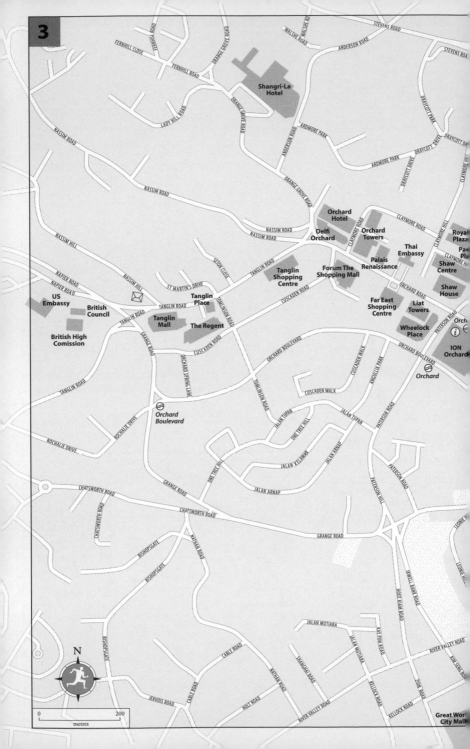

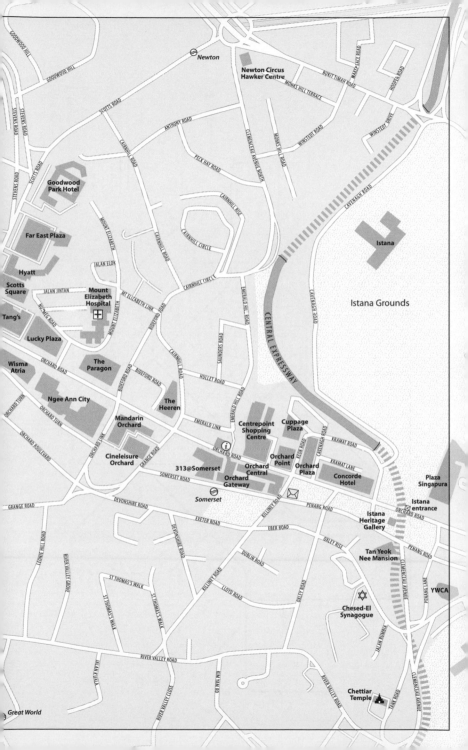

THE MRT SYSTEM

KEY

East–West line
North–South line
North–East line / under construction
Circle line
Downtown line
Thomson–East coast line
(to open in stages from 2019)
Interchange station
Station
Station under development